350
DreamHOMESource
ONE-STORY
HOME PLANS

350 One-Story Home Plans

DreamHOMESource

hanley▲wood

Published by Hanley Wood
One Thomas Circle, NW, Suite 600
Washington, DC 20005

Distribution Center
29333 Lorie Lane
Wixom, Michigan 48393

Group Publisher, Andrew Schultz
Associate Publisher, Editorial Development, Jennifer Pearce
Managing Editor, Hannah McCann
Senior Editor, Nate Ewell
Associate Editor, Simon Hyoun
Senior Plan Merchandiser, Morenci C. Clark
Plan Merchandiser, Nicole Phipps
Proofreader/Copywriter, Dyana Weis
Graphic Artist, Joong Min
Plan Data Team Leader, Susan Jasmin
Production Manager, Brenda McClary

Vice President, Retail Sales, Scott Hill
National Sales Manager, Bruce Holmes
Director, Plan Products, Matt Higgins

Most Hanley Wood titles are available at quantity discounts with bulk purchases for educational, business,
or sales promotional use. For information, please contact Bruce Holmes at bholmes@hanleywood.com.

VC Graphics, Inc.
Creative Director, Veronica Vannoy
Graphic Designer, Jennifer Gerstein
Graphic Designer, Denise Reiffenstein

Photo Credits
Front Cover, Main and Back Cover, Left: Design HPK1600151, for details see page 160.
Photo © 1995 Donald A. Gardner, Inc., Photography courtesy of Donald A. Gardner Architects, Inc.
Front Cover, Lower Right and Back Cover, Top: Design HPK1600001,
for details see page 6 and 313. Photo courtesy of Stephen Fuller, Inc.

10 9 8 7 6 5 4 3 2 1

Library of Congress Control Number: 2005927712

ISBN-13: 978-1-931131-47-6
ISBN-10: 1-931131-47-3

350
DreamHOMESource
ONE-STORY
HOME PLANS

ONLINE EXTRA!

PASSAGEWAY

For access to bonus home plans, articles, online ordering, and more go to: **www.hanley woodbooks.com/350onestoryhomeplans**

Features of this site include:

- A dynamic link that lets you search and view bonus home plans
- Online related feature articles
- Built-in tools to save and view your favorite home plans
- A dynamic web link that allows you to order your home plan online
- Contact details for the Hanley Wood Home Plan Hotline
- Free subscriptions to Hanley Wood Home Plan e-news

hanley▲wood

CONTENTS

Number One Choice

Photo by Laurence Taylor; see more of this home on p. 263.

What you're bound to notice while looking through our collection of one-story home designs is that it encompasses a wide variety of architectural styles and an even wider range of square footages. Of course, certain styles have traditionally favored one-story variations. The Southwestern styles—Spanish Colonial, Mission, Pueblo—that arose in the open spaces of the North American frontier, as well as the Mediterranean styles—inspired by the residential architecture of southern Spain, Italy, France, Morocco, and Greece—prominent in the Southeastern states, all feature the low-slung, ground-hugging profile of a one-story elevation. But to appreciate the rising popularity of single-level design in other styles and regions of the country, we must discuss the practical advantages that a one-story home can offer.

THE ONE-STORY ADVANTAGE

The built-in convenience of a home with its rooms on one floor is that it requires no stair climbing—a feature that many seniors and persons with disabilities will appreciate. The clustering of the master suite, living room, kitchen, and dining area recommends one-story designs as ideal empty-nester homes.

Larger one-story homes are also quieter than multilevel homes of comparable square footage. There's no noise from upstairs foot traffic and the rooms at the center of the plan are well-insulated from exterior sound. In addition, the absence of an upper story more easily allows designers to implement ceiling treatments such as coffering and tray ceilings—beautifully effected in our feature home.

OUTDOOR OPPORTUNITY

Finally, many one-story homes offer exciting indoor/outdoor possibilities, such as between family rooms and courtyards, or between breakfast nooks and patios. Freed of the need for boxy rooms and right-angle walls, these homes can allow many parts of the plan—from gathering and sleeping areas to work spaces—direct access to outdoor zones without the expense of second-floor decks and balconies. Implement full-height panoramic windows and sliding glass doors to achieve truly dramatic vistas of the surrounding landscape.

HOW TO USE THIS BOOK

Following this introduction, our feature stories will explore in greater detail all the advantages of one-story design. When

considering a home plan, take time to visualize the flow of interior spaces and imagine how the design would feel to you. The rest of the book is divided into four sections organized by square footage. Smaller homes are ideal for first-time buyers and larger plans for luxury lovers—but of course, the decision is yours. Lastly, take full advantage of your one-story home plan by selecting a matching landscape design (and other projects), found in section five.

MAKE IT YOURS

Every plan discussed in this book is available to own. Turn to page 376 to learn how to order a plan and what you will receive with your purchase. Materials lists, customization, home automation, and other options are also explained in this part of the book, fol-

AS MUCH AS THEY ARE CONVENIENT AND COMFORTABLE, single-story designs draw inspiration from established architectural styles to produce graceful and dramatic living spaces.

lowed by the list of prices on page 382. Please note that the plans are organized by plan number, not by page number.

LET US HELP

Few other experiences are as challenging or rewarding as building a new home. Any time you have a question or simply would like a second opinion about a home, please feel free to contact our representatives at 1-800-521-6797.

Crowd Pleaser

An easy-living design turns a long day's journey into comfort.

This Georgian-style home, originally conceived as a gift by the designer to his parents, shows an attentive eye to style and an innovative layout. At front, a porch with Chippendale detailing and four Doric-style columns hosts a paneled entry with a fanlight transom—an attractive complement to the mix of shingles, brick, and stucco that adorns the rest of the exterior. With its distinguished looks and robust presence, the home attains an air of confidence that suits it for any prominent lot in the neighborhood.

Homeowners who enjoy entertaining will appreciate the arrangement of the foyer and formal dining room that allows guests to enjoy the fireplace centered at the rear of the family room. The wide-open interior is also an invitation to natural light, which enters by way of

1 HANDSOME COLUMNS introduce a welcoming gabled entry—as well as the home's Colonial heritage.

② **ACCESS THE VERSATILE DECK** via the master bedroom, nook, or mudroom. A modest pool completes the design.

③ **FAMILY DINING** is cozy and casual in the breakfast nook. Full-height windows, French doors, and a skylight keep things bright.

the sunroom, carefully placed skylights, and a set of French doors leading out to a side deck and pool area. Overnight guests will find privacy and convenience in the second bedroom, which splits a bath with the nearby office; separate vanities and a compartmented bath make sharing easy.

Complementing the home's good manners is a perfectly planned kitchen that cherishes a family's casual spirit. The breakfast nook and island kitchen

All photos by B. Massey Photographers, courtesy of Stephen Fuller, Inc. To see more of this home, turn to page 313.

④ A DECORATIVE CEILING AND LARGE WINDOWS establish an attractive height in the master bedroom. Found at the top of the plan, the suite provides quiet comfort and exclusive views of the rear landscape.

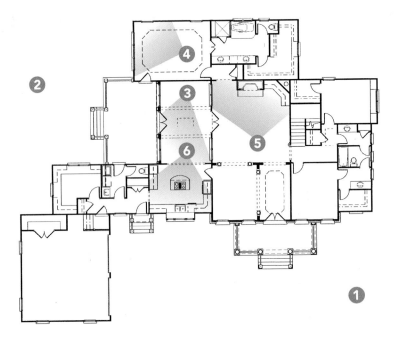

provide spaces for informal dining. The nearby second entry helps to employ the utility areas and the garage to everyday kitchen chores, such as bringing in groceries from the car or stocking the pantry. The side deck, with access to a half-bath and bar areas, is an ideal space for outdoor dining.

Finally, the master suite provides a replenishing retreat from a long day of work and play. The bedroom features a decorative tray ceiling, panoramic views to the side of the plan, and private access to the deck. The master bath delivers a long list of amenities—dual vanities, whirlpool tub, compartmented toilet, steam shower—and is attended by a very generous walk-in closet. A brief entryway serves to separate and secure the space for the fortunate homeowners.

The expansive layout of the floorplan suggests numerous opportunities for outdoor living. A cutting garden at the front of the home, just outside the kitchen, could be picture perfect. In the master suite, owners may appreciate a garden facing the windowed tub. Finally, consider how visiting grandchildren will love splashing in the outdoor pool, accessible from the side deck.

5 SINGLE-LEVEL DESIGN finds full expression in the family room, where built-in shelves, a centerpiece fireplace, and a coffered ceiling establish the home's formal side.

6 THE COUNTRY-STYLE island kitchen serves the home's everyday occasions. Clustering the kitchen with the utility room, garage, and deck allows it to work smarter and harder.

Open Opportunity

Nothing is more glorious than enjoying an outdoor space that is as comfortable and inviting as your favorite indoor rooms. So designing these outdoor areas has taken on a new importance. These are spaces that are created just for pleasure—and should be a pleasure to create. Whether you prefer feasting outdoors, catching some sun, enjoying the landscape, socializing, or lounging pool-side, you can design a space that's tailor-made for you, your family, and friends.

The new family room isn't centered around the television anymore; outdoor rooms are the hottest new spot for feasts, celebrations, and family fun.

As you enter the plans selection and customization stage of your new home, now is the time to plan your outdoor space. When designing outdoor rooms, special emphasis should naturally be placed on this space that's meant for pure enjoyment. Landscape Designer Susan Raucher of Creative Touch landscaping in Southampton, New York, advises: "The outdoor areas are really an extension of your home and should reflect your taste, color preferences, and favorite activities." If it's a pool you crave, design options are nearly limitless. But before you dive in, think about your yard and what the focus of your pool will be, warns the National Spa and Pool Institute. Do you need a pool to accommodate large groups, or will it be more of a private spot intended for personal relaxation? Is it meant for exercise, or as a gathering spot for splashing kids?

A LIMESTONE AND GRANITE HEARTH is a luxurious touch that creates a cozy atmosphere. Wrought-iron furniture and weather-proof cushions are appropriate for outdoor use.

Lydia Gould Bessler (3)

Once you've determined the pool's primary function, consult with a professional builder, who can walk you through the design phase with the assistance of computer-aided design technology. This way, you'll be able to visualize your pool and your backyard space before the first bulldozer arrives.

Susan Raucher also stresses that you should think about the purpose of a space before you decide upon the design. "The type of use is key in planning your outdoor living design," she explains. "How often

ARTS & CRAFTS FLAIR and well-designed lighting have turned this pool (top) into a stylish oasis. A sleek profile and earth-tone surface materials let the pool (inset) fit with its surroundings.

IN A COVERED OUTDOOR ROOM, you have more flexibility with materials since furniture won't be exposed directly to harsh elements. This northern California space mirrors a traditional indoor room.

you entertain and how you use the property are also important." For example, if you enjoy entertaining, make sure your outdoor rooms can accommodate plenty of seating—comfy couches and plush armchairs encourage conversation. Weatherproof fabrics are important for easy maintenance and eliminate the task of removing and storing cushions with each approaching rain. If you want to have plenty of alfresco meals, you'll also want to invest in a weatherproof table and chairs.

Because outdoor dining is so enjoyable, many spaces now include a full outdoor kitchen featuring a deluxe grill, a bar cart, sink, and refrigerator. Luxury features like fire pits and outdoor hearths beautifully complete an outdoor living area, reflecting the design of a traditional living room and

Trellis Structures

THIS FORMAL GARDEN PERGOLA instantly creates a shady outdoor room and adds architectural interest to the backyard.

updating it. A custom-built pergola can protect from direct sunlight, while adding a romantic element. Whether you prefer a space that is open to enjoy the starry sky or sheltered from the elements to encourage year-round use, there are a multitude of products from which to choose. To make your garden, backyard, pool, patio, or deck a comfortable destination to while away your free time with family and friends, you'll need a few accessories, from furniture to fencing to lighting and outdoor appliances. Take a look at any recent Hanley Wood home magazine to see a review of the latest products and ideas, all of which will enhance your outdoor living space—making it more functional, more beautiful, and more fun.

OUTDOOR SPACES combine the comfort of your home with the beauty of the natural environment. Take cues from the design of your home. Look to where the plan interacts with the landscape. The slightest effort can create an enjoyable alfresco setting.

Small Dreams—Beautiful Designs for First-Time Builders

P lans in this square-foot range are ideal for those looking to build a smart, flexible, cost-efficient, and energy-saving home that is no larger than what the family needs or what the plot allows. Of course, a smaller home should feel snug, not cramped—a challenging balance for designers to attain.

One space-saving strategy is to forgo formal spaces such as separate dining rooms, which can cut up a floor plan into uncomfortable squares. Instead, smartly built smaller homes call for rooms that flow easily between household hotspots and perform "on demand." For instance, a peninsula counter in the kitchen allows the space to function flexibly as a dining area, prep space, breakfast bar, and serving buffet for larger meals. Adding another set of doors to the rear porch would introduce attractive possibilities for outdoor dining. In all smaller designs, judicious placement of porches and balconies is a great way to add both character and area to the home.

A SMALL INTERIOR WINDOW (above) allows the bedroom and bath to share ambient light--a smart way to compensate for obstructed windows (right) or other small-lot challenges. In both examples, a coordinated decorating scheme let's minimal spaces feel great.

Sam Gray

A good principle to remember is that a well-designed small space can create a sense of order through travel paths and visual paths as well as with physical structures such as walls. This will allow areas of the home to retain definition without

Tony Giammarino

Mark Samu

being closed off. As far as interior design is concerned, give thought to proper lighting and color combinations. Controlling the amount of contrast between adjoining spaces will establish the proportions that feel right. If there's room in your budget, invest in a lighting specialist.

Lastly, put to work what you'll save by building small. Let your home communicate a sense of intimacy and regard for meaningful details by incorporating quality materials and artful touches, like those pictured here. Whether you're building a primary residence or vacation home, you'll be amazed at how a smaller than average home can fit just right.

BUILT-IN BOOKCASES, media shelves, and art niches are space-efficient features that forestall clutter, preserving floor space and allowing rooms to flow comfortably.

WITH BRICK, WOOD, AND SIDING, this home will captivate interest right away. An efficient layout reveals two family bedrooms—or use one as a study—at the front of the home; the master suite is tucked at the rear for privacy. The master bath will soothe and revitalize, and the large walk-in closet is sure to please. The family room opens to the dining room, with easy access to the open kitchen. The convenient laundry room is hidden in one wall of the kitchen.

HOME PLAN

HPK1600007

Style: Transitional

Square Footage: 1,151

Bedrooms: 3

Bathrooms: 2

Width: 39' - 3"

Depth: 42' - 1"

Foundation: Slab

eplans.com

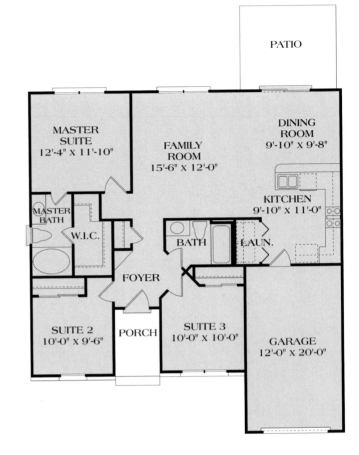

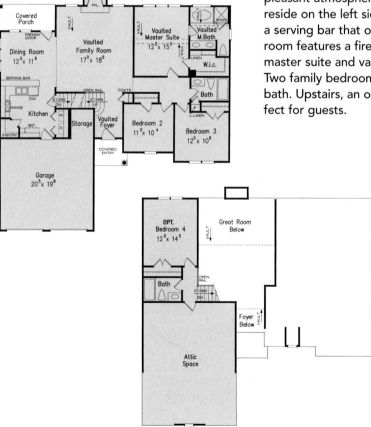

THIS ADORABLE THREE-BEDROOM HOME will provide a pleasant atmosphere for your family. The communal living areas reside on the left side of the plan. The L-shaped kitchen includes a serving bar that opens to the dining area. The vaulted family room features a fireplace and leads to the sleeping quarters. A master suite and vaulted master bath will pamper homeowners. Two family bedrooms reside across the hall and share a full hall bath. Upstairs, an optional fourth bedroom and full bath are perfect for guests.

HOME PLAN

HPK1600008

Style: Country Cottage

Square Footage: 1,477

Bonus Space: 283 sq. ft.

Bedrooms: 3

Bathrooms: 2

Width: 51' - 0"

Depth: 51' - 4"

Foundation: Crawlspace, Unfinished Walkout Basement

eplans.com

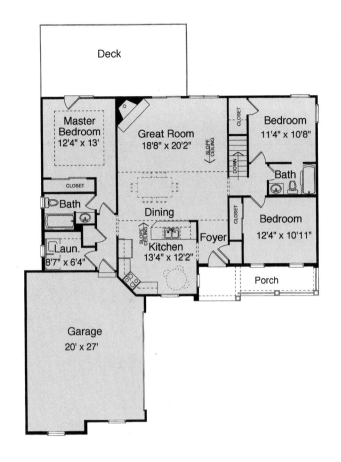

STONE AND SIDING, A FRONT PORCH, and multiple gables decorate the exterior of this charming one-floor plan. The interior offers options that include a kitchen that can accommodate a small dining area or can be designed to offer more cabinets and a larger great room. The gas fireplace can be located in the corner or on the rear wall. The master bedroom enjoys a raised-center ceiling and a private bath. This delightful home is designed with an unfinished walk-out basement that can be decorated to provide additional living space.

HPK1600009

HOME PLAN

Style: Country Cottage

Square Footage: 1,390

Bedrooms: 3

Bathrooms: 2

Width: 50' - 0"

Depth: 55' - 8"

Foundation: Unfinished Walkout Basement

eplans.com

Deck

Master Bedroom
12'-4" x 13'-0"

Great Room
18'-8" x 17'-4"

Bedroom
11'-4" x 10'-8"

Bath

Dining

Bath

Kitchen
13'-4" x 9'-11"

Foyer

Bedroom
12'-4" x 10'-10"

Laun.

Porch

Garage
20'-0" x 26'-2"

Bath

Optional Library

OPTIONAL LAYOUT

HOME PLAN

HPK1600010

Style: Country Cottage

Square Footage: 1,315

Bedrooms: 3

Bathrooms: 2

Width: 50' - 0"

Depth: 54' - 8"

Foundation: Unfinished Walkout Basement

eplans.com

THIS COUNTRY-STYLE HOUSE SEEMS BIGGER than it is, because the open layout draws the dining and great rooms together with the kitchen. This spaciousness continues as the great room opens through a French door to a wide deck facing the backyard. The deck can also be entered through the master suite, which enjoys a private bath. Two other bedrooms, located on the right side, share a bath. One could be used as a library. The courtyard between the garage doors and the foyer, along with the rustic brick-and-siding facade, will draw appreciative looks from passersby.

HOMEOWNERS CAN WAIT OUT RAINY DAYS on the front covered porch of this home and likewise enjoy sunny afternoons on the rear deck. They'll find spacious shelter inside in the large great room, easily accessible from the kitchen with a breakfast nook. With a corner fireplace and rear deck access, the great room will be buzzing with activity. Two secondary bedrooms—make one a library—share a full hall bath. The master suite is graciously appointed with a private bath and walk-in closet.

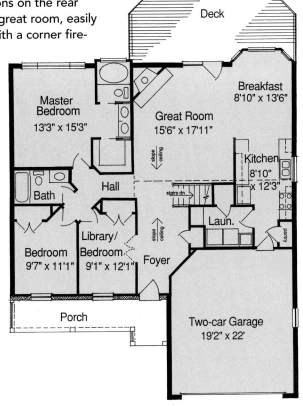

HOME PLAN

HPK1600011

Style: Country Cottage

Square Footage: 1,422

Bedrooms: 3

Bathrooms: 2

Width: 45' - 0"

Depth: 51' - 4"

Foundation: Unfinished Walkout Basement

eplans.com

COMPACT AND PERFECT FOR STARTERS OR EMPTY-NESTERS, this is a wonderful single-level home. The beautiful facade is supplemented by a stylish and practical covered porch. Just to the left of the entry is a roomy kitchen with bright windows and convenient storage. The octagonal dining room shares a three-sided fireplace with the living room. A covered patio to the rear enhances outdoor living. A fine master suite enjoys a grand bath and is complemented by a secondary bedroom and full bath.

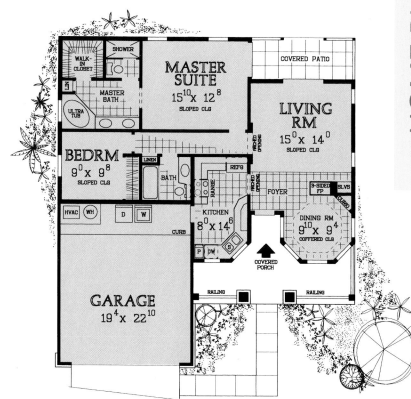

HOME PLAN

 # HPK1600012

Style: **Country Cottage**
Square Footage: **1,118**
Bedrooms: **2**
Bathrooms: **2**
Width: **44' - 4"**
Depth: **47' - 4"**
Foundation: **Slab**

eplans.com

HOME PLAN

HPK1600013

Style: Country Cottage

Square Footage: 1,373

Bedrooms: 3

Bathrooms: 2

Width: 50' - 4"

Depth: 45' - 0"

Foundation: Unfinished Walkout Basement, Crawlspace

eplans.com

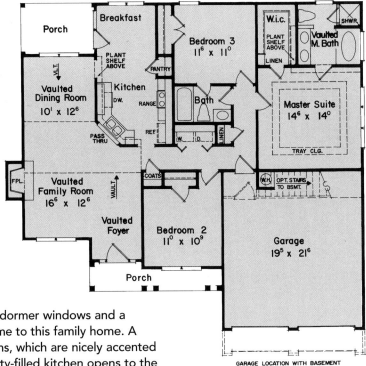

GARAGE LOCATION WITH BASEMENT

A STEEP GABLE ROOFLINE punctuated with dormer windows and a columned front porch give a traditional welcome to this family home. A vaulted ceiling tops the family and dining rooms, which are nicely accented with a fireplace and bright windows. An amenity-filled kitchen opens to the breakfast room. The master suite has a refined tray ceiling and a vaulted bath. Two family bedrooms, a laundry center, and a full bath—with private access from Bedroom 3—complete this stylish plan.

©1999 Donald A. Gardner, Inc.

B. NATHAN

THIS BEAUTIFUL COUNTRY HOUSE FEATURES light-filled dormers and varied rooflines. A family can appreciate and enjoy the front and rear covered porches where they can sit and enjoy the view. The great room, dining room, and kitchen comprise one large open area—the great room boasts a cathedral ceiling, a fireplace, and built-in shelves. The luxurious master bedroom includes a walk-in closet, private bath, and oversized tub. A cathedral ceiling also graces the front bedroom. A bonus room adds space for a game or media room.

HOME PLAN

HPK1600014

Style: Country

Square Footage: 1,425

Bonus Space: 424 sq. ft.

Bedrooms: 3

Bathrooms: 2

Width: 61' - 0"

Depth: 51' - 8"

eplans.com

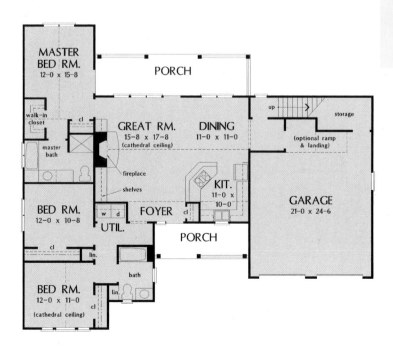

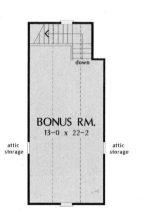

HPK1600015

Style: Traditional
Square Footage: 1,359
Bedrooms: 3
Bathrooms: 2
Width: 57' - 0"
Depth: 42' - 0"

HOME PLAN

eplans.com

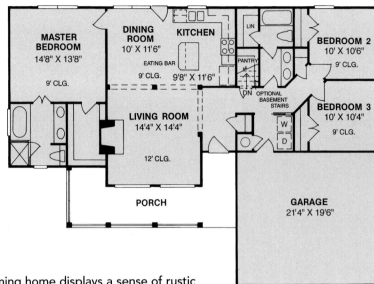

LIKE A PETITE RANCH HOUSE, this welcoming home displays a sense of rustic charm. Inside, it is the picture of comfort, with open spaces and thoughtful planning. Enter from the front porch to the foyer; on the left, columns and an archway lead to the hearth-warmed living room. A gracious introduction the dining room reveals tons of natural light, and an open kitchen with a space-saving island. Sleeping quarters are separated for privacy, with a lovely master suite on the left, and two secondary bedrooms on the right. A side-loading two-car garage completes the plan.

THIS FARMHOUSE-STYLE HOME SQUEEZES SPACE-EFFICIENT FEATURES into its compact design. A cozy front porch opens into a vaulted great room and its adjoining dining room. Twin dormer windows above fill this area with natural light and accentuate the high ceilings. A warm hearth in the great room adds to its coziness. The U-shaped kitchen has a breakfast bar that's open to the dining room and a sink overlooking a flower box. A nearby side-door accesses the handy laundry room. Vaulted bedrooms are positioned along the back of the plan. They contain wall closets and share a full bath that includes a soaking tub. An open-rail staircase leads to the basement, which can be developed into living or sleeping space at a later time.

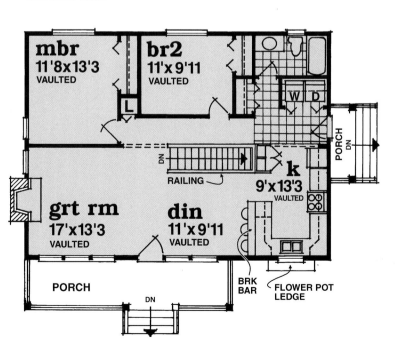

HOME PLAN

HPK1600016

Style: Traditional

Square Footage: 1,557

Bedrooms: 3

Bathrooms: 2

Width: 46' - 0"

Depth: 40' - 0"

Foundation: Unfinished Walkout Basement

eplans.com

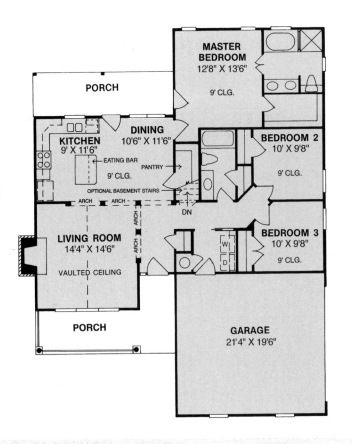

PORCH

KITCHEN
9' X 11'6"

EATING BAR

9' CLG.

OPTIONAL BASEMENT STAIRS

ARCH — ARCH

LIVING ROOM
14'4" X 14'6"

VAULTED CEILING

PORCH

DINING
10'6" X 11'6"

PANTRY

ARCH

ARCH

DN

MASTER
BEDROOM
12'8" X 13'6"

9' CLG.

BEDROOM 2
10' X 9'8"

9' CLG.

W
D

BEDROOM 3
10' X 9'8"

9' CLG.

GARAGE
21'4" X 19'6"

TRADITIONAL STYLING ON THIS ONE-STORY home begins with a welcoming front porch. From the foyer, arches lead to the vaulted living room, warmed by a fireplace. The island kitchen and dining area are ahead and access a rear porch. The master suite is situated for privacy and accommodates a spa bath. Two additional bedrooms share a full bath to complete the plan.

HOME PLAN

HPK1600017

Style: Traditional

Square Footage: 1,263

Bedrooms: 3

Bathrooms: 2

Width: 42' - 0"

Depth: 54' - 0"

eplans.com

HOME PLAN

#HPK1600018

Style: Traditional

Square Footage: 1,377

Bonus Space: 322 sq. ft.

Bedrooms: 3

Bathrooms: 2

Width: 57' - 8"

Depth: 44' - 0"

eplans.com

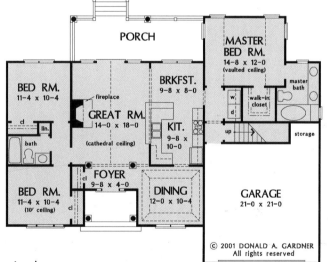

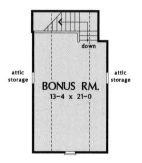

THIS DELIGHTFUL SUMMER COTTAGE offers a simple layout, favorable to any family. The foyer is flanked by an elegant dining room boasting a tray ceiling and two family bedrooms that share a hall bath. The great room is enhanced by a cathedral ceiling and a warming fireplace. The gourmet kitchen is conveniently located and ready to serve the breakfast area, which showcases great views of the rear porch. The master suite boasts elegance with its vaulted ceiling, large walk-in closet, and pampering private bath. Just around the corner from the master retreat is a conveniently located laundry room.

EQUALLY GRACIOUS OUTSIDE AND INSIDE, this one- or two-bedroom cottage has a post-and-rail covered porch hugging one wing, with convenient access through double doors or pass-through windows in the dining room and kitchen. The columned entry foyer has a sloped ceiling and leads past a second bedroom or media room into a great room with a sloped ceiling, fireplace, and low wall along the staircase that leads to the attic. The master suite fills the right wing and features a plant shelf in the bedroom and a garden tub in the master bath, plus a large walk-in closet and laundry facilities.

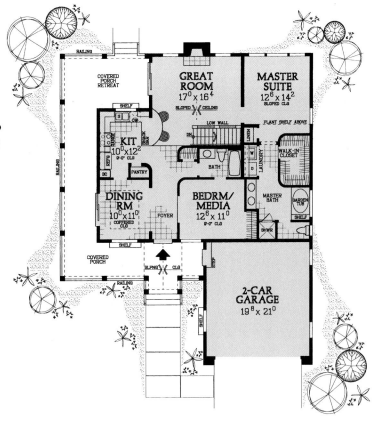

HOME PLAN

(#) HPK1600019

Style: Country Cottage

Square Footage: 1,295

Bedrooms: 2

Bathrooms: 2

Width: 48' - 0"

Depth: 59' - 0"

Foundation: Unfinished Basement

eplans.com

Floor Plan Labels

Patio
24-0x12-7

Owner's
Bedroom
13-0x15-9

Kitchen
9-1x11-11

Greatroom
14-5x17-5

Bedroom
12-1x11-11

Bath
14-7x8-0

Dining
12-1x11-11

Foyer

Bath

Storage
9-0x6-10

Laun.
5-6x6-7

Porch
10-8x6-0

Bedroom
12-1x11-0

Garage
20-5x20-11

Laundry

Garage

Basement Stair
Location

HOME PLAN

(#) HPK1600020

Style: Traditional

Square Footage: 1,392

Bedrooms: 3

Bathrooms: 2

Width: 52' - 6"

Depth: 52' - 8"

Foundation: Unfinished
Basement, Crawlspace,
Slab

eplans.com

YOU'LL LOVE THE UNASSUMING ELEGANCE of this traditional neighborhood home. A portico-style porch opens through French doors to a foyer with an impressive cathedral ceiling. To the left, a sloped ceiling and tasteful columns define the dining room. An L-shaped kitchen flows effortlessly into the great room, perfect for entertaining. Here, a cathedral ceiling and cozy fireplace are inviting. Two bedrooms, nearly identical, share a full bath. Separated for privacy, the master suite enjoys a sloped ceiling and a pampering private bath. An expansive rear patio extends living areas.

FAMILY RM
VAULTED CLG
12⁴ x 12⁰

MASTER BEDRM
VAULTED CLG
13⁰ x 12⁰

MASTER BATH

BEDRM
VAULTED CLG
10⁰ x 10⁸

COVERED PORCH

SNACK BAR

PANTRY

DW

KIT
12⁴ x 10⁰

SINK

R

REFG

D   W

LAUNDRY

LINEN

PLANT SHELF ABOVE

BATH

BEDRM
VAULTED CLG
10⁰ x 10⁸

BAY WINDOW

DINING

LIVING RM
VAULTED CLG
13¹⁰ x 19⁰

PLANT SHELF ABOVE

F.A.U.   W.H

ENTRY

HALF WALL

CURB

COVERED PORCH

GARAGE
21⁴ x 23⁸

HOME PLAN

(#) HPK1600021

Style: Farmhouse

Square Footage: 1,389

Bedrooms: 3

Bathrooms: 2

Width: 44' - 8"

Depth: 54' - 6"

Foundation: Slab

eplans.com

TWO EXTERIORS, ONE FLOOR PLAN—what more could you ask? Simple rooflines and an inviting porch enhance the floor plan. A formal living room has a warming fireplace and a delightful bay window. The U-shaped kitchen shares a snack bar with the bayed family room. Note the sliding glass doors to the rear yard here. Three bedrooms include two family bedrooms served by a full bath and a lovely master suite with its own private bath.

©1998 Donald A. Gardner, Inc.

HOME PLAN

(#) **HPK1600022**

Style: Country Cottage

Square Footage: 1,428

Bonus Space: 313 sq. ft.

Bedrooms: 3

Bathrooms: 2

Width: 52' - 8"

Depth: 52' - 4"

eplans.com

© 1998 Donald A Gardner, Inc.

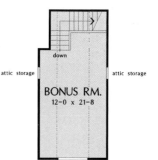

STUNNING ARCHED WINDOWS framed by bold front-facing gables add to the tremendous curb appeal of this modest home. Topped by a cathedral ceiling and with porches on either side, the great room is expanded further by its openness to the dining room and kitchen. Flexibility, which is so important in a home this size, is found in the versatile bedroom/study as well as the bonus room over the garage. The master suite is positioned for privacy at the rear of the home, with a graceful tray ceiling, walk-in closet, and private bath. An additional bedroom and a hall bath complete the plan.

THIS TRADITIONAL DESIGN IS PERFECT FOR THOSE who want all their living space on one level. A covered porch welcomes guests and ushers them into the vaulted great room where a fireplace warms the room. An open dining space sits across from the efficient kitchen for easy serving and clean-up. Two family bedrooms are split to the right of the plan. A full hall bath sits between the bedrooms and is convenient for guests. On the left, the master suite enjoys privacy, a walk-in closet, and a full bath with dual vanities.

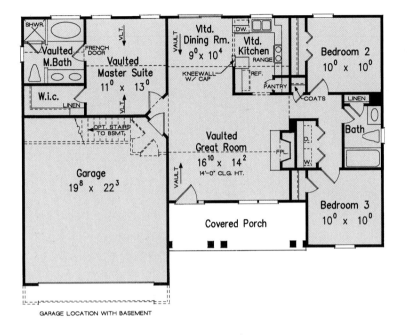

GARAGE LOCATION WITH BASEMENT

HOME PLAN

HPK1600023

Style: Country Cottage

Square Footage: 1,080

Bedrooms: 3

Bathrooms: 2

Width: 50' - 0"

Depth: 36' - 0"

Foundation: Crawlspace, Unfinished Walkout Basement

eplans.com

© 1994 Donald A. Gardner Architects, Inc.

A GREAT ROOM THAT STRETCHES INTO THE DINING ROOM makes this design perfect for entertaining. A cozy fireplace, stylish built-ins, and a cathedral ceiling further this casual yet elegant atmosphere. A rear deck extends living possibilities. The ample kitchen features an abundance of counter and cabinet space and an angled cooktop and serving bar that overlooks the great room. Two bedrooms, a hall bath, and a handy laundry room make up the family sleeping wing; the master suite is privately located at the rear of the plan.

HOME PLAN

HPK1600024

Style: **Farmhouse**
Square Footage: **1,346**
Bedrooms: **3**
Bathrooms: **2**
Width: **65' - 0"**
Depth: **44' - 2"**

eplans.com

HOMES UNDER 1,500 SQUARE FEET

MASTER BED RM.
14-8 x 13-0

DECK

master bath

walk-in closet

w/d

UTIL.

lin.   sto.   cl

bath

cl

GREAT RM.
15-8 x 15-0

DINING
11-4 x 11-0

(cathedral ceiling)

fireplace

FOYER
6-8 x 5-8

KIT.
11-4 x 12-4

GARAGE
21-0 x 21-0

© 1994 Donald A. Gardner Architects, Inc.

BED RM.
10-0 x 10-4

BED RM.
10-0 x 10-4

cl

PORCH

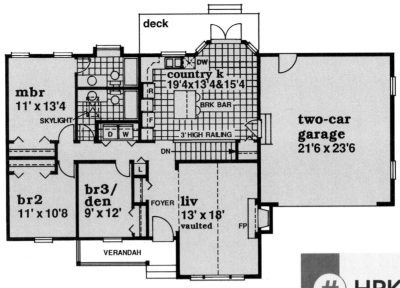

SMALLER IN SIZE BUT BIG ON LIVABILITY, this one-story home has amenities and options usually found only in larger homes. Begin with the covered veranda and its entry to a central foyer. On the right is a vaulted living room with central fireplace. On the left is a bedroom—or make it a den. A hall closet holds coats and other outdoor gear. The country kitchen lives up to its name. It features an open-railed stair to the basement, an L-shaped work counter, a breakfast snack island, and a bayed breakfast nook with double-door access to the backyard. The two family bedrooms share a full main bath; the master suite has a private bath. A two-car garage sits to the side of the plan.

HOME PLAN

HPK1600025

Style: Ranch

Square Footage: 1,360

Bedrooms: 3

Bathrooms: 2

Width: 64' - 0"

Depth: 38' - 0"

Foundation: Crawlspace, Unfinished Basement

eplans.com

A COLUMNED FRONT PORCH WITH FRENCH DOORS and nine-over-nine sashed windows grace the exterior of this traditional bungalow. Inside you'll find a fireplace and formal dining room, a master bedroom with cathedral ceilings and attached bath, and a living room with a vaulted ceiling. The kitchen features a separate pantry with serving/preparation island and convenient access to the two-car garage. A screened porch is annexed to the dining room, providing expansive rear views.

HOME PLAN

HPK1600026

Style: Bungalow

Square Footage: 1,419

Bedrooms: 3

Bathrooms: 2

Width: 49' - 4"

Depth: 48' - 0"

Foundation: Unfinished Walkout Basement

eplans.com

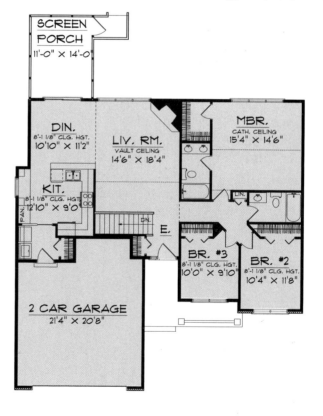

SCREEN PORCH
11'-0" × 14'-0"

DIN.
8'-1 1/8" CLG. HGT.
10'10" × 11'2"

LIV. RM.
VAULT CEILING
14'6" × 18'4"

MBR.
CATH. CEILING
15'4" × 14'6"

KIT.
8'-1 1/8" CLG. HGT.
12'10" × 9'0"

BR. #3
8'-1 1/8" CLG. HGT.
10'0" × 9'10"

BR. #2
8'-1 1/8" CLG. HGT.
10'4" × 11'8"

2 CAR GARAGE
21'4" × 20'8"

THIS STELLAR SINGLE-STORY SYMMETRICAL HOME offers plenty of living space for any family. The front porch and rear deck make outdoor entertaining delightful. The living and dining rooms are open and spacious for family gatherings. A well-organized kitchen with an abundance of cabinetry and a built-in pantry completes the functional plan. Three bedrooms reside on the left side of the plan.

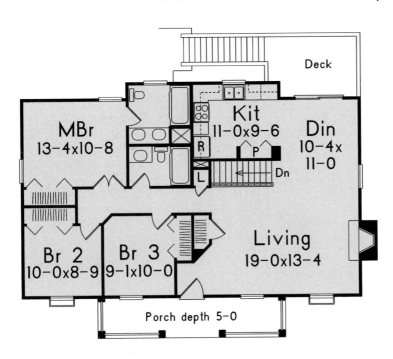

HPK1600027

Style: Traditional

Square Footage: 1,140

Bedrooms: 3

Bathrooms: 2

Width: 44' - 0"

Depth: 27' - 0"

Foundation: Unfinished Basement

HOME PLAN

eplans.com

S. NATHAN

THIS CHARMING COUNTRY HOME UTILIZES MULTIPANE WINDOWS, columns, dormers, and a covered porch to offer a welcoming front exterior. Inside, the great room with a dramatic cathedral ceiling commands attention; the kitchen and breakfast room are just beyond a set of columns. The tier-ceilinged dining room presents a delightfully formal atmosphere for dinner parties or family gatherings. A tray ceiling in the master bedroom contributes to its pleasant atmosphere, as do the large walk-in closet and the gracious private bath with a garden tub and a separate shower. The secondary bedrooms are located at the opposite end of the house for privacy.

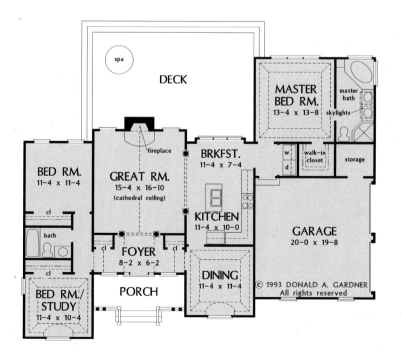

HPK1600028

Style: Traditional
Square Footage: 1,498
Bedrooms: 3
Bathrooms: 2
Width: 59' - 8"
Depth: 46' - 8"

HOME PLAN

eplans.com

THIS ABSOLUTELY CHARMING VICTORIAN-STYLE RANCH HOME is warm and inviting, yet the interior is decidedly up-to-date. An assemblage of beautiful windows surrounds the main entry, flooding the entrance foyer and adjoining great room with an abundance of shaded light. An elegant 10-foot stepped ceiling is featured in the great room, as is a corner fireplace and rear wall of French-style sliding doors. The beautiful multisided breakfast room features a 16-foot ceiling adorned with high clerestory windows, which become the exterior "turret." A private master suite includes a compartmented bath, dressing alcove, very large walk-in closet, 10-foot stepped ceiling, and beautiful bay window overlooking the rear.

HOME PLAN

(#) HPK1600029

Style: Farmhouse

Square Footage: 1,466

Bedrooms: 3

Bathrooms: 2

Width: 60' - 0"

Depth: 39' - 10"

Foundation: Unfinished Basement, Slab, Crawlspace

eplans.com

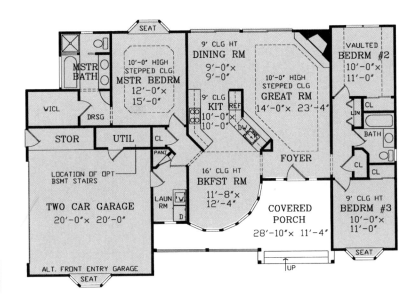

HOME PLAN

HPK1600030

Style: Country Cottage

Square Footage: 972

Bedrooms: 2

Bathrooms: 1

Width: 30' - 0"

Depth: 35' - 0"

Foundation: Unfinished Basement

eplans.com

EYE-CATCHING EXTERIOR DETAILS distinguish this small Victorian design. Inside, natural light flows through the living area from the turret's windows, where there's a sitting bay. The living room and dining room make one open space, which is helpful for entertaining. A sliding door in the dining room leads to the backyard. An angled kitchen provides plenty of workspace. The master bedroom and a second bedroom share a full bath.

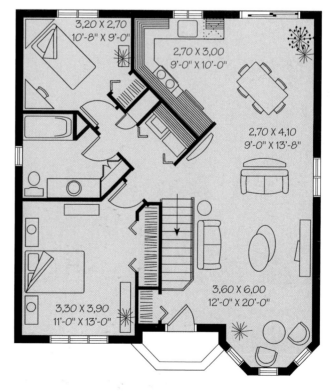

3,20 X 2,70
10'-8" X 9'-0"

2,70 X 3,00
9'-0" X 10'-0"

2,70 X 4,10
9'-0" X 13'-8"

3,30 X 3,90
11'-0" X 13'-0"

3,60 X 6,00
12'-0" X 20'-0"

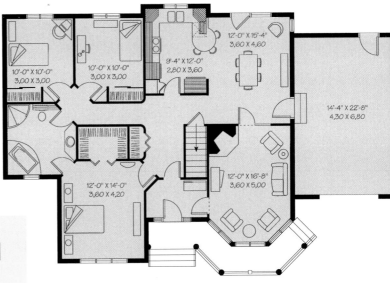

HPK1600031

Style: Country Cottage

Square Footage: 1,370

Bedrooms: 3

Bathrooms: 1

Width: 58' - 0"

Depth: 36' - 0"

Foundation: Unfinished Basement

eplans.com

THE COVERED PORCH WRAPS AROUND THE TURRET, giving this home an inviting look. The bright Palladian window floods the master bedroom with natural light. The living room boasts a fireplace, making this room the perfect gathering area. The L-shaped kitchen is connected to the dining room and offers a rounded bar area. The dining room accesses the backyard. Each family bedroom holds ample closet space. The master bedroom privately accesses the family bath and features a spacious walk-in closet.

THIS SWEET FOLK VICTORIAN COTTAGE, decorated with a bit of gingerbread trim, features a unique bay-windowed foyer with a generously sized coat closet. Additional windows—the elegant arched window in the front bedroom and four tall windows in the family room—fill this design with natural light. The family room adjoins a skylit kitchen, which provides a compact pantry and opens to a dining room with sliding glass doors to the backyard. Two bedrooms, both with long wall closets, share a bath that includes an angled vanity, corner shower, and comfortable tub.

3,00 X 2,70
10'-0" X 9'-0"

2,40 X 3,90
8'-0" X 13'-0"

2,40 X 4,40
8'-0" X 14'-8"

3,30 X 3,60
11'-0" X 12'-0"

4,50 X 3,60
15'-0" X 12'-0"

HOME PLAN

HPK1600032

Style: Victorian

Square Footage: 958

Bedrooms: 2

Bathrooms: 1

Width: 30' - 0"

Depth: 35' - 4"

Foundation: Unfinished Basement

eplans.com

THIS ENCHANTING SUMMER COTTAGE DESIGN offers a simple layout for guest quarters or vacationing getaways. Decorative flower boxes and traditional siding grace the exterior. A petite storage room is located to the immediate right of the entry. The kitchen/eating area accesses the side of the home through a lovely set of double doors. The sitting room is a quiet retreat for any occasion. The bedroom features ample closet space. The efficient hall bath is complete with laundry facilities.

2,70 X 3,30
9'-0" X 12'-0"

3,20 X 3,60
10'-8" X 12'-0"

2,70 X 3,30
9'-0" X 12'-0"

HOME PLAN

HPK1600033

Style: Country

Square Footage: 784

Bedrooms: 1

Bathrooms: 1

Width: 28' - 0"

Depth: 28' - 0"

Foundation: Slab

eplans.com

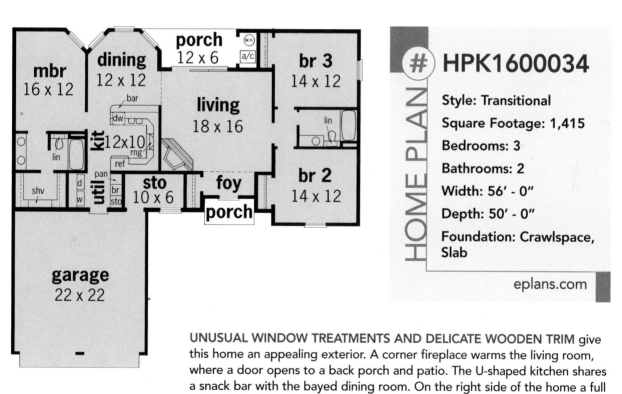

HOME PLAN

**HPK1600034**

Style: Transitional

Square Footage: 1,415

Bedrooms: 3

Bathrooms: 2

Width: 56' - 0"

Depth: 50' - 0"

Foundation: Crawlspace, Slab

eplans.com

UNUSUAL WINDOW TREATMENTS AND DELICATE WOODEN TRIM give this home an appealing exterior. A corner fireplace warms the living room, where a door opens to a back porch and patio. The U-shaped kitchen shares a snack bar with the bayed dining room. On the right side of the home a full hall bath links two secondary bedrooms. The master suite offers a full bath with double sinks and a walk-in closet with built-in shelves. The two-car garage includes a storage area.

TWIN BAY WINDOWS, AN ELEGANT PALLADIAN WINDOW, and corner quoins help create symmetry to this spectacular Southern home. The formal dining room and living room are filled with natural light from the bay windows that each maintain. The more casual family room also enjoys wonderful views with its generous window wall. The island kitchen serves both the dining room and the breakfast nook with ease and efficiency. Three bedrooms and a full bath join the lavish master suite on the second floor where the master bedroom delights with a tray ceiling. A second staircase leads from the kitchen to the second-floor utility room. A bonus room over the two-car garage offers an option for future development.

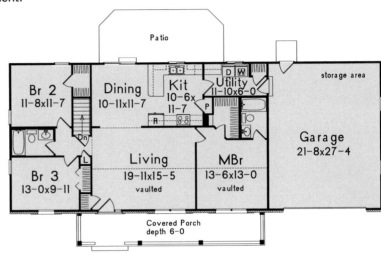

HOME PLAN

HPK1600035

Style: Traditional

Square Footage: 1,400

Bedrooms: 3

Bathrooms: 2

Width: 72' - 0"

Depth: 28' - 0"

Foundation: Crawlspace, Unfinished Basement

eplans.com

BRIGHT AND INVITING, THIS NEIGHBORHOOD HOME enjoys natural light and a flowing floor plan designed for today's busy family. Enter to find a grand vaulted ceiling, punctuated by arched dormer windows. An activity room begins the plan, offering a great place for family gatherings. Open and thoroughly modern, the kitchen serves the dining room, which opens to the rear terrace for alfresco dining. Near the laundry room, a home office affords peace and quiet. Sleeping quarters are arranged on the left; two secondary bedrooms share a full bath, as a master suite delights in a sloped ceiling, spa bath, and walk-in closet.

HOME PLAN

 # HPK1600036

Style: Country Cottage

Square Footage: 1,402

Bedrooms: 3

Bathrooms: 2

Width: 64' - 0"

Depth: 31' - 2"

Foundation: Crawlspace, Slab

eplans.com

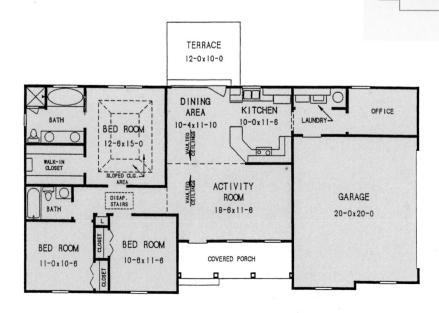

TERRACE
12-0x10-0

DINING AREA
10-4x11-10

KITCHEN
10-0x11-6

LAUNDRY

OFFICE

BATH

BED ROOM
12-6x15-0

WALK-IN CLOSET

SLOPED CLG. AREA

VAULTED CEILINGS

BATH

DISAP. STAIRS

VAULTED CEILINGS

ACTIVITY ROOM
18-6x11-6

GARAGE
20-0x20-0

BED ROOM
11-0x10-6

CLOSET

CLOSET

BED ROOM
10-6x11-6

COVERED PORCH

THIS ONE-LEVEL HOME WITH A FRONT PORCH showcases an angled fireplace and sloped ceilings. The great room combines with the dining area, creating an open, spacious effect. A door leads to a raised deck for a favorable indoor/outdoor relationship. The master suite provides a large walk-in closet and deluxe bath with a unique half-moon tub and a separate shower. A bedroom accessed from the foyer creates an optional den.

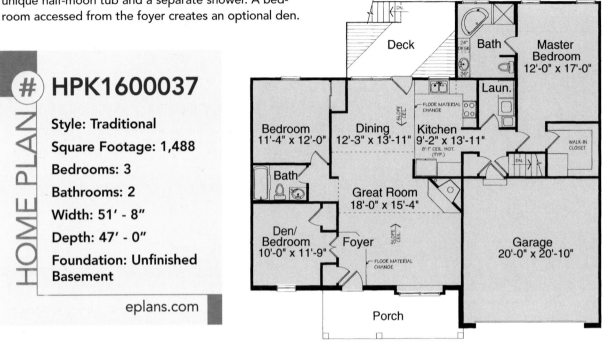

HOME PLAN

HPK1600037

Style: **Traditional**

Square Footage: **1,488**

Bedrooms: **3**

Bathrooms: **2**

Width: **51' - 8"**

Depth: **47' - 0"**

Foundation: **Unfinished Basement**

eplans.com

Photo courtesy of Ron & Donna Kolb-Exposures Unlimited. This home,

THE FASCINATING CLERESTORY WINDOW above the front covered porch of this home grows on you, beckoning you to find out what wonders are housed inside. Surely, the openness of this plan is its most intriguing quality. The vault-ceiling activity room flows naturally into the kitchen, graced by ample counter and cabinet space, and then into the bayed dining area. Off the kitchen is a handy laundry, a utility room, storage space, and entry to the garage. On the other side of the house reside three bedrooms and two baths. The huge oval bathtub and twin vanities set below a vaulted ceiling make the master suite special. Extra space is available above the garage for another bedroom, study, or whatever you need.

HOME PLAN

HPK1600038

Style: Country Cottage

Square Footage: 1,294

Bonus Space: 374 sq. ft.

Bedrooms: 3

Bathrooms: 2

Width: 64' - 6"

Depth: 29' - 10"

Foundation: Crawlspace, Slab

eplans.com

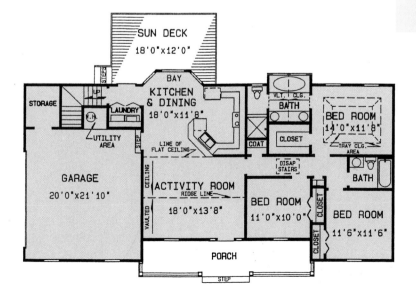

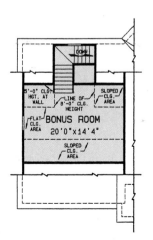

SIMPLE COUNTRY COTTAGE CHARM IS
EXPRESSED with carriage-style garage doors on
this narrow-lot design. The foyer opens to a living
room with a full vaulted ceiling, rising to soaring
heights for a feeling of expanded space. The dining
area is elegantly defined by columns and a ceiling-
height plant shelf. The country-style kitchen features wide windows facing the front property.
Bedrooms are designed for privacy; the master
suite hosts a dramatic vaulted ceiling and a private
spa bath. Not to be missed: a rear patio that is
perfect for summer barbecues.

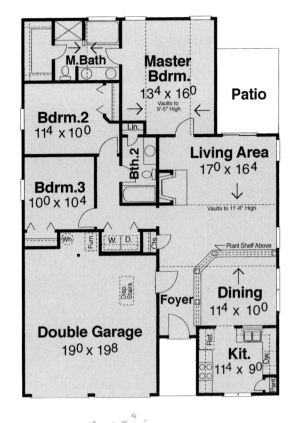

HOME PLAN

HPK1600039

Style: Country Cottage

Square Footage: 1,365

Bedrooms: 3

Bathrooms: 2

Width: 37' - 0"

Depth: 53' - 0"

Foundation: Unfinished
Basement, Slab

eplans.com

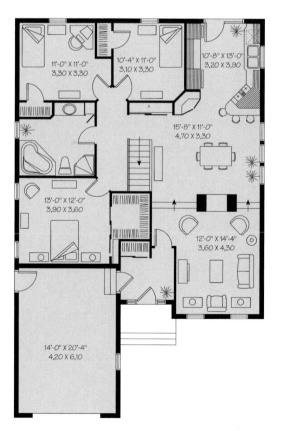

THIS CHARMING COUNTRY HOME WILL BRING PLENTY OF COMFORT and convenience to your family. From the sunken living room with a see-through fireplace into the dining area, to the lavish bath enjoyed by three bedrooms, you will be amazed at what this plan offers. Guests will know right off that they have come to a special place when they enter the foyer with its cathedral ceiling and sunken floor. The entire right side of the house seamlessly draws all the living areas together, enhancing spaciousness. Especially striking is the peninsular snack bar between the well-equipped kitchen and sunlit dining room.

HOME PLAN

HPK1600040

Style: Traditional

Square Footage: 1,393

Bedrooms: 3

Bathrooms: 1

Width: 36' - 0"

Depth: 56' - 0"

Foundation: Unfinished Basement

eplans.com

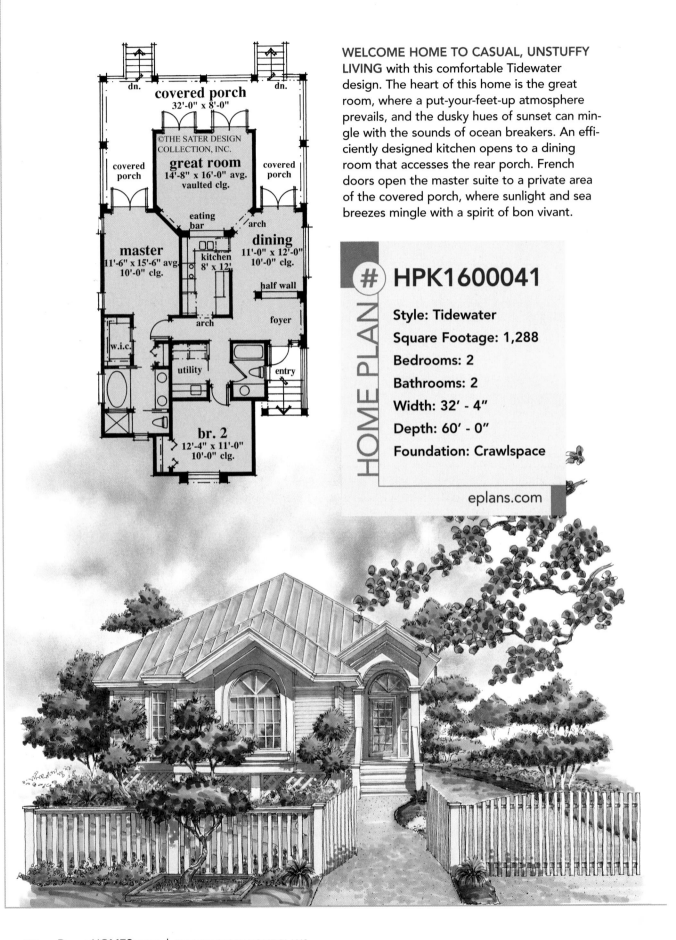

covered porch
32'-0" x 8'-0"

dn.

dn.

©THE SATER DESIGN COLLECTION, INC.

great room
14'-8" x 16'-0" avg.
vaulted clg.

covered porch

covered porch

eating bar

arch

master
11'-6" x 15'-6" avg.
10'-0" clg.

kitchen
8' x 12'

dining
11'-0" x 12'-0"
10'-0" clg.

half wall

w.i.c.

foyer

arch

utility

entry

br. 2
12'-4" x 11'-0"
10'-0" clg.

WELCOME HOME TO CASUAL, UNSTUFFY LIVING with this comfortable Tidewater design. The heart of this home is the great room, where a put-your-feet-up atmosphere prevails, and the dusky hues of sunset can mingle with the sounds of ocean breakers. An efficiently designed kitchen opens to a dining room that accesses the rear porch. French doors open the master suite to a private area of the covered porch, where sunlight and sea breezes mingle with a spirit of bon vivant.

HOME PLAN

HPK1600041

Style: Tidewater

Square Footage: 1,288

Bedrooms: 2

Bathrooms: 2

Width: 32' - 4"

Depth: 60' - 0"

Foundation: Crawlspace

eplans.com

HERE IS A RUSTIC COTTAGE THAT PROVIDES PLENTY OF AMENITIES. An open interior takes full advantage of outdoor views and allows flexible space. The family room boasts a fireplace and vistas that extend to the rear property. The dining room features a double window and French-door access to the sundeck. Wrapping counters in the kitchen provide plenty of space for food preparation. The master suite provides a compartmented bath, front-property views, and two wardrobes. The secondary bedrooms share a hall with linen storage.

HPK1600042

Style: Traditional

Square Footage: 1,208

Bedrooms: 3

Bathrooms: 2

Width: 48' - 0"

Depth: 29' - 0"

Foundation: Unfinished Basement

eplans.com

HOMES UNDER 1,500 SQUARE FEET

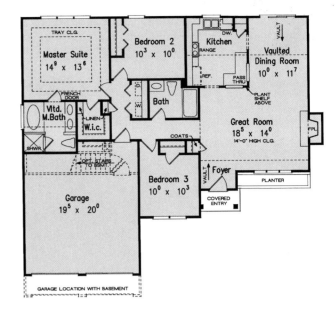

HOME PLAN

HPK1600043

Style: Traditional

Square Footage: 1,287

Bedrooms: 3

Bathrooms: 2

Width: 51' - 4"

Depth: 43' - 0"

Foundation: Unfinished Walkout Basement

eplans.com

SIMPLICITY IS BEST—ESPECIALLY when it comes to designing a quality home that won't break your budget. Stylish and efficient, this floor plan is sure to meet the needs of your family. The vaulted foyer reveals a great room, accented by a 14-foot ceiling, warming fireplace, and picturesque planter window. Pass-throughs in the L-shaped kitchen assist in serving the vaulted dining area. A short hall leads to two bedrooms that share a full bath, and a master suite that enjoys a walk-in closet with dual linens and a vaulted spa bath.

THIS BRICK COTTAGE WOULD FIT into any neighborhood and is a darling addition to a narrow space. A coat closet is conveniently located near the front entrance. The living room is creatively set apart from the dining room by a set of short stairs. The open kitchen features a breakfast bar and is within steps of the dining room. A sun room enjoys the natural light pouring through a wall of windows. Two bedrooms share a full hall bath.

HPK1600044

Style: Contemporary

Square Footage: 1,145

Bedrooms: 2

Bathrooms: 1

Width: 36' - 0"

Depth: 43' - 0"

Foundation: Unfinished Basement

HOME PLAN

eplans.com

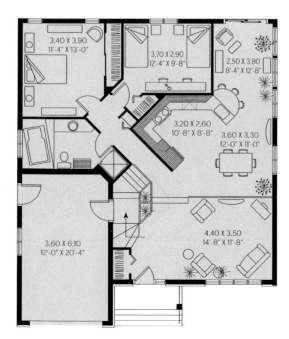

3,40 X 3,90
11'-4" X 13'-0"

3,70 X 2,90
12'-4" X 9'-8"

2,50 X 3,80
8'-4" X 12'-8"

3,20 X 2,60
10'-8" X 8'-8"

3,60 X 3,30
12'-0" X 11'-0"

3,60 X 6,10
12'-0" X 20'-4"

4,40 X 3,50
14'-8" X 11'-8"

HOMES UNDER 1,500 SQUARE FEET

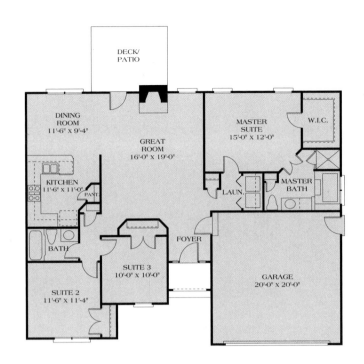

DECK/
PATIO

DINING
ROOM
11'-6" x 9'-4"

GREAT
ROOM
16'-0" x 19'-0"

MASTER
SUITE
15'-0" x 12'-0"

W.I.C.

KITCHEN
11'-6" x 11'-0"

PANT

LAUN.

MASTER
BATH

BATH

FOYER

SUITE 3
10'-0" x 10'-0"

GARAGE
20'-0" x 20'-0"

SUITE 2
11'-6" x 11'-4"

HPK1600045

HOME PLAN

Style: Colonial

Square Footage: 1,383

Bedrooms: 3

Bathrooms: 2

Width: 50' - 0"

Depth: 49' - 0"

Foundation: Crawlspace,
Slab, Crawlspace

eplans.com

SHUTTERED WINDOWS, AN ARCHED PORTICO, and elegant, wooden entrance greet visitors to this abode. You can enter the foyer via the garage or stoop in this home. From this vantage, the great room and dining room create the appearance of one large room. A laundry room and master suite are on the right-hand side, with a huge walk-in closet located in the bedroom. To the left of the great room lie the kitchen with walk-in pantry, dining room, and deck access. Two family bedrooms are located at the other end, sharing a bath, and separated from the kitchen.

QUAINT COTTAGE STYLE GRACES THE EXTERIOR of this lovely home. The three bedrooms are made up of two familiy suites, which share a hall bath, and a master bedroom on the opposite side of the home. The master suite includes a private bath with two linen closets, a garden tub, and a walk-in closet. A family room with a fireplace is open to a dining area, which overlooks the rear patio deck. The kitchen accesses a laundry room, which conveniently connects to the garage.

HOME PLAN

(#) HPK1600046

Style: Transitional

Square Footage: 1,395

Bedrooms: 3

Bathrooms: 2

Width: 44' - 11"

Depth: 50' - 1"

Foundation: Slab

eplans.com

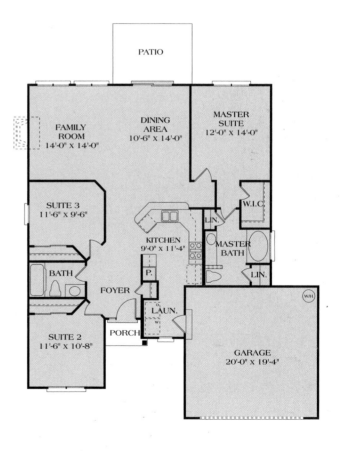

PATIO

FAMILY ROOM 14'-0" x 14'-0"

DINING AREA 10'-6" x 14'-0"

MASTER SUITE 12'-0" x 14'-0"

SUITE 3 11'-6" x 9'-6"

W.I.C

LIN.

KITCHEN 9'-0" x 11'-4"

MASTER BATH

LIN.

BATH

FOYER

P.

LAUN.

SUITE 2 11'-6" x 10'-8"

PORCH

GARAGE 20'-0" x 19'-4"

W/H

HOMES UNDER 1,500 SQUARE FEET

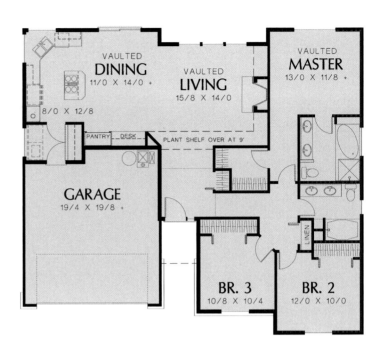

HOME PLAN

⊕ HPK1600047

Style: Country Cottage

Square Footage: 1,467

Bedrooms: 3

Bathrooms: 2

Width: 49' - 0"

Depth: 43' - 0"

Foundation: Crawlspace

eplans.com

THIS CHARMING TRADITIONAL DESIGN BOASTS A COZY, compact floor plan. Vaulted ceilings add spaciousness to the dining area, living room, and master bedroom. The kitchen is open to the dining room and includes an island cooktop and corner sink. A service entry leads to the two-car garage and holds the laundry alcove and a storage closet. The master suite is as gracious as those found in much larger homes, with a walk-in closet and a bath with a spa tub, separate shower, and double sinks.

© 2000 Donald A. Gardner, Inc.

HOME PLAN

(#) HPK1600048

Style: Country

Square Footage: 1,399

Bonus Space: 296 sq. ft.

Bedrooms: 3

Bathrooms: 2

Width: 58' - 0"

Depth: 44' - 4"

eplans.com

OPEN GABLES, A COVERED PORCH, and shuttered windows bring out the country flavor of this three-bedroom home. Inside, the great room enjoys a cathedral ceiling and a fireplace. Decorative columns set off the formal dining room, which is only steps away from the well-outfitted kitchen. Here, a window sink, a pantry, and a cooktop island overlooking the great room make an ideal food-preparation environment. Two family bedrooms located to the right of the plan share a full bath. The secluded master suite is highlighted by dual vanities, a compartmented shower and toilet, separate tub, walk-in closet, and cathedral ceiling.

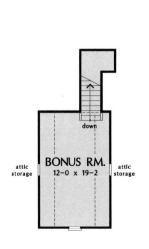

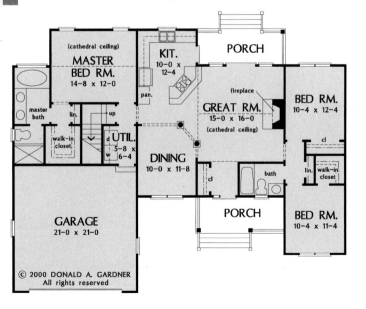

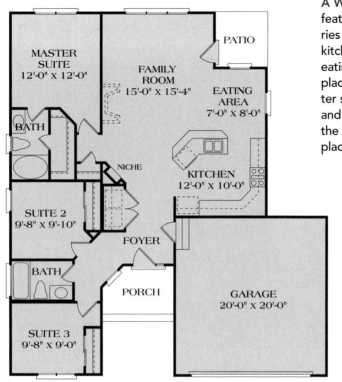

MASTER SUITE
12'-0" x 12'-0"

FAMILY ROOM
15'-0" x 15'-4"

PATIO

EATING AREA
7'-0" x 8'-0"

BATH

NICHE

KITCHEN
12'-0" x 10'-0"

SUITE 2
9'-8" x 9'-10"

FOYER

BATH

PORCH

GARAGE
20'-0" x 20'-0"

SUITE 3
9'-8" x 9'-0"

A WELCOMING PORCH LEADS TO AN ENTRY that features a sidelight and transom. Inside, the foyer carries guests past a utility closet and niche, to the island kitchen with a snack bar. The kitchen opens to the eating area and the family room (with an optional fireplace) accessible to the rear patio. The secluded master suite provides privacy and features a master bath and walk-in closet. Suites 2 and 3 are separated from the living area and share a full hall bath. The well-placed garage entrance opens to the foyer.

HOME PLAN

HPK1600049

Style: Traditional
Square Footage: 1,204
Bedrooms: 3
Bathrooms: 2
Width: 43' - 1"
Depth: 47' - 1"
Foundation: Slab

eplans.com

HOME PLAN

(#) HPK1600050

Style: Bungalow

Square Footage: 1,392

Bedrooms: 3

Bathrooms: 2

Width: 44' - 0"

Depth: 52' - 6"

Foundation: Unfinished Basement, Crawlspace

eplans.com

TRADITIONAL CORNER COLUMNS ADD PRESTIGE to this three-bedroom ranch home. The vaulted living room features a gas fireplace and a built-in media center. An open kitchen with a work island adjoins the dining room, which contains a large bay window and double French doors leading to the rear deck. An abundance of natural light from the skylights in the main hallways adds dramatic effects. The master suite is appointed with His and Hers wall closets and a private bath. Family bedrooms share a full hall bath. The laundry room has space for a full-size washer and dryer with cabinets overhead. The crawlspace option allows for a convenient homework space between the dining room and living room.

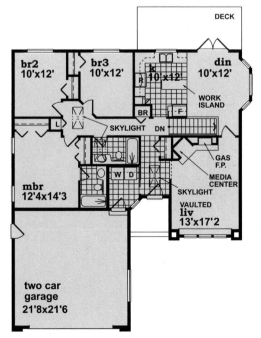

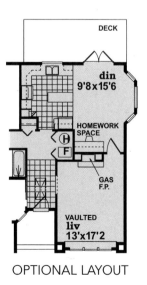

OPTIONAL LAYOUT

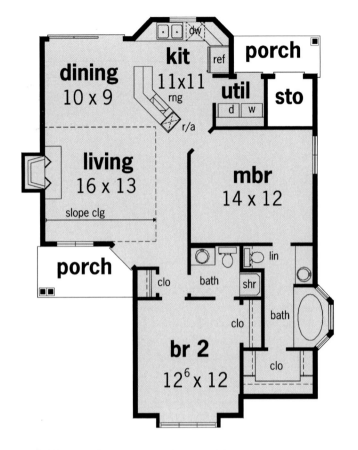

dining
10 x 9

kit
11x11

ref

porch

rng

util

d w

sto

living
16 x 13

r/a

mbr
14 x 12

slope clg

porch

clo

bath

lin

shr

clo

bath

br 2
12⁶ x 12

clo

THIS SNUG HOME USES SPACE EFFICIENTLY, with no wasted square footage. Brightened by a clerestory window, the living room features a sloped ceiling and a warming fireplace. A spacious master suite enjoys a walk-in closet and a lavish bath with a garden tub set in a bay. The secondary bedroom has access to the hall bath. Wood trim and eye-catching windows make this home charming as well as practical.

HPK1600051

HOME PLAN

Style: Country Cottage
Square Footage: 984
Bedrooms: 2
Bathrooms: 2
Width: 33' - 9"
Depth: 43' - 0"
Foundation: Crawlspace, Slab, Unfinished Basement

eplans.com

THIS FACADE IS ACCENTED BY WOOD TRIM, hipped rooflines, and muntin windows. A unique angled doorway draws visitors into the entry, where they are greeted with a spacious living room. This room features an 11-foot box ceiling, a bar with glass shelves and access to a covered back porch. The kitchen offers a pantry, built-in shelves, and a snack bar. The master suite includes a large sitting area, walk-in closet, and private bath. An additional bedroom provides a walk-in closet and an adjacent bath.

HOME PLAN

HPK1600052

Style: Country Cottage

Square Footage: 1,150

Bedrooms: 2

Bathrooms: 2

Width: 38' - 0"

Depth: 52' - 0"

Foundation: Slab, Crawlspace

eplans.com

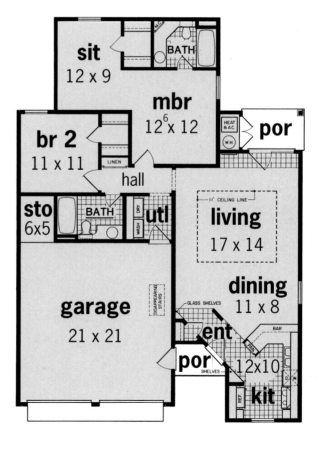

sit 12 x 9

BATH

mbr 12⁶ x 12

por

br 2 11 x 11

LINEN

hall

HEAT & A.C.
W.H.

living 17 x 14
11' CEILING LINE

sto 6x5

BATH

DRY

utl

WASH

garage 21 x 21

DISAPPEARING STAIRS

GLASS SHELVES

dining 11 x 8

ent

BAR

por

SHELVES

kit 12x10

REF.

HOMES UNDER 1,500 SQUARE FEET

A FRENCH FACADE ACCENTUATES THE COZY APPEAL
of this home with corner quoins, shuttered windows, transoms, and a stucco finish. The foyer introduces the spacious and open living room, which flows into the dining room and kitchen. A fireplace warms this area. The U-shaped kitchen features a window sink and a pantry. The kitchen is also within a few steps of the dining area. Two family bedrooms to the left of the plan share a full hall bath. The master bedroom sports a bright sitting bay, a walk-in closet with built-ins, and a roomy bath.

HPK1600053

Plan: HPK1600053

Style: Traditional

Square Footage: 1,442

Bedrooms: 3

Bathrooms: 2

Width: 54' - 0"

Depth: 50' - 0"

Foundation: Crawlspace, Slab

eplans.com

HPK1600054

HOME PLAN

Style: Contemporary

Square Footage: 1,426

Bedrooms: 3

Bathrooms: 2

Width: 42' - 0"

Depth: 56' - 0"

Foundation: Unfinished Basement

eplans.com

THIS CHARMING CONTEMPORARY FEATURES A STUCCO FACADE exterior with columned front stoop, and many pleasant amenities inside. You'll discover an intimate floor plan that doesn't sacrifice modernity or convenience. The kitchen, directly off the foyer, features a snappy double-door entry. The sunny living room is warmed by a fireplace in winter and offers sliding glass doors to the patio. A handy laundry unit is back toward the kitchen. Two bedrooms with shared bath nestle behind the living room. The master suite adjoins the corner bedroom, and offers a large closet and twin vanities in the bath. Immediately to the left of the entrance hall is the garage, also accessible from outside. All in all, a sweet little charmer!

HOME PLAN

HPK1600055

Style: Floridian

Square Footage: 1,487

Bedrooms: 3

Bathrooms: 2

Width: 58' - 0"

Depth: 58' - 0"

Foundation: Slab

eplans.com

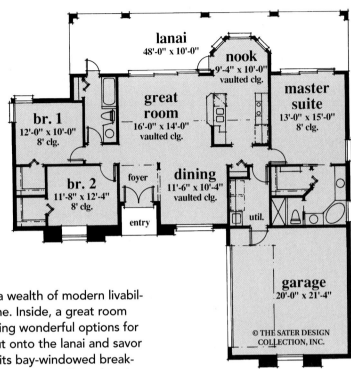

STUCCO STYLING, ELEGANT ARCHES, and a wealth of modern livability is presented in this compact one-story home. Inside, a great room with a vaulted ceiling opens to the lanai, offering wonderful options for either formal or informal entertaining. Step out onto the lanai and savor the outdoors from the delightful kitchen with its bay-windowed breakfast nook. Two secondary bedrooms (each with its own walk-in closet) share a full bath. Finally, enjoy the lanai from the calming master suite, which includes a pampering bath with a corner tub, separate shower, and large walk-in closet.

HPK1600056

Style: Country Cottage

Square Footage: 1,429

Bedrooms: 3

Bathrooms: 2

Width: 49' - 0"

Depth: 53' - 0"

Foundation: Slab, Unfinished Walkout Basement, Crawlspace

eplans.com

HOME PLAN

THIS HOME'S GRACIOUS EXTERIOR is indicative of the elegant, yet extremely livable floor plan inside. Volume ceilings that crown the family living areas combine with an open floor plan to give the modest square footage a more spacious feel. The formal dining room is set off from the foyer and vaulted family room with stately columns. The spacious family room has a corner fireplace, rear-yard door, and serving bar from the open galley kitchen. A bay-windowed breakfast nook flanks the kitchen on one end, and a laundry center and wet bar/serving pantry leads to the dining room on the other. The split-bedroom plan allows the amenity-rich master suite maximum privacy. A pocket door off the family room leads to the hall housing the two family bedrooms and a full bath.

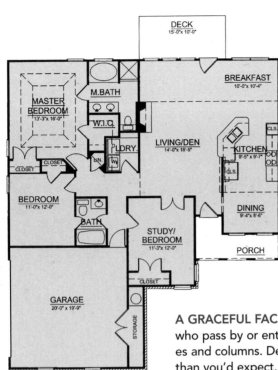

HPK1600057

Style: Colonial

Square Footage: 1,464

Bedrooms: 3

Bathrooms: 2

Width: 46' - 4"

Depth: 51' - 0"

Foundation: Slab, Unfinished Basement

eplans.com

A GRACEFUL FACE TO THIS TRADITIONAL HOME WILL WELCOME ALL who pass by or enter its doors. Particularly inviting are the front-porch arches and columns. Despite its modest square footage, the layout offers more than you'd expect. A spacious living room or den and dining area adjoin the kitchen. The row of windows along the back guarantee that the breakfast area will get plenty of sunlight, and there's lots of space for plants. Three bedrooms—one could be a study—and two full baths and a half-bath are also found in this one-story plan. To top it off there's also a laundry and a two-car garage with storage space.

IF YOU'RE LOOKING FOR A HOME WITH OPTIONS, you've found it! For a charming country facade, choose horizontal siding. Or do you prefer the stately warmth of brick? Either way, you will have a well-planned home with your personal touch. Inside, the foyer can serve as a mudroom, with a coat closet and defining railing. The living room offers expansive views and flows into the dining room. A U-shaped kitchen provides space for a breakfast nook. Identical bedrooms, or make one an office, share a full bath. The master bedroom enjoys a private bath.

HOME PLAN

**HPK1600058**

Style: Bungalow
Square Footage: 1,484
Bedrooms: 3
Bathrooms: 2
Width: 53' - 6"
Depth: 28' - 0"
Foundation: Crawlspace, Unfinished Basement

eplans.com

HOMES UNDER 1,500 SQUARE FEET

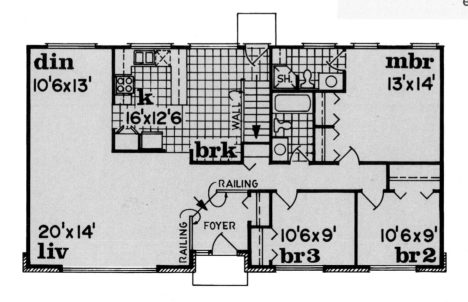

din
10'6x13'

k
16'x12'6

brk

WALL

SH.

mbr
13'x14'

RAILING

20'x14'
liv

RAILING

FOYER

10'6x9'
br3

10'6x9'
br2

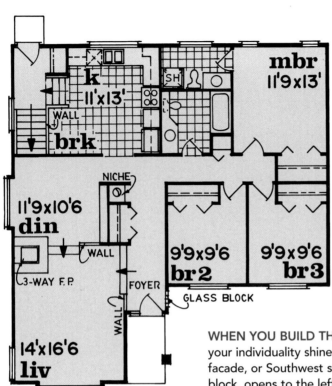

 # HOME PLAN **HPK1600059**

Style: Bungalow

Square Footage: 1,434

Bedrooms: 3

Bathrooms: 2

Width: 41' - 4"

Depth: 42' - 4"

Foundation: Unfinished Basement, Crawlspace

eplans.com

WHEN YOU BUILD THIS THREE-BEDROOM COTTAGE, you can let your individuality shine through; choose a brick-and-siding country facade, or Southwest stucco. Inside, the foyer, accented with glass block, opens to the left to the bright living room with a three-way fireplace that shares its warmth with the dining room. The efficient kitchen allows for a breakfast area, perfect for casual meals. Twin bedrooms share a full bath at the front of the home. The master bedroom includes a shower bath.

FROM THE HIGH CEILING IN THE ENTRY AND GREAT ROOM to the snack bar in the open kitchen, there's a great deal to enjoy with this home. The great room features a fireplace, transoms, and great views to the rear property. This area provides plenty of space for entertaining guests or enjoying casual family time. The kitchen flows into the breakfast room and shares a snack bar. Two family bedrooms are to the left of the entry, and share a full bath. One of the bedrooms could serve as a den with French doors off the entry. The opulent master suite features a double-sink vanity, walk-in closet, box-bay window, and tiered ceiling.

HOME PLAN

 # HPK1600060

Style: Traditional

Square Footage: 1,347

Bedrooms: 3

Bathrooms: 2

Width: 42' - 0"

Depth: 54' - 0"

eplans.com

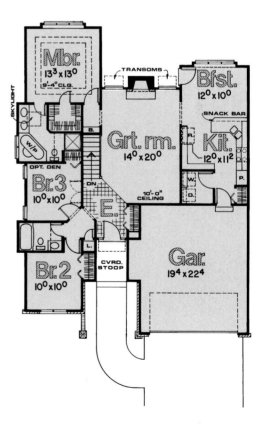

THIS TRADITIONAL BRICK HOME flaunts a touch of European flavor with its corner quoins. It also presents great curb appeal from the wide muntin window to the sidelight and transom in the entry. The spacious living room includes a warming fireplace. The dining room and U-shaped kitchen are connected by the snack bar and easily access a covered patio. Two family bedrooms reside along the extended hallway. At the end of the hall is the master bedroom, which presents a deluxe private bath and a walk-in closet. The utility room acts as a passage to the two-car garage.

HOME PLAN

(#) HPK1600061

Style: Traditional

Square Footage: 1,405

Bedrooms: 3

Bathrooms: 2

Width: 40' - 0"

Depth: 60' - 8"

Foundation: Slab

eplans.com

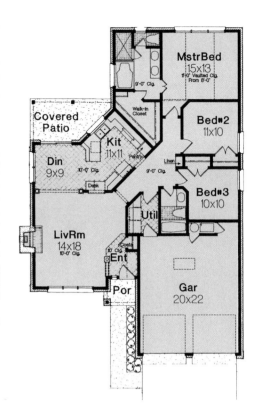

ALTERNATE EXTERIOR

ALTERNATE EXTERIOR

ALTERNATE EXTERIORS

THIS UNIQUE LITTLE HOUSE HAS MANY ATTRAC-
TIVE FEATURES. The living room has a cathedral ceiling with a wood burning fireplace. The kitchen/dinette
has a nice island and adjoining utility room. The master
bedroom also features a cathedral ceiling, and is
enhanced by a spacious walk-in closet and a private
bath with a compartmented shower and tub. Two additional bedrooms and a bath make up the opposite side
of the home. This plan has three different elevations to
choose from.

HPK1600062

HOME PLAN

Style: Traditional

Square Footage: 1,317

Bedrooms: 3

Bathrooms: 2

Width: 45' - 0"

Depth: 52' - 4"

Foundation: Slab

eplans.com

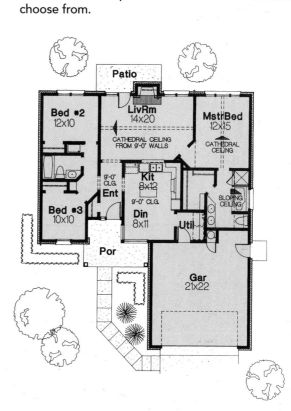

GABLED ROOFLINES, SHUTTERS, AND SIDING—ALL elements of a fine facade. The foyer opens directly to the vaulted great room, where a fireplace waits to warm cool winter evenings. Nearby, the efficient kitchen easily accesses the dining room. Two secondary bedrooms share a full hall bath. The deluxe master suite offers a vaulted bath and a spacious walk-in closet. A laundry room is located in between the master suite and the two-car garage.

HOME PLAN

HPK1600063

Style: Country Cottage

Square Footage: 1,232

Bedrooms: 3

Bathrooms: 2

Width: 46' - 0"

Depth: 44' - 4"

Foundation: Unfinished Walkout Basement, Crawlspace, Slab

eplans.com

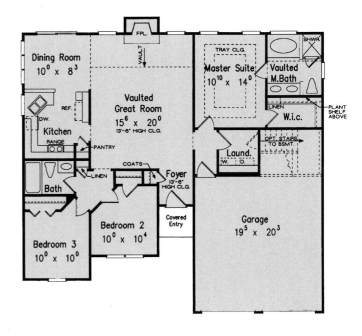

LOOKING FOR THE PERFECT STARTER HOME? How about a great retreat? For anyone who wants a budget-friendly plan, this brick-and-siding design is a dream come true. The foyer is adorned by columns and a half-wall that gracefully separate it from the living room. The kitchen flows easily from here, with a step-saving layout and sliding glass doors that let the light in. Four bedrooms line the left side of the house and share a marvelous spa bath.

HOME PLAN

HPK1600064

Style: Contemporary

Square Footage: 1,433

Bedrooms: 4

Bathrooms: 1

Width: 30' - 0"

Depth: 50' - 0"

Foundation: Unfinished Basement

eplans.com

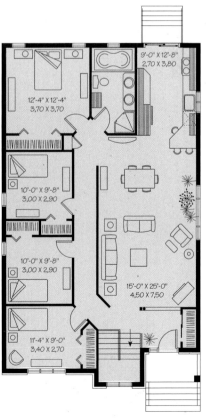

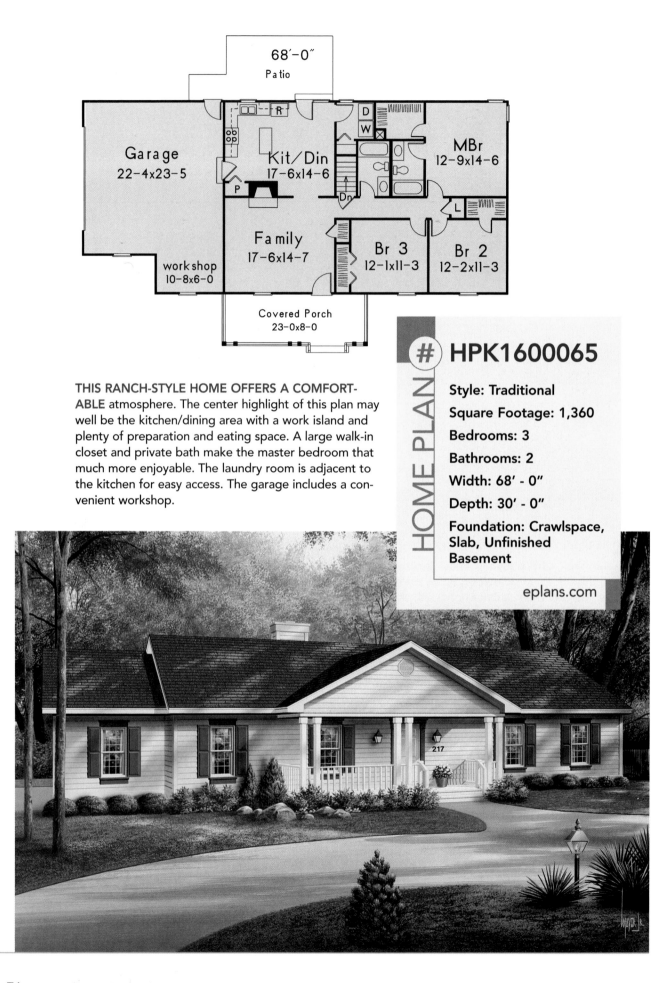

68'-0"
Patio

Garage
22-4x23-5

Kit/Din
17-6x14-6

MBr
12-9x14-6

Family
17-6x14-7

Br 3
12-1x11-3

Br 2
12-2x11-3

workshop
10-8x6-0

Covered Porch
23-0x8-0

THIS RANCH-STYLE HOME OFFERS A COMFORT-
ABLE atmosphere. The center highlight of this plan may
well be the kitchen/dining area with a work island and
plenty of preparation and eating space. A large walk-in
closet and private bath make the master bedroom that
much more enjoyable. The laundry room is adjacent to
the kitchen for easy access. The garage includes a convenient workshop.

HPK1600065

HOME PLAN

Style: Traditional

Square Footage: 1,360

Bedrooms: 3

Bathrooms: 2

Width: 68' - 0"

Depth: 30' - 0"

Foundation: Crawlspace,
Slab, Unfinished
Basement

eplans.com

ALTERNATE EXTERIORS

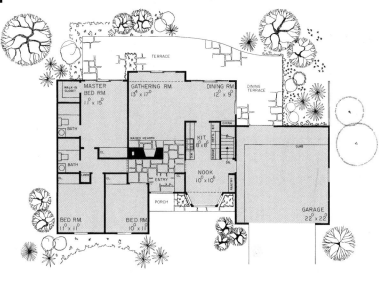

THIS DESIGN OFFERS YOU A CHOICE of three distinctively different exteriors. Blueprints show details for all three options. A study of the floor plan reveals a fine measure of livability. In less than 1,400 square feet, you'll find amenities often found in much larger homes. In addition to the two eating areas and the open planning of the gathering room, the indoor/outdoor relationships are of great interest. The basement may be developed at a later date for recreational activities.

(#) HPK1600066

HOME PLAN

Style: Contemporary

Square Footage: 1,366

Bedrooms: 3

Bathrooms: 2

Width: 65' - 0"

Depth: 37' - 4"

Foundation: Unfinished Basement

eplans.com

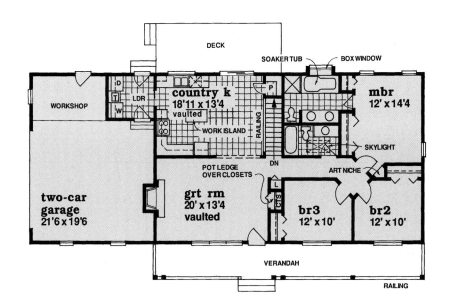

OPTIONAL LAYOUT

AN EYEBROW DORMER AND A LARGE VERANDA give guests a warm country greeting outside; inside, vaulted ceilings lend a sense of spaciousness to this three-bedroom home. A bright country kitchen boasts an abundance of counter space and cupboards. The front entry is sheltered by a broad veranda. Built-in amenities adorn the interior, including a pot ledge over the entry coat closet, an art niche, a skylight, and a walk-in pantry and island workstation in the kitchen. A box-bay window and a spa-style tub highlight the master suite. The two-car garage provides a workshop area.

HOME PLAN

HPK1600067

Style: Ranch

Square Footage: 1,408

Bedrooms: 3

Bathrooms: 2

Width: 70' - 0"

Depth: 34' - 0"

Foundation: Unfinished Basement, Crawlspace

eplans.com

HPK1600068

HOME PLAN

Style: Ranch

Square Footage: 1,298

Bedrooms: 3

Bathrooms: 2

Width: 70' - 0"

Depth: 36' - 0"

Foundation: Crawlspace, Unfinished Basement

eplans.com

A FRONT VERANDA, CEDAR LATTICE, AND SOLID STONE chimney enhance the appeal of this one-story country-style home. The open plan begins with the great room, which includes a fireplace and a plant ledge over the wall separating the living space from the country kitchen. The U-shaped kitchen provides an island work counter and sliding glass doors to the rear deck and a screened porch. The master suite also has a wall closet and a private bath with window seat.

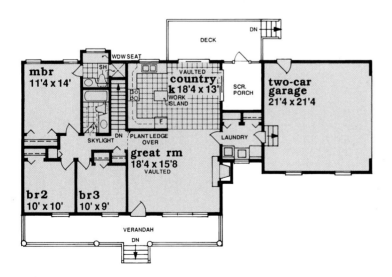

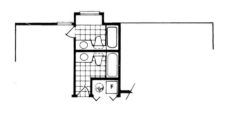

OPTIONAL LAYOUT

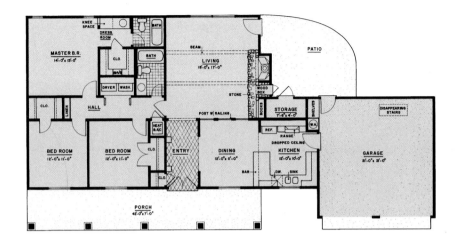

THIS CHARMING RANCH-STYLE HOME HAS
MUCH to offer in livability. The entry leads to the
vaulted living room where the stone fireplace is
easy to enjoy and provides a warm welcome on
chilly evenings. There's an ingenious pass-through
wood box so owners can replenish the fuel supply
without venturing outside. The formal dining room
adjoins the efficient kitchen with its convenient
garage access. The pampering master suite boasts
a dressing room and a full bath; two additional family bedrooms share a second full bath.

HOME PLAN # HPK1600069

Style: Farmhouse

Square Footage: 1,395

Bedrooms: 3

Bathrooms: 2

Width: 73' - 0"

Depth: 37' - 0"

Foundation: Crawlspace,
Slab, Unfinished
Basement

eplans.com

© 1987 Donald A. Gardner, Architects, Inc.

(#) **HPK1600070**

Style: Key West

Square Footage: 1,426

Bedrooms: 3

Bathrooms: 2 ½

Width: 67' - 6"

Depth: 36' - 8"

eplans.com

RUSTIC CHARM ABOUNDS IN THIS AMENITY-FILLED, three-bedroom plan. From the central living area with its cathedral ceiling and fireplace to the sumptuous master suite, this plan has it all. Be sure to notice the large walk-in closet in the master bedroom, the pampering whirlpool tub, and the separate toilet compartment. Two other bedrooms have a connecting bath with a vanity for each. The house wraps around a screened porch with skylights—a grand place for eating and entertaining. The spacious rear deck has plenty of room for a hot tub.

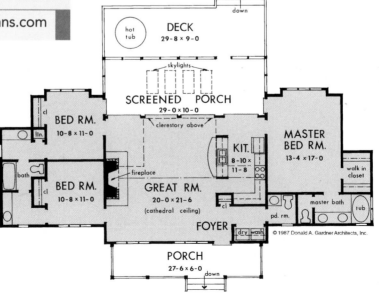

© 1987 Donald A. Gardner Architects, Inc.

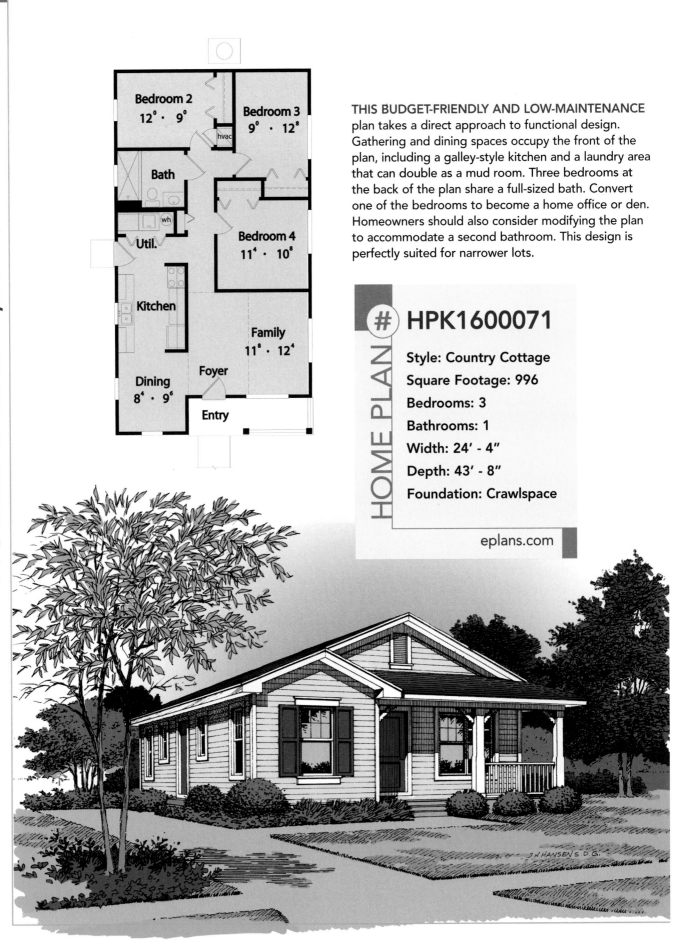

Bedroom 2
12⁰ · 9⁰

Bedroom 3
9⁰ · 12⁸

hvac

Bath

wh

Util.

Kitchen

Bedroom 4
11⁴ · 10⁸

Family
11⁸ · 12⁴

Dining
8⁴ · 9⁶

Foyer

Entry

THIS BUDGET-FRIENDLY AND LOW-MAINTENANCE plan takes a direct approach to functional design. Gathering and dining spaces occupy the front of the plan, including a galley-style kitchen and a laundry area that can double as a mud room. Three bedrooms at the back of the plan share a full-sized bath. Convert one of the bedrooms to become a home office or den. Homeowners should also consider modifying the plan to accommodate a second bathroom. This design is perfectly suited for narrower lots.

HOME PLAN

HPK1600071

Style: Country Cottage

Square Footage: 996

Bedrooms: 3

Bathrooms: 1

Width: 24' - 4"

Depth: 43' - 8"

Foundation: Crawlspace

eplans.com

MULTIPANE WINDOWS WITH QUAINT SHUTTERS add a touch of charm to this cozy country plan that is just right for a small family or empty-nesters. A covered front porch shelters visitors from inclement weather. An ample living room/dining room area leads the way to a rear kitchen overlooking a unique flagstone terrace—great for outdoor grilling or summertime entertainment. Two full baths serve three bedrooms—one a master suite. The kitchen includes an informal eating space.

HOME PLAN

HPK1600072

Style: Farmhouse

Square Footage: 1,080

Bedrooms: 3

Bathrooms: 2

Width: 36' - 0"

Depth: 34' - 0"

Foundation: Unfinished Basement

eplans.com

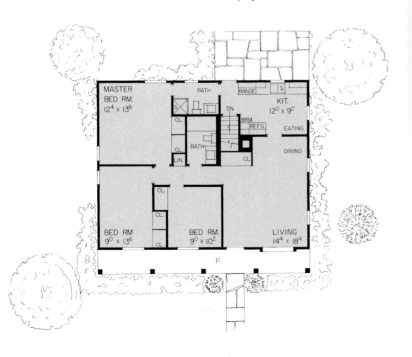

HPK1600073

Style: NW Contemporary

Square Footage: 1,292

Bedrooms: 3

Bathrooms: 2

Width: 52' - 0"

Depth: 34' - 0"

Foundation: Crawlspace

eplans.com

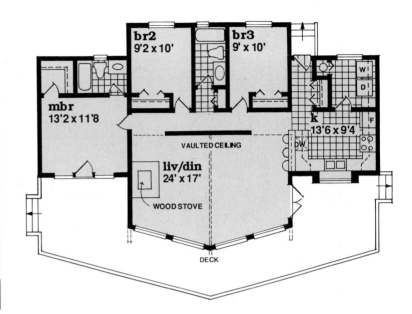

THE CASUAL LIVING SPACE OF THIS COZY HOME offers room to kick off your shoes or put on a bash, and is highlighted by a woodstove. The master suite nestles to the left of the living area and boasts a walk-in closet. Two secondary bedrooms allow space for guests and family members. The kitchen provides a snack counter.

A QUIET, AESTHETICALLY PLEASANT, AND COMFORTABLE one-story country home answers the requirements of modest-income families. The entrance to the house is sheltered by the front porch, which leads to the hearth-warmed living room. The master suite is arranged with a large dressing area that has a walk-in closet plus two linear closets and space for a vanity. The main part of the bedroom contains a media center. The adjoining, fully equipped kitchen includes the dinette, which can comfortably seat six people and leads to the rear terrace through six-foot sliding glass doors.

HOME PLAN #

HPK1600074

Style: Country Cottage

Square Footage: 1,366

Bedrooms: 3

Bathrooms: 2

Width: 71' - 4"

Depth: 35' - 10"

Foundation: Slab, Unfinished Basement, Crawlspace

eplans.com

HOMES UNDER 1,500 SQUARE FEET

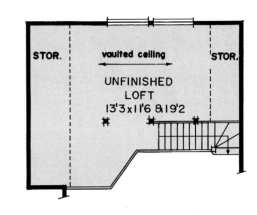

UNFINISHED
LOFT
13'3 x 11'6 & 19'2

HOME PLAN

(#) HPK1600075

Style: Vacation

Square Footage: 680

Bonus Space: 419 sq. ft.

Bedrooms: 1

Bathrooms: 1

Width: 26' - 6"

Depth: 28' - 0"

Foundation: Crawlspace

eplans.com

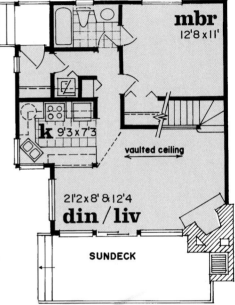

mbr
12'8 x 11'

k 9'3 x 7'3

vaulted ceiling

21'2 x 8' & 12'4
din / liv

SUNDECK

FULL WINDOW WALLS PROVIDE THE LIVING AND DINING rooms of this rustic vacation home with natural light. A full sun-deck with a built-in barbecue sits just outside the living area and is entered through sliding glass doors. The entire living space has a vaulted ceiling to gain spaciousness and to allow for the full-height windows. The efficient U-shaped kitchen has a pass-through counter to the dining area and a corner sink with windows overhead. A master bedroom is on the first floor and has the use of a full bath. A loft on the second floor overlooks the living room. It provides an additional 419 square feet not included in the total. Use it for an additional bedroom or as a studio.

HPK1600076

Style: Vacation

Square Footage: 1,404

Bonus Space: 256 sq. ft.

Bedrooms: 2

Bathrooms: 2

Width: 54' - 7"

Depth: 46' - 6"

Foundation: Crawlspace

HOME PLAN

eplans.com

THIS RUSTIC CRAFTSMAN-STYLE COTTAGE provides an open interior with good flow to the outdoors. The front covered porch invites casual gatherings; inside, the dining area is set for both everyday and formal occasions. Meal preparations are a breeze with a cooktop/snack-bar island in the kitchen. A centered fireplace in the great room shares its warmth with the dining room. A rear hall leads to the master bedroom and a secondary bedroom; upstairs, a loft has space for computers.

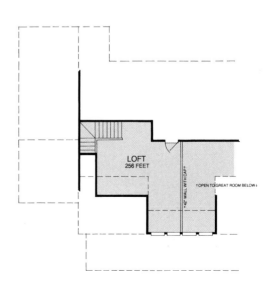

HOME PLAN

HPK1600077

Style: NW Contemporary

Square Footage: 1,495

Bedrooms: 3

Bathrooms: 2

Width: 58' - 6"

Depth: 33' - 0"

Foundation: Crawlspace

eplans.com

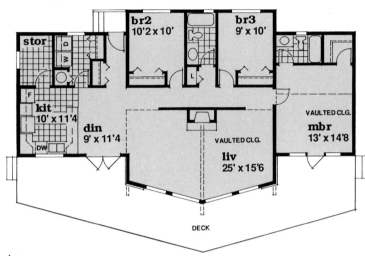

THIS THREE-BEDROOM COTTAGE has just the right rustic mix of vertical wood siding and stone accents. High vaulted ceilings are featured throughout the living room and master bedroom. The living room also has a fireplace and full-height windows overlooking the deck. The dining room has double-door access to the deck. A convenient kitchen includes a U-shaped work area with storage space.

HOME PLAN

HPK1600078

Style: NW Contemporary

Square Footage: 1,230

Bedrooms: 3

Bathrooms: 2

Width: 55' - 6"

Depth: 33' - 0"

Foundation: Crawlspace, Unfinished Basement

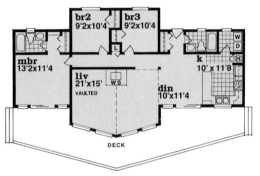

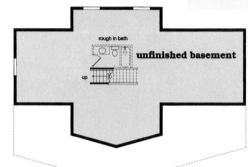

HOME PLAN

HPK1600079

Style: NW Contemporary

Square Footage: 1,405

Bedrooms: 3

Bathrooms: 2

Width: 62' - 0"

Depth: 29' - 0"

Foundation: Crawlspace, Unfinished Basement

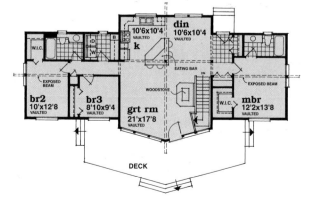

Elbow Room—Homes for the Growing Family

AN INSPIRED MIX of old wood and plain metal lets this kitchen (above) shine. Notice the space-smart touches, such as a sliding door and a movable island. Both kitchens welcome guests and make room for casual meals.

In contrast to starter homes, plans within the 1,501 to 2,000 square-foot range—sometimes called "family-sized" homes—find space toward one or two additional bedrooms to accommodate an arriving baby or home office. Formal spaces tend to gain more definition as separate rooms—such as dining rooms or foyers—but maintaining flow-through and spaciousness remain important goals. Porches and decks still provide supplemental space for larger gatherings and contribute favorably to the exterior architecture.

The concept of the master suite as a privileged and secluded part of the home arrives with the family-sized home. Look for a fully trimmed master suite that resides away from the most highly trafficked parts of the home and the other bedrooms. Ideally, the plan should comprise a large bedroom facing the rear and side of the plan, a master bath designed for two, and an ample walk-in closet. To preserve the master bath for exclusive use by the homeowners, the half-bath/powder room is often placed near the foyer.

Well-designed homes of this size will find easy access to natural light from exterior windows without having to incorporate special accommodations, such as skylights or additional dormers. Homeowners can take advantage of natural lighting situations by replacing an extra bedroom with a study or library.

Mark Samu (2)

HOME PLAN
HPK1600080

Style: Santa Fe
Square Footage: 1,883
Bedrooms: 3
Bathrooms: 2
Width: 66' - 2"
Depth: 59' - 8"

© 2002 Donald A. Gardner, Inc.

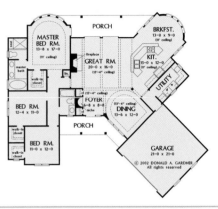

HOME PLAN
HPK1600081

Style: Santa Fe
Square Footage: 1,895
Bedrooms: 3
Bathrooms: 2
Width: 65' - 10"
Depth: 59' - 9"

© 2002 Donald A. Gardner, Inc.

HOME PLAN

HPK1600082

Style: Traditional

Square Footage: 1,746

Bedrooms: 3

Bathrooms: 2

Width: 58' - 0"

Depth: 59' - 4"

Foundation: Slab

eplans.com

WOODEN WINDOW ACCENTS BRING A RUSTIC FLAVOR to this warm Santa Fe design. Double doors open to the foyer: to the right, a vaulted dining room is enhanced by bright multipane windows. The study opens to the left through stylish French doors. Ahead, the vaulted great room ushers in natural light. An efficient kitchen easily serves the bayed breakfast nook for simple casual meals. Two family bedrooms share a full bath, creating a quiet zone for the master suite. A corner whirlpool tub, oversized walk-in closet, and sliding-glass-door access to the lanai make this retreat a true haven.

THIS CLASSIC STUCCO DESIGN provides a cool retreat in any climate. From the covered porch, enter the skylit foyer to find an arched ceiling leading to the central gathering room with its raised-hearth fireplace and terrace access. A connecting corner dining room is conveniently located near the amenity-filled kitchen. The large master suite includes terrace access and a private bath with a whirlpool tub, a separate shower, and plenty of closet space. A second bedroom and a study that can be converted to a bedroom complete this wonderful plan.

HOME PLAN

HPK1600083

Style: Santa Fe
Square Footage: 2,000
Bedrooms: 3
Bathrooms: 2 ½
Width: 75' - 0"
Depth: 55' - 0"
Foundation: Slab

eplans.com

GRACEFUL CURVES

WELCOME YOU into the courtyard of this Santa Fe home. Inside, a gallery directs traffic to the work zone on the left or the sleeping zone on the right. The wide covered rear porch is accessible from the dining room, the gathering room with fireplace, and the secluded master bedroom. The master bath features a whirlpool tub, separate shower, double vanity, and a spacious walk-in closet. Two additional bedrooms share a full bath with separate vanities. Extra storage space is provided in the two-car garage.

HOME PLAN #

HPK1600084

Style: Santa Fe
Square Footage: 1,934
Bedrooms: 3
Bathrooms: 2 ½
Width: 61' - 6"
Depth: 67' - 4"
Foundation: Slab

eplans.com

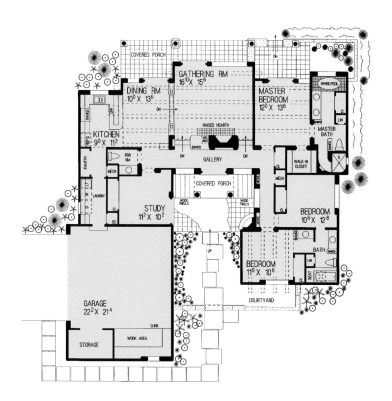

CLEAN LINES AND PLENTY OF WINDOWS
add style to this contemporary Pueblo design. A fireplace makes the expansive entry courtyard even more welcoming. Inside, another fireplace, a wet bar, and a curved wall of windows enhance the great room. The kitchen easily serves the formal dining room and the breakfast area, which opens to a covered rear veranda. A split-bedroom plan places the master suite, with its indulgent dual-vanity bath and walk-in closet, to the right of the plan; two family bedrooms sit to the left of the plan.

HOME PLAN

(#) HPK1600085

Style: SW Contemporary

Square Footage: 1,950

Bedrooms: 3

Bathrooms: 2

Width: 65' - 4"

Depth: 60' - 0"

Foundation: Slab

eplans.com

HOME PLAN

HPK1600086

Style: SW Contemporary

Square Footage: 1,899

Bedrooms: 3

Bathrooms: 2

Width: 43' - 4"

Depth: 79' - 6"

Foundation: Slab

eplans.com

LONG AND SLENDER, THIS PUEBLO-STYLE HOME is perfect for a narrow lot. A facade graced with stepped rooflines and vigas brings the Southwest to your neighborhood. The well-lit entry begins with a columned living room—enclose the space for a generous bedroom. Ahead, the wet bar and dining room are ready to serve guests in style. Continue through arches to the hearth-warmed great room and breakfast nook, both with veranda access. The secluded master suite is located to the far left, splendid with an indulgent bath and private patio.

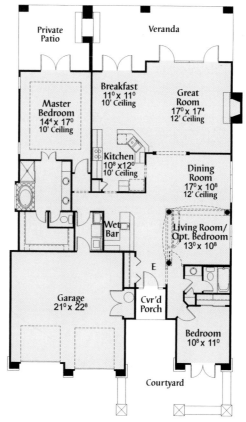

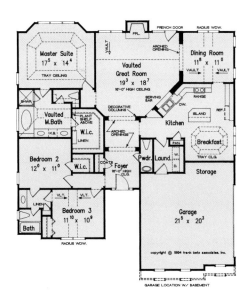

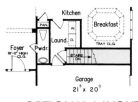

OPTIONAL LAYOUT

ARCHED OPENINGS, DECORATIVE COLUMNS, and elegant ceiling details throughout highlight this livable floor plan. The country kitchen includes a spacious work area, preparation island, serving bar to the great room, and a breakfast nook with a tray ceiling. Set to the rear for gracious entertaining, the dining room opens to the great room. Note the warming fireplace and French-door access to the backyard in the great room. The master suite is beautifully appointed with a tray ceiling, bay window, compartmented bath, and walk-in closet. Two family bedrooms, a laundry room, and a powder room complete this gracious design.

HOME PLAN

HPK1600087

Style: Country Cottage

Square Footage: 1,884

Bedrooms: 3

Bathrooms: 2 ½

Width: 50' - 0"

Depth: 55' - 4"

Foundation: Slab, Crawlspace, Unfinished Walkout Basement

eplans.com

GENTLE ARCHED LINTELS HARMONIZE with the high hipped roof to create an elevation that is both welcoming and elegant. This efficient plan minimizes hallway space in order to maximize useable living areas. A favorite feature of this home is the "elbow-bend" galley kitchen that has easy access to the dining room and breakfast room—plus a full-length serving bar open to the great room. The master suite has a cozy sitting room and a compartmented bath. Two family bedrooms share a full hall bath.

(#) HPK1600088

HOME PLAN

Style: Traditional
Square Footage: 1,575
Bedrooms: 3
Bathrooms: 2
Width: 50' - 0"
Depth: 52' - 6"
Foundation: Crawlspace, Unfinished Walkout Basement

eplans.com

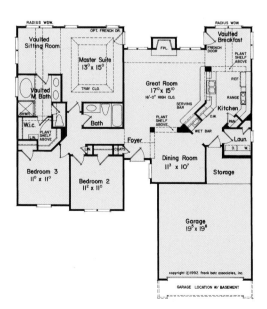

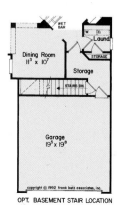

THIS NARROW-LOT PLAN HAS ALL THE APPEAL AND ROMANCE of a European cottage. The front porch welcomes you to a charming set of double doors. Two family bedrooms, a hall bath, a laundry room, and the two-car garage with storage are located at the front of the plan. The island kitchen easily serves the dining room, which accesses a private garden and the casual breakfast room. The spacious family room offers a warming fireplace, built-ins, and back-porch access. The plan is completed by the master suite, which features a private bath and walk-in closet.

HOME PLAN

HPK1600089

Style: European Cottage
Square Footage: 1,964
Bedrooms: 3
Bathrooms: 2
Width: 38' - 10"
Depth: 90' - 1"
Foundation: Slab

eplans.com

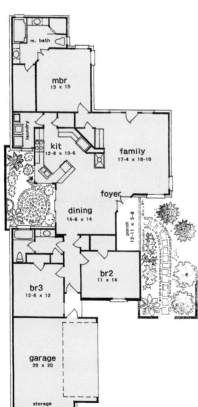

HOME PLAN

 # HPK1600090

Style: European Cottage

Square Footage: 1,823

Bedrooms: 3

Bathrooms: 2

Width: 38' - 10"

Depth: 94' - 10"

Foundation: Slab

eplans.com

THIS HOME'S LONG, NARROW FOOTPRINT is ideal for a slim lot. A beautiful facade using stucco, brick, shuttered windows, and steepled rooftops is as inviting as the floor plan. A courtyard entrance is flanked by the open dining and family spaces. Two family bedrooms are split from the master suite, which fosters privacy. The master bedroom, at the rear of the home, enjoys simple luxuries in the dual-vanity bath.

A GRAND DOUBLE BANK OF WINDOWS looking in on the formal dining room mirrors the lofty elegance of the extra-tall vaulted ceiling inside. From the foyer, an arched entrance to the great room visually frames the fireplace on the back wall. The wraparound kitchen has plenty of counter and cabinet space, along with a handy serving bar. The luxurious master suite features a front sitting room for quiet times and a large spa-style bath. Two family bedrooms share a hall bath.

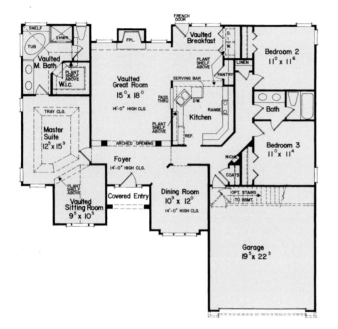

HOME PLAN

HPK1600091

Style: Country Cottage

Square Footage: 1,715

Bedrooms: 3

Bathrooms: 2

Width: 55' - 0"

Depth: 49' - 0"

Foundation: Unfinished Walkout Basement, Slab, Crawlspace

eplans.com

EUROPEAN STYLE SHINES FROM THIS HOME'S FACADE in the form of its stucco detailing, hipped rooflines, fancy windows, and elegant entryway. Inside, decorative columns and a plant shelf define the formal dining room, which works well with the vaulted family room. The efficient kitchen offers a serving bar to both the family room and the deluxe breakfast room. Located apart from the family bedrooms for privacy, the master suite is sure to please with its many amenities, including a vaulted sitting area and a private covered porch. The two secondary bedrooms share a full hall bath.

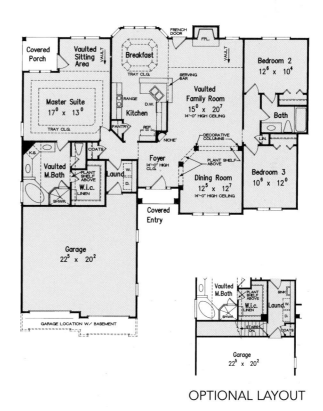

OPTIONAL LAYOUT

HOME PLAN

HPK1600092

Style: European Cottage

Square Footage: 1,779

Bedrooms: 3

Bathrooms: 2

Width: 57' - 0"

Depth: 56' - 4"

Foundation: Unfinished Walkout Basement, Crawlspace

eplans.com

THIS COMPACT ONE-STORY HAS PLENTY OF LIVING in it. The master suite features an optional sun-washed sitting area with views to the rear of the home. A vaulted great room with fireplace conveniently accesses the kitchen via a serving bar. Meals can also be taken in the cozy breakfast area. For formal occasions the dining room creates opulence with its decorative columns. Two family bedrooms flank the right of the home with a shared bath, linen storage, and easy access to laundry facilities.

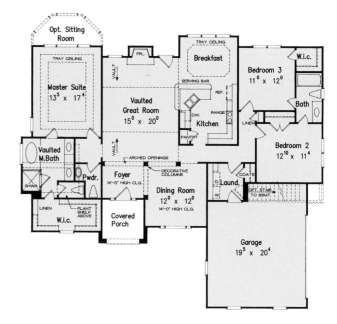

HOME PLAN
HPK1600093

Style: Country Cottage

Square Footage: 1,832

Bedrooms: 3

Bathrooms: 2 ½

Width: 59' - 6"

Depth: 52' - 6"

Foundation: Crawlspace, Slab, Unfinished Walkout Basement

eplans.com

CORNER QUOINS, FRENCH SHUTTERS, and rounded windows provide an Old World feel to this modern cottage design. A stunning brick facade hints at the exquisite beauty of the interior spaces. The great room is warmed by a fireplace and accesses the rear porch. The casual kitchen/dinette area provides pantry space. The master suite offers a private bath and enormous walk-in closet. Two family bedrooms on the opposite side of the home share a full hall bath and linen storage. A double garage and laundry room are located nearby.

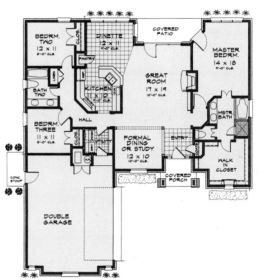

HOME PLAN

HPK1600094

Style: Traditional

Square Footage: 1,834

Bedrooms: 3

Bathrooms: 2

Width: 55' - 0"

Depth: 60' - 4"

Foundation: Slab

eplans.com

ALTERNATE EXTERIOR

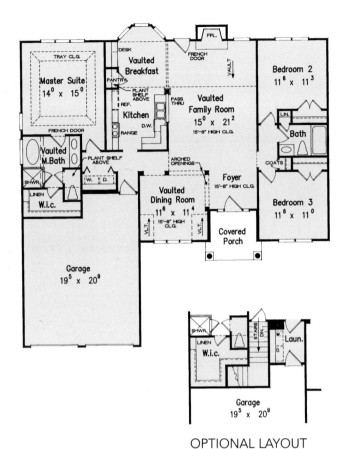

OPTIONAL LAYOUT

A LOVELY FACADE OPENS THIS ONE-STORY HOME, with gable ends and dormer windows as decorative features. The interior features vaulted family and dining rooms—a fireplace in the family room offers warmth. Defined by columns, the formal dining experience is enhanced. The kitchen attaches to a bayed breakfast nook with a vaulted ceiling. A split floor plan has the family bedrooms on the right side and the master suite on the left. The master bedroom has a tray ceiling, vaulted bath, and walk-in closet.

HPK1600095

HOME PLAN

Style: Traditional

Square Footage: 1,575

Bedrooms: 3

Bathrooms: 2

Width: 52' - 0"

Depth: 52' - 6"

Foundation: Crawlspace, Slab, Unfinished Walkout Basement

eplans.com

DECK

BEDROOM NO. 3
11'-6" X 11'-0"

BREAKFAST
11'-4" X 8'-6"

GREAT ROOM
14'-0" X 17'-6"

KITCHEN
11'-4" X 10'-0"

MASTER
BEDROOM
12'-4" X 15'-6"

BATH

FOYER
6'-6" X 5'-0"

DN

HIS

BEDROOM NO. 2
11'-0" X 12'-2"

DINING ROOM
11'-4" X 10'-6"

PWDR

MASTER
BATH

STOOP

LAUNDRY

HERS

TWO-CAR GARAGE
20'-4" X 19'-4"

HPK1600096

Style: French

Square Footage: 1,684

Bedrooms: 3

Bathrooms: 2 ½

Width: 55' - 6"

Depth: 57' - 6"

**Foundation: Finished
Walkout Basement**

HOME PLAN

eplans.com

CHARMING AND COMPACT, this home is as beautiful as it is practical. The impressive arch over the double front door is repeated with an arched window in the formal dining room. This room opens to a spacious great room with a fireplace and is near the kitchen and bayed breakfast area. Split sleeping arrangements put the master suite at the right of the plan and two family bedrooms at the left.

COUNT ON THE CENTER-HALL DESIGN AND OPEN FLOOR PLANNING of this design to meet your livability needs for years to come. The great room serves both informal and formal occasions and is close enough to the formal dining room and the less formal breakfast room to make entertaining easy. Further enhancements in the great room include a fireplace and double doors opening to the rear deck. The breakfast room boasts a bay window. The master suite features a tray ceiling and a bath with plenty of closet space, a garden whirlpool tub, and double sinks.

HPK1600097

HOME PLAN #

Style: Traditional

Square Footage: 1,733

Bedrooms: 3

Bathrooms: 2 ½

Width: 55' - 6"

Depth: 57' - 6"

Foundation: Finished Walkout Basement

eplans.com

Deck

Bedroom #3
11⁶ x 11⁰

Great Room
14⁰ x 17⁶

Breakfast
11⁴ x 8⁶

Kitchen
11⁴ x 10⁰

Master Bedroom
12⁴ x 15⁶

Bedroom #2
11⁴ x 14⁸

Dining Room
11⁴ x 10⁶

Two Car Garage
20⁴ x 19⁴

HOME PLAN

(#) HPK1600098

Style: Traditional

Square Footage: 1,733

Bedrooms: 3

Bathrooms: 2 ½

Width: 55' - 6"

Depth: 57' - 6"

Foundation: Finished Walkout Basement

eplans.com

DELIGHTFULLY DIFFERENT, THIS BRICK ONE-STORY HOME has everything for the active family. The foyer opens to a formal dining room, accented with four columns, and a great room with a fireplace and French doors to the rear deck. The efficient kitchen has an attached light-filled breakfast nook. The master bath features a tray ceiling, His and Hers walk-in closets, a double-sink vanity, and a huge garden tub. The two-car garage is accessed through the laundry room.

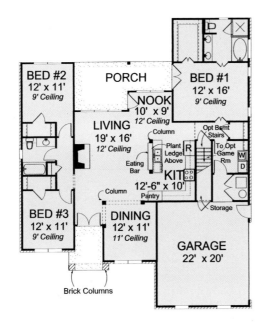

VARYING ROOFLINES AND STRONG BRICK COLUMNS leading to the entrance provide bold first impressions to visitors of this home. Come inside to find a practical and inviting floor plan filled with thoughtful touches. Secluded to the far left of the plan are two bedrooms which share a full bath; the master suite is tucked away in the back right corner of the plan with an enormous walk-in closet and master bath. Living spaces are open to each other, with the kitchen easily serving the nook and living room—adorned with a lovely plant ledge—and a dining room nearby. Venture upstairs to the optional game room and finish it at your leisure.

HOME PLAN

HPK1600099

Style: European Cottage
Square Footage: 1,595
Bonus Space: 312 sq. ft.
Bedrooms: 3
Bathrooms: 2
Width: 49' - 0"
Depth: 60' - 0"
Foundation: Slab

eplans.com

HOME PLAN

HPK1600100

Style: Ranch

Square Footage: 1,782

Bedrooms: 3

Bathrooms: 2

Width: 52' - 0"

Depth: 59' - 4"

eplans.com

SYMMETRICAL GABLES OFFSET A HIP ROOF AND ARCH-TOP WINDOWS and complement a stately brick exterior with this traditional design. Inside, the formal dining room opens from an elegant tiled entry and offers space for quiet, planned occasions as well as traditional festivities. The casual living area shares a three-sided fireplace with the breakfast area and hearth room, while the kitchen offers a convenient snack bar for easy meals. A nine-foot ceiling enhances the master suite, which features a whirlpool tub, twin vanities, an ample walk-in closet, and a compartmented toilet. Split sleeping quarters offer privacy to both the master and the family bedrooms, which share a full bath.

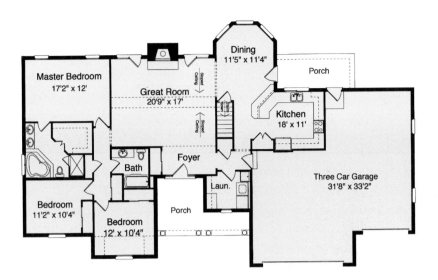

Master Bedroom 17'2" x 12'

Great Room 20'9" x 17'

Dining 11'5" x 11'4"

Porch

Kitchen 18' x 11'

Bath

Foyer

Laun.

Three Car Garage 31'8" x 33'2"

Bedroom 11'2" x 10'4"

Bedroom 12' x 10'4"

Porch

(#) HPK1600101

Style: Traditional

Square Footage: 1,755

Bedrooms: 3

Bathrooms: 2

Width: 78' - 6"

Depth: 47' - 7"

Foundation: Unfinished Basement

eplans.com

A SUNBURST WINDOW SET WITHIN A BRICK EXTERIOR and multigabled roof lends a vibrant aura to this three-bedroom home. The slope-ceilinged great room features a fireplace with French doors at each side. The nearby bay-windowed dining room accesses the rear porch—a perfect place for a barbe-cue grill. Conveniently placed near the garage for fast unloading, the U-shaped kitchen is sure to please. The master suite enjoys a walk-in closet and a luxurious bath including a separate shower, whirlpool tub, and twin-sink vanity. The two family bedrooms benefit from front-facing windows and share a full bath.

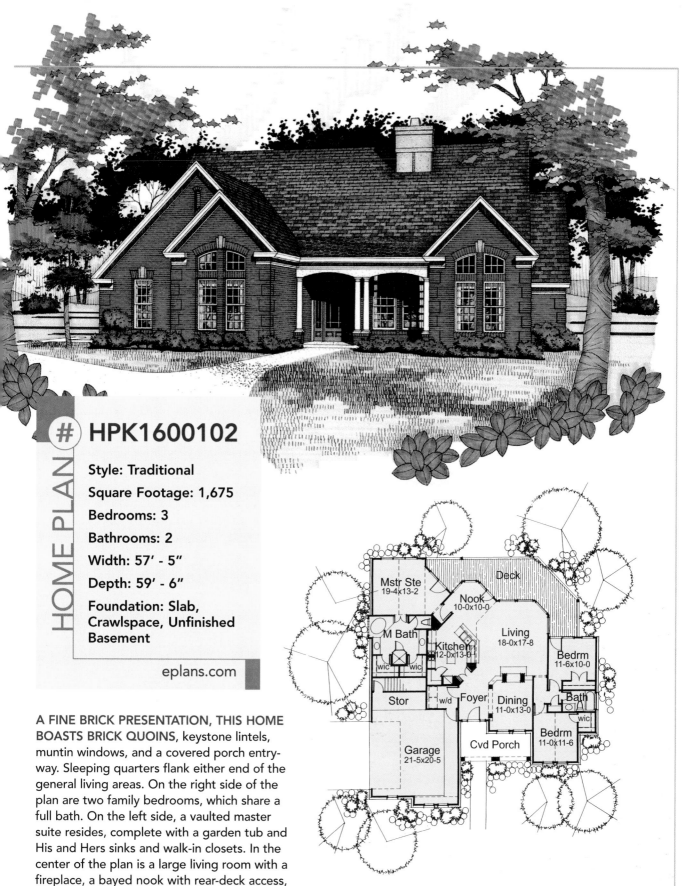

HOME PLAN

HPK1600102

Style: Traditional

Square Footage: 1,675

Bedrooms: 3

Bathrooms: 2

Width: 57' - 5"

Depth: 59' - 6"

Foundation: Slab, Crawlspace, Unfinished Basement

eplans.com

A FINE BRICK PRESENTATION, THIS HOME BOASTS BRICK QUOINS, keystone lintels, muntin windows, and a covered porch entry-way. Sleeping quarters flank either end of the general living areas. On the right side of the plan are two family bedrooms, which share a full bath. On the left side, a vaulted master suite resides, complete with a garden tub and His and Hers sinks and walk-in closets. In the center of the plan is a large living room with a fireplace, a bayed nook with rear-deck access, a dining room with a pillared entrance, and a large kitchen. Storage space is provided just off the garage.

MULTIPLE GABLES, A TRANSOM OVER THE ENTRY DOOR, and a brick-and-stone exterior combine to create an exciting front on this beautiful one-story home. The open foyer offers a view through the great room to the rear yard. A dramatic fireplace and sloped ceiling decorate the fashionable great room. The spacious kitchen and breakfast room feature a favorable indoor/outdoor relationship. The first-floor master bedroom with a tray ceiling, private bath, and extra-large walk-in closet pampers homeowners with its size and luxury. Two additional bedrooms complete this spectacular home.

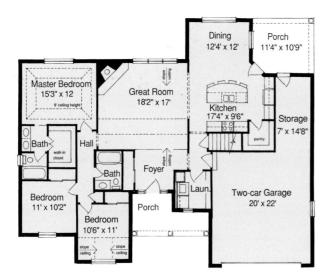

HPK1600103

HOME PLAN

Style: Transitional

Square Footage: 1,593

Bedrooms: 3

Bathrooms: 2

Width: 60' - 0"

Depth: 48' - 10"

Foundation: Unfinished Basement

eplans.com

WITH ITS BRICK FACADE AND GABLES, this home brings great curb appeal to any neighborhood. This one-story home features a great room with a cozy fireplace, a laundry room tucked away from the spacious kitchen, and a breakfast area accessing the screened porch. Completing this design are two family bedrooms and an elegant master bedroom suite featuring an ample walk-in closet. A dressing area in the master bathroom is shared by a dual vanity and a step-up tub.

HOME PLAN

HPK1600104

Style: Craftsman

Square Footage: 1,759

Bedrooms: 3

Bathrooms: 2

Width: 82' - 10"

Depth: 47' - 5"

Foundation: Unfinished Basement

eplans.com

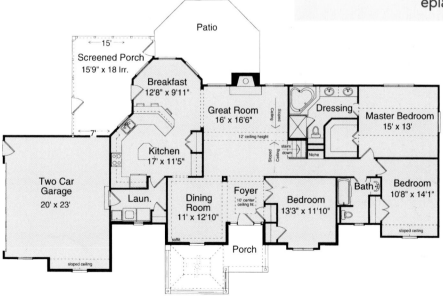

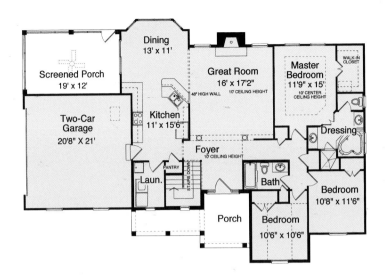

HPK1600105

Style: Craftsman

Square Footage: 1,611

Bedrooms: 3

Bathrooms: 2

Width: 66' - 4"

Depth: 43' - 10"

Foundation: Unfinished Basement

eplans.com

A STONE-AND-SIDING EXTERIOR EASILY COM-BINES with the front covered porch on this three-bedroom ranch home. Inside, columns define the great room, which holds a warming fireplace framed by windows. The bay window in the dining room pours light into the nearby kitchen. Access the screened porch via the dining room to expand the possible living space. The master suite enjoys a walk-in closet and a luxurious bath, including a separate shower and whirlpool tub. Two family bedrooms share a full bath and views of the front yard. Note the two-car, side-access garage—perfect for a corner lot.

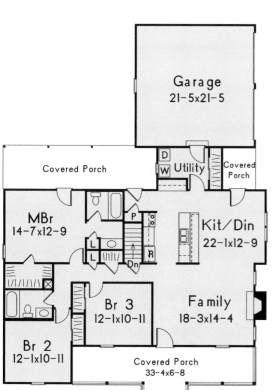

HOME PLAN

HPK1600106

Style: Traditional

Square Footage: 1,501

Bedrooms: 3

Bathrooms: 2

Width: 48' - 0"

Depth: 57' - 4"

Foundation: Crawlspace, Slab, Unfinished Basement

eplans.com

THIS RANCH-STYLE HOME PROVIDES AN INVITING FRONT COVERED PORCH with rustic accents. Inside, the family room provides a lovely fireplace and is open to a kitchen/dining area that accesses a rear covered porch. Nearby, a utility room leads into the two-car garage. The master bedroom provides spacious views of the rear property and privately accesses the rear covered porch. This bedroom also features a walk-in closet and a full bath with linen storage. Bedrooms 2 and 3 share a full hall bath.

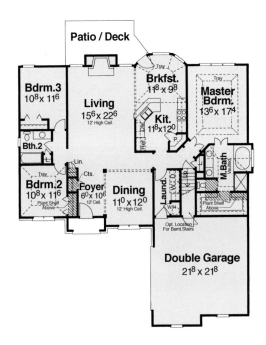

Patio / Deck

Bdrm.3
10⁸ x 11⁶

Living
15⁶ x 22⁶
12' High Ceil.

Brkfst.
11⁸ x 9⁸

Master Bdrm.
13⁶ x 17⁴

Kit.
11⁸ x 12⁰

Bth.2

Lin.

Bdrm.2
10⁸ x 11⁶
Plant Shelf Above

Foyer
6⁰ x 10⁶
12' Ceil.

Dining
11⁰ x 12⁰
12' High Ceil.

Laund.

M.Bath
Vaulted

Plant Shelf Above

Opt. Location For Bsmt.Stairs

Double Garage
21⁸ x 21⁸

Bonus
13⁴ x 23⁸
Vaulted

HPK1600107

Style: Traditional

Square Footage: 1,869

Bonus Space: 336 sq. ft.

Bedrooms: 3

Bathrooms: 2

Width: 54' - 0"

Depth: 60' - 6"

Foundation: Unfinished Walkout Basement, Crawlspace, Slab

HOME PLAN

eplans.com

A RUSTIC EXTERIOR OF SHINGLES, SIDING, AND STONE PROVIDES a sweet country look. Inside, the foyer is flanked by a dining room and family bedrooms. Bedrooms 2 and 3 share a full hall bath. The master suite, located on the opposite side of the home for privacy, boasts a tray ceiling and a pampering bath with an oversized tub. The kitchen opens to a breakfast room that accesses the rear sun deck. The enormous living room is warmed by a central fireplace. The laundry room and double-car garage complete this plan.

REAR EXTERIOR

HPK1600108

Style: Traditional

Square Footage: 1,977

Bonus Space: 430 sq. ft.

Bedrooms: 3

Bathrooms: 2

Width: 69' - 8"

Depth: 59' - 6"

eplans.com

A TWO-STORY FOYER WITH A PALLADIAN WINDOW above sets the tone for this sunlit home. Columns mark the passage from the foyer to the great room, where a central fireplace and built-in cabinets are found. A screened porch with four skylights above and a wet bar provides a pleasant place to start the day or wind down after work. The kitchen is flanked by the formal dining room and the breakfast room. Hidden quietly at the rear, the master suite includes a bath with dual vanities and skylights. Two family bedrooms (one an optional study) share a bath that has twin sinks.

© 1994 Donald A. Gardner Architects, Inc.

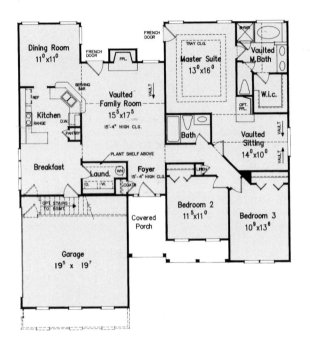

ASYMMETRICAL GABLES, A COLUMNED PORCH, and an abundance of windows brighten the exterior of this compact home. An efficient kitchen boasts a pantry and a serving bar that it shares with the formal dining room and the vaulted family room. A sunny breakfast room and nearby laundry room complete the living zone. Be sure to notice extras such as the focal-point fireplace in the family room and a plant shelf in the laundry room. The sumptuous master suite offers a door to the backyard, a vaulted sitting area, and a pampering bath. Two family bedrooms share a hall bath.

HPK1600109

HOME PLAN

Style: Southern Colonial

Square Footage: 1,671

Bedrooms: 3

Bathrooms: 2

Width: 50' - 0"

Depth: 51' - 0"

Foundation: Slab, Crawlspace, Unfinished Walkout Basement

eplans.com

HOME PLAN

HPK1600110

Style: Country Cottage

Square Footage: 1,583

Bonus Space: 544 sq. ft.

Bedrooms: 3

Bathrooms: 2

Width: 54' - 0"

Depth: 47' - 0"

Foundation: Crawlspace, Unfinished Walkout Basement, Slab

eplans.com

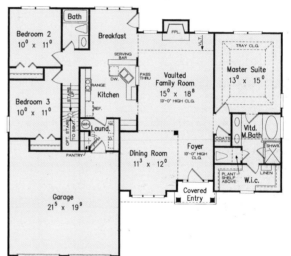

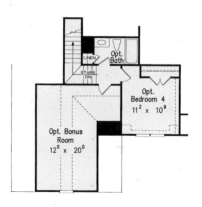

THIS COMFORTABLE COTTAGE IS WELL SUITED TO AN ALPINE ENVIRONMENT, yet, with its flexible interior and superior architecture, can be built anywhere. Open living and dining space is anchored by a decorative column and a fireplace surrounded by views. A well-planned kitchen features a food-preparation island and a serving bar. A triple window in the breakfast area brightens the kitchen; a French door allows access to the rear property. To the right of the plan, the master suite boasts a vaulted bath, a plant shelf, and a walk-in closet. Two secondary bedrooms share a full bath.

HOME PLAN (#)

HPK1600111

Style: Traditional

Square Footage: 1,815

Bedrooms: 3

Bathrooms: 2 ½

Width: 60' - 0"

Depth: 60' - 6"

Foundation: Finished Walkout Basement

eplans.com

WITH ZONED LIVING AT THE CORE OF THIS FLOOR PLAN, livability takes a convenient turn. Living areas are to the left of the plan; sleeping areas are to the right. The formal dining room is open to the central hallway and foyer and features graceful columned archways to define its space. The great room contains angled corners and a magnificent central fireplace and offers ample views to the rear grounds. Steps away is a well-lit breakfast room with private rear-porch access and an adjoining C-shaped kitchen with a unique angled counter space and sink. Sleeping quarters are clustered around a private hallway, which offers a guest bath. The master suite includes a resplendent bath with a garden tub, dual lavatories, and a walk-in closet. Two family bedrooms share a full bath that features a compartmented toilet and tub.

AS AT HOME IN A DEVELOPMENT AS IT IS IN AN ORCHARD, this design combines country charm with Craftsman appeal. A Palladian-style window fills the study/bedroom with light, and a stone wall and cozy front porch recall times past. A sole column and tray ceiling distinguish the dining room that opens to a great room, which features French doors to the rear porch and a striking two-room fireplace. An angled counter separates the kitchen from the great room and breakfast nook. With a master bath, two full additional baths, an optional study/bedroom, and a bonus room, this home has plenty of space for growing families.

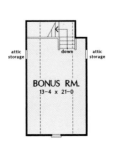

HOME PLAN

HPK1600112

Style: Craftsman
Square Footage: 1,952
Bonus Space: 339 sq. ft.
Bedrooms: 4
Bathrooms: 3
Width: 50' - 0"
Depth: 60' - 0"

eplans.com

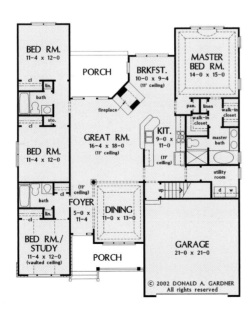

SHINGLES AND VERTICAL SIDING COMBINE WITH MULTIPLE ROOFLINES and gables on a hipped roof to create an eye-catching appeal for this three-bedroom home. All on one floor, this home provides plenty of room with ease of accessibility. Just inside the entry, the great room features a warming fireplace and a built-in media center. The dining room and island kitchen have an excellent view of this focal point in the great room. The master suite and a den fill the left side of the plan while two family bedrooms share a full bath to the right. Note the shop area or third-car parking within the garage.

HOME PLAN

HPK1600113

Style: Traditional

Square Footage: 1,852

Bedrooms: 3

Bathrooms: 2

Width: 70' - 0"

Depth: 45' - 0"

Foundation: Crawlspace

eplans.com

EUROPEAN STYLE INFLUENCES THE EXTERIOR of this distinctive ranch home. Appealing rooflines and a covered porch with repeating arches provide stunning curb appeal. Inside, an impressive 10-foot-high entry greets family and friends. An open concept pervades the kitchen/dinette area. Picture your family enjoying the bayed eating area, wrapping counters, desk, island, and wet bar/servery—ideal for entertaining. The decorative hutch space adds appeal to a formal dining room. Bright windows frame a fireplace in the great room. Sure to please is the service entry to the laundry/mud room with soaking sink and counter space. Bedroom 2 can easily be converted into a private den. A boxed ceiling decorates the master suite, and three windows provide natural lighting. Dual sinks, a walk-in closet, whirlpool tub, and cedar-lined window seat enhance the master bath.

HOME PLAN

HPK1600114

Style: Traditional
Square Footage: 1,850
Bedrooms: 3
Bathrooms: 2
Width: 62' - 0"
Depth: 48' - 0"

eplans.com

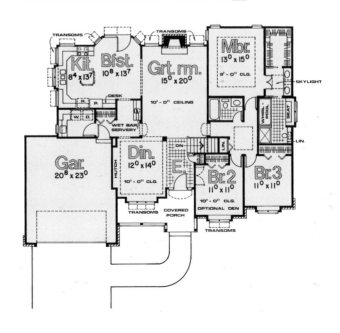

THIS CHARMING ONE-STORY PLAN FEATURES A FACADE that is accented by a stone pediment and a shed-dormer window. Inside, elegant touches grace the efficient floor plan. Vaulted ceilings adorn the great room and master bedroom, and a 10-foot tray ceiling highlights the foyer. One of the front bedrooms makes a perfect den; another accesses a full hall bath with a linen closet. The great room, which opens to the porch, includes a fireplace and a media niche. The dining room offers outdoor access and built-ins for ultimate convenience.

HOME PLAN

HPK1600115

Style: Country Cottage

Square Footage: 1,580

Bedrooms: 3

Bathrooms: 2 ½

Width: 50' - 0"

Depth: 48' - 0"

Foundation: Crawlspace

eplans.com

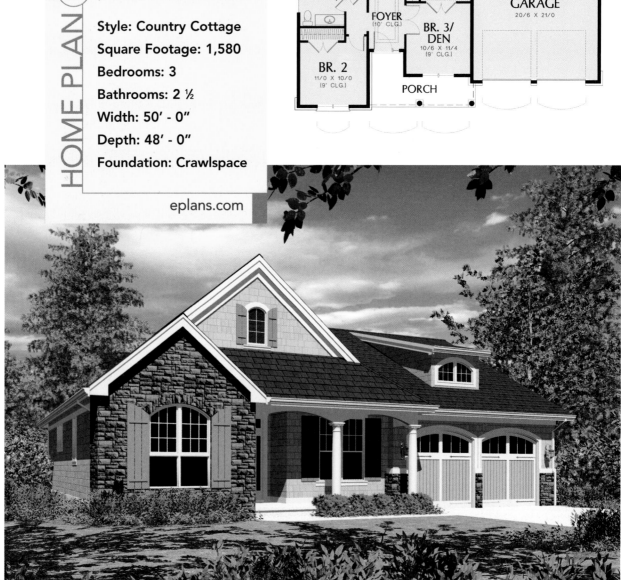

HPK1600116

HOME PLAN

Style: Craftsman

Square Footage: 1,724

Bonus Space: 375 sq. ft.

Bedrooms: 3

Bathrooms: 2

Width: 53' - 6"

Depth: 58' - 6"

Foundation: Crawlspace, Unfinished Walkout Basement, Slab

eplans.com

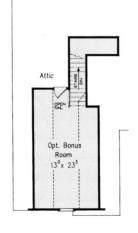

THIS DOWN-HOME, ONE-STORY PLAN HAS ALL THE COMFORTS and necessities for solid family living. The vaulted family room, along with the adjoining country-style kitchen and breakfast nook, is at the center of the plan. The extended hearth fireplace flanked by radius windows will make this a cozy focus for family get-togethers and entertaining visitors. A formal dining room is marked off by decorative columns. The resplendent master suite assumes the entire right wing, where it is separated from two bedrooms located on the other side of the home. Built-in plant shelves in the master bath create a garden-like environment. Additional space is available for building another bedroom or study.

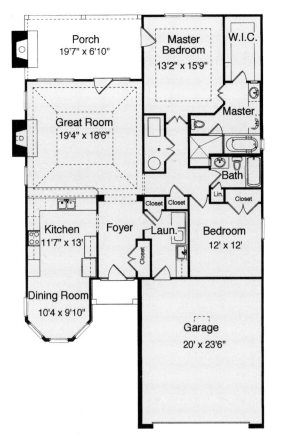

Porch
19'7" x 6'10"

Master Bedroom
13'2" x 15'9"

W.I.C.

Master

Great Room
19'4" x 18'6"

Bath

Closet   Closet   Closet

Lin.

Closet

Kitchen
11'7" x 13'

Foyer

Laun.

Bedroom
12' x 12'

Closet

Dining Room
10'4" x 9'10"

Garage
20' x 23'6"

A BRICK-AND-STONE EXTERIOR WITH SHAKE SIDING DECORATES the front of this delightful home. The large great room enjoys an 11-foot ceiling, gas fireplace, and access to the rear porch. The master bedroom suite offers a luxury bath with a dual-bowl vanity, whirlpool tub, and large walk-in closet. Access to the rear porch from the master suite is an unexpected feature. This home, designed for a narrow lot, offers spaciousness and luxurious living.

HOME PLAN

(#) HPK1600117

Style: European Cottage

Square Footage: 1,612

Bedrooms: 2

Bathrooms: 2

Width: 42' - 0"

Depth: 67' - 4"

Foundation: Slab, Unfinished Basement

eplans.com

THIS HOME BOASTS A CHARMING EXTERIOR AND AN EFFICIENT INTERIOR. A covered porch leads to a foyer with access to the living room on the right, or to the other half of the house on the left. Proceed through the living room—with fireplace and vaulted ceilings—to the kitchen, dining room and pantry area, to the first bedroom, with private double vanity bath, and rear porch access. Three other bedrooms are housed on the other side of the floor plan, along with the garage and optional basement area.

HOME PLAN

HPK1600118

Style: Traditional

Square Footage: 1,560

Bedrooms: 4

Bathrooms: 2

Width: 44' - 0"

Depth: 58' - 0"

eplans.com

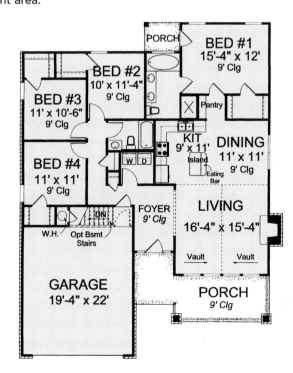

THIS RUSTIC BEAUTY PROVIDES A PRACTICAL FLOOR PLAN. The great room is warmed by a fireplace and enhanced by a cathedral ceiling. Another cathedral ceiling adds a spacious feel to the master bedroom. Additional luxuries in the master suite include a private bath, two walk-in closets, and access to a covered porch (also accessible from the great room). Two additional bedrooms share a hall bath, with the utility room conveniently nearby. A bonus room is available for extra storage.

HOME PLAN

(#) HPK1600119

Style: Craftsman
Square Footage: 1,608
Bonus Space: 437 sq. ft.
Bedrooms: 3
Bathrooms: 2
Width: 40' - 8"
Depth: 62' - 8"

eplans.com

©1998 Donald A. Gardner Architects, Inc.   B. NATHAN

HOME PLAN

HPK1600120

Style: Country Cottage
Square Footage: 1,544
Bonus Space: 320 sq. ft.
Bedrooms: 3
Bathrooms: 2
Width: 63' - 0"
Depth: 43' - 0"

eplans.com

THIS HOME WOULD LOOK GOOD IN ANY NEIGH-BORHOOD. From the covered front porch to the trio of gables, this design has a lot of appeal. Inside, the Craftsman styling continues with built-in shelves and a warming fireplace in the great room and plenty of windows to bring in the outdoors. The U-shaped kitchen offers easy access to the formal dining area. Expansion is possible with an optional bonus room, adding a second level. A tray ceiling adorns the master bedroom, along with His and Hers walk-in closets and a pampering bath complete with a twin-sink vanity and a separate shower and garden tub. Expansion is possible with an optional bonus room, adding a second level.

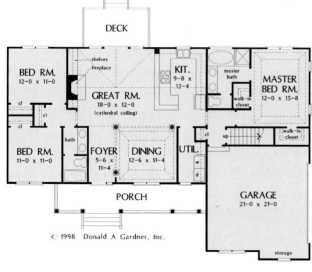

© 1998   Donald A Gardner, Inc.

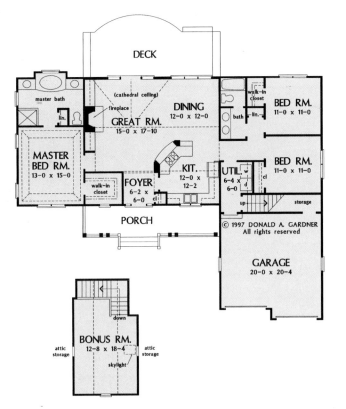

DECK

master bath

GREAT RM.
15-0 x 17-10
(cathedral ceiling)
fireplace
lin.

DINING
12-0 x 12-0

walk-in closet
bath
lin.

BED RM.
11-0 x 11-0

MASTER BED RM.
13-0 x 15-0

walk-in closet

FOYER
6-2 x
6-0
cl

KIT.
12-0 x
12-2

UTIL.
6-4 x
6-0
w
d
cl

BED RM.
11-0 x 11-0

up
storage

PORCH

© 1997 DONALD A. GARDNER
All rights reserved

GARAGE
20-0 x 20-4

down
BONUS RM.
12-8 x 18-4
attic storage
attic storage
skylight

THE FOYER OPENS TO A SPACIOUS GREAT ROOM with a fireplace and a cathedral ceiling in this lovely traditional home. Sliding doors open to a rear deck from the great room, posing a warm welcome to enjoy the outdoors. The U-shaped kitchen features an angled peninsula counter with a cooktop. A private hall leads to the family sleeping quarters, which includes two bedrooms and a full bath with a double-bowl lavatory. Sizable bonus space above the garage provides a skylight.

HPK1600121

HOME PLAN

Style: Traditional

Square Footage: 1,517

Bonus Space: 287 sq. ft.

Bedrooms: 3

Bathrooms: 2

Width: 61' - 4"

Depth: 48' - 6"

eplans.com

© 1997 Donald A. Gardner Architects, Inc.

FRONT EXTERIOR

HOME PLAN

HPK1600122

Style: Traditional
Square Footage: 1,971
Bonus Space: 358 sq. ft.
Bedrooms: 3
Bathrooms: 3
Width: 62' - 6"
Depth: 57' - 2"

eplans.com

THIS CRAFTSMAN COTTAGE COMBINES STONE, siding, and cedar shake to create striking curb appeal. The interior features an open floor plan with high ceilings, columns, and bay windows to visually expand space. Built-in cabinetry, a fireplace, and a kitchen pass-through highlight and add convenience to the great room. The master suite features a tray ceiling in the bedroom and a bath with garden tub, separate shower, dual vanities, and a walk-in closet. On the opposite side of the home is another bedroom that could be used as a second master suite. Above the garage, a bonus room provides ample storage and space to grow.

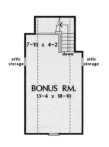

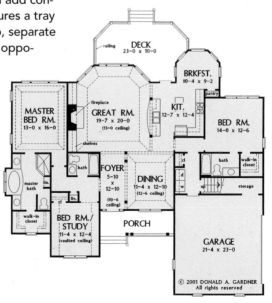

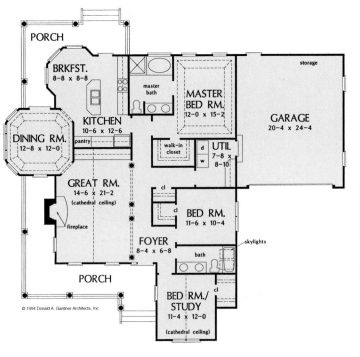

PORCH

BRKFST.
8-8 x 8-8

master
bath

MASTER
BED RM.
12-0 x 15-2

storage

KITCHEN
10-6 x 12-6

pantry

GARAGE
20-4 x 24-4

DINING RM.
12-8 x 12-0

walk-in
closet

d   UTIL
w   7-8 x
     8-10

GREAT RM.
14-6 x 21-2
(cathedral ceiling)

cl

fireplace

cl

BED RM.
11-6 x 10-4

FOYER
8-4 x 6-8

skylights

bath

PORCH

© 1994 Donald A. Gardner Architects, Inc.

BED RM./
STUDY
11-4 x 12-0

(cathedral ceiling)

INVITING PORCHES ARE JUST THE BEGINNING OF THIS LOVELY COUNTRY home. To the left of the foyer, a columned entry supplies a classic touch to a spacious great room that features a cathedral ceiling, built-in bookshelves, and a fireplace that invites you to share its warmth. An octagonal dining room with a tray ceiling provides a perfect setting for formal occasions. The adjacent kitchen is designed to easily serve both formal and informal areas. It includes an island cooktop and a built-in pantry, with the sunny breakfast area just a step away. The master suite, separated from two family bedrooms by the walk-in closet and utility room, offers privacy and comfort.

HOME PLAN

HPK1600123

Style: Farmhouse

Square Footage: 1,737

Bedrooms: 3

Bathrooms: 2

Width: 65' - 10"

Depth: 59' - 8"

eplans.com

REAR EXTERIOR

HOME PLAN

HPK1600124

Style: Farmhouse

Square Footage: 1,787

Bonus Space: 326 sq. ft.

Bedrooms: 3

Bathrooms: 2

Width: 66' - 2"

Depth: 66' - 8"

eplans.com

CATHEDRAL CEILINGS BRING A FEELING OF SPACIOUSNESS to this home. The great room features a fireplace, cathedral ceilings, and built-in bookshelves. The kitchen is designed for efficient use with its food preparation island and pantry. The master suite provides a welcome retreat with a cathedral ceiling, a walk-in closet, and a luxurious bath. Two additional bedrooms, one with a walk-in closet, share a skylit bath. A second-floor bonus room is perfect for a study or a play area.

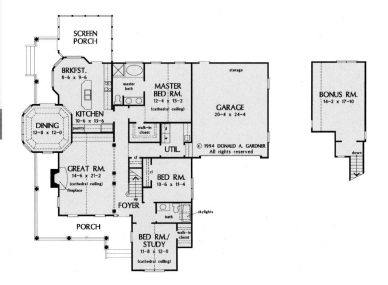

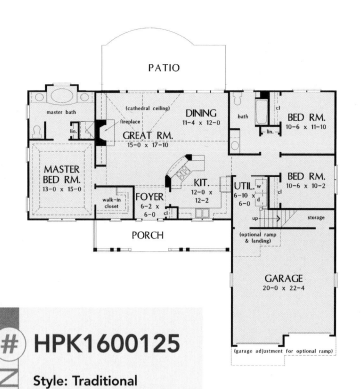

PATIO

master bath

(cathedral ceiling)

DINING
11-4 x 12-0

bath

cl

BED RM.
10-6 x 11-10

fireplace

lin.

lin.

GREAT RM.
15-0 x 17-10

down

skylight

attic
storage

attic
storage

BONUS RM.
12-8 x 20-4

MASTER
BED RM.
13-0 x 15-0

KIT.
12-0 x
12-2

UTIL.
6-10 x
6-0

BED RM.
10-6 x 10-2

w
d

cl

walk-in
closet

FOYER
6-2 x
6-0

cl

up

storage

PORCH

(optional ramp
& landing)

GARAGE
20-0 x 22-4

(garage adjustment for optional ramp)

THIS TRADITIONAL HOME ENJOYS A CRAFTSMAN'S TASTE with its detail to the exterior. The heart of this home is the massive great room which features cathedral ceilings, a warming fireplace with built-ins, and access to the rear patio, formal dining room and gourmet kitchen. Two family bedrooms share the right wing of this home along with a full bath and a conveniently located utility room. A tray ceiling illuminates the master bedroom, which enjoys a large walk-in closet and a private bath featuring a pampering Roman tub with vanities on each side. The attic can be made into a bonus room with a skylight.

©1999 Donald A. Gardner, Inc.

A HIPPED DORMER ON THE EXTERIOR AND A TRAY CEILING inside provides highlights to the dining room of this traditional craftsman. Escape to the privacy of your master suite and its own whirlpool tub (four extra bathrooms throughout the house means no sharing!). The kitchen is tucked away from traffic, but within view of the amply-spaced eating area. The main floor of this house has an additional covered porch in the rear corner leading off of the garage. Both the den and family bedroom feature built-in desks. These conveniences are mirrored upstairs with a ready-to-use book-case, hutch, wine storage, and bar. Entertain upstairs in style, and still have plenty of space available for all of your storage needs.

HOME PLAN

 # HPK1600126

Style: Craftsman
Square Footage: 1,899
Bedrooms: 2
Bathrooms: 2 ½
Width: 62' - 0"
Depth: 68' - 8"

eplans.com

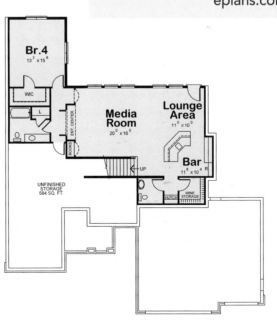

USING WOOD AND STONE FOR THE FACADE, this traditional home boasts a large receiving porch and free-flowing interior spaces. The spacious living room is open to the adjacent dining room and has a built-in fireplace and entertainment center. The master suite is secluded for privacy and features a bath with a separate tub and shower and a walk-in closet.

HPK1600127

HOME PLAN

Style: Traditional

Square Footage: 1,770

Bedrooms: 3

Bathrooms: 2

Width: 64' - 0"

Depth: 48' - 0"

Foundation: Slab, Crawlspace

eplans.com

THIS CHARMING ONE-STORY TRADITIONAL HOME greets visitors with a covered porch. A uniquely shaped galley-style kitchen shares a snack bar with the spacious gathering room where a fireplace is the focal point. The dining room furnishes sliding glass doors to the rear terrace, as does the master bedroom. This bedroom area also includes a luxury bath with a whirlpool tub and separate dressing room. Two additional bedrooms, one that could double as a study, are located at the front of the home. The two-car garage features a large storage area and can be reached through the service entrance or from the rear terrace.

HOME PLAN

HPK1600128

Style: Farmhouse

Square Footage: 1,830

Bedrooms: 3

Bathrooms: 2

Width: 75' - 0"

Depth: 43' - 5"

Foundation: Unfinished Basement

eplans.com

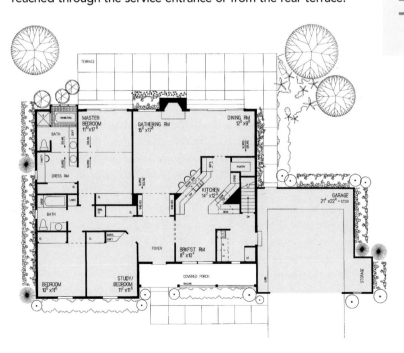

RUSTIC IN NATURE, THIS HILLSIDE HOME OFFERS A SUR-ROUNDING DECK and upper-level balcony on the exterior to complement its horizontal siding and stone detailing. The entry opens to a staircase leading up to the main level or down to fin-ish-later space in the basement. The kitchen is at the heart of the home and has miles of counter space and a pass-through bar to the dining room. Both the living and dining rooms have sliding glass doors to the deck. A corner fireplace warms and lights both areas. The master bedroom sits to the right of the plan and has a private bath and deck access. Two additional bedrooms with a shared bath sit to the left of the plan. One of these bedrooms has deck access.

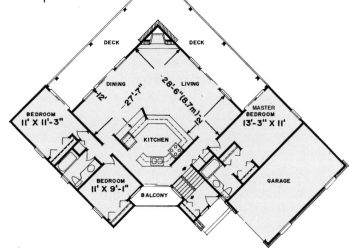

HPK1600129

HOME PLAN

Style: Bungalow

Square Footage: 1,530

Bedrooms: 3

Bathrooms: 2

Width: 77' - 7"

Depth: 61' - 0"

Foundation: Unfinished Basement

eplans.com

© 1997 Donald A. Gardner Architects, Inc.

HOME PLAN

(#) HPK1600130

Style: Contemporary

Square Footage: 1,680

Bedrooms: 3

Bathrooms: 2

Width: 62' - 8"

Depth: 59' - 10"

eplans.com

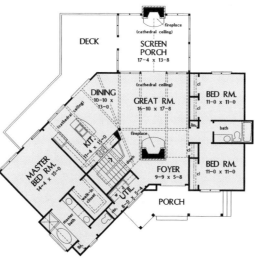

DECK

fireplace
(cathedral ceiling)

SCREEN
PORCH
17-4 x 13-8

(cathedral ceiling)

DINING
10-10 x
13-0

GREAT RM.
16-10 x 17-8

BED RM.
11-0 x 11-0

bath

KIT.
11-4 x 15-0

fireplace

MASTER
BED RM.
14-4 x 15-0

FOYER
9-9 x 5-8

BED RM.
11-0 x 11-0

walk-in
closet

UTIL.
8-0 x 5-4

master
bath

PORCH

GARAGE
22-0 x 22-0

THIS RUSTIC RETREAT IS UPDATED WITH CONTEMPORARY ANGLES and packs a lot of living into a small space. The covered front porch leads to a welcoming foyer. The beam-ceilinged great room opens directly ahead and features a fireplace, a wall of windows, and access to the screened porch (with its own fireplace!) and is adjacent to the angled dining area. A highly efficient island kitchen is sure to please with tons of counter and cabinet space. Two family bedrooms, sharing a full bath, are located on one end of the plan; the master suite is secluded for complete privacy at the other end.

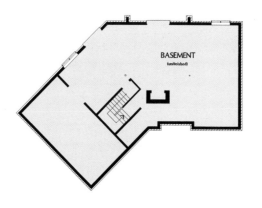

BASEMENT
(unfinished)

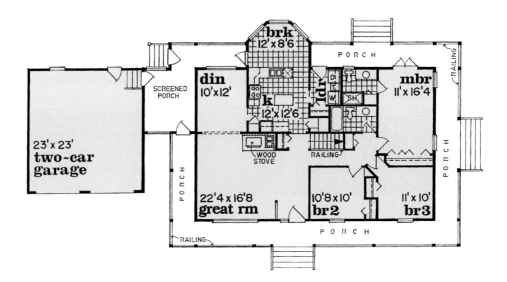

THIS POPULAR DESIGN BEGINS WITH A WRAP-AROUND COVERED PORCH made even more charming with turned-wood spindles. The entry opens directly to the great room, which is warmed by a wood stove. The adjoining dining room offers access to a screened porch for outdoor after-dinner leisure. A country kitchen features a center island and a breakfast bay for casual meals. Family bedrooms share a full bath that features a soaking tub. The two-car garage connects to the plan via the screened porch.

HOME PLAN

HPK1600131

Style: Farmhouse

Square Footage: 1,541

Bedrooms: 3

Bathrooms: 2

Width: 87' - 0"

Depth: 44' - 0"

Foundation: Crawlspace, Unfinished Basement

eplans.com

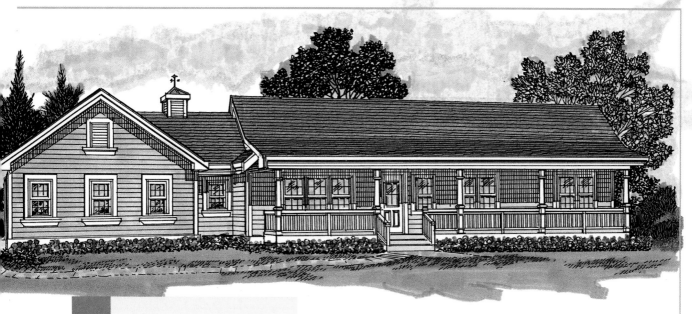

HPK1600132

HOME PLAN #

Style: Ranch

Square Footage: 1,652

Bedrooms: 3

Bathrooms: 2

Width: 78' - 6"

Depth: 48' - 0"

Foundation: Crawlspace, Unfinished Basement

eplans.com

THIS LONG, LOW RANCH HOME HAS OUT-DOOR LIVING on two porches—one to the front and one to the rear. Vaulted ceilings in the great room, kitchen, and master bedroom add a dimension of extra space. A fireplace warms the great room, which opens to the country kitchen. The fine master suite also has doors to the rear porch and is graced by a walk-in closet, plus a full bath with a garden tub and dual vanity. The two-car garage contains space for a freezer and extra storage cabinets that are built in.

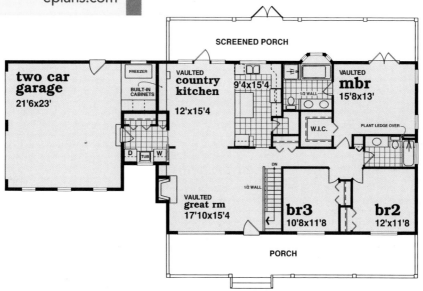

THE WIDE FRONT STEPS, COLUMNED PORCH, and symmetrical layout give this charming home a Georgian appeal. The large kitchen, with its walk-in pantry, island/snack bar, and breakfast nook, will gratify any cook. The central great room offers radiant French doors on both sides of the fireplace. Outside those doors is a comfortable covered porch with two skylights. To the left of the great room reside four bedrooms—three secondary bedrooms and a master bedroom. The master bedroom enjoys a walk-in closet, twin-vanity sinks, a separate shower and tub, and private access to the rear porch.

HOME PLAN

 # HPK1600133

Style: Colonial

Square Footage: 1,997

Bedrooms: 4

Bathrooms: 2 ½

Width: 56' - 4"

Depth: 67' - 4"

Foundation: Crawlspace, Slab, Unfinished Basement

eplans.com

PILLARS, BEAUTIFUL TRANSOMS, AND SIDELIGHTS set off the entry door and draw attention to this comfortable home. The foyer leads to a formal dining room and a great room with a ribbon of windows pouring in light. To the left of the kitchen is a roomy laundry area, with lots of storage space for those extra household supplies. Privacy is assured with a master suite—a large walk-in closet and full bath with separate shower and large tub add to the pleasure of this wing. Two family bedrooms occupy the right side of the design and share a full bath.

HOME PLAN # HPK1600134

Style: Traditional

Square Footage: 1,836

Bedrooms: 3

Bathrooms: 2

Width: 65' - 8"

Depth: 55' - 0"

Foundation: Crawlspace, Slab, Unfinished Basement

eplans.com

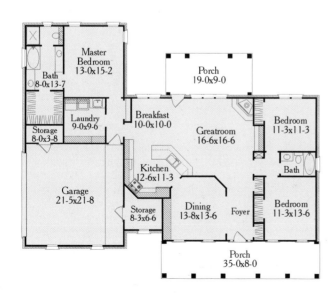

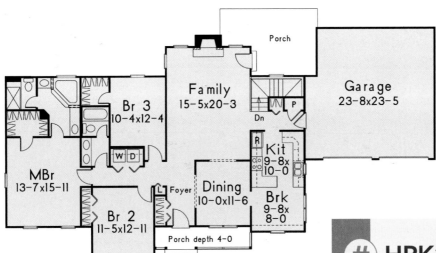

THE STEEP SIDE-GABLED ROOF IS VERY DISTINCTIVE, offering plenty of curb appeal for this one-story home. Outside, the shutters sharply emphasize the windows on all sides of the house. Inside, windows enhance the enormous family room, which enjoys a fireplace and access to the rear porch. The deluxe master bath is accented by the step-up corner tub flanked by double vanities. Spacious closets are found throughout the home.

HOME PLAN

HPK1600135

Style: Traditional

Square Footage: 1,708

Bedrooms: 3

Bathrooms: 2

Width: 80' - 0"

Depth: 42' - 0"

Foundation: Crawlspace, Unfinished Basement

eplans.com

Owner's Bedroom
12-11x15-4

Bath
6-0x16-10

Stor.

Porch
15-4x5-0

Dining
10-11x12-7

Bedroom
13-9x10-0

Greatroom
15-6x18-11

Bath

Kitchen
10-11x14-1

Garage
19-1x20-4

Bedroom
13-9x11-0

Basement Option

Porch
26-8x5-8

HOME PLAN

 # HPK1600136

Style: Traditional

Square Footage: 1,643

Bedrooms: 3

Bathrooms: 2

Width: 62' - 2"

Depth: 51' - 4"

Foundation: Crawlspace, Slab, Unfinished Basement

eplans.com

TWO COVERED PORCHES LEND A RELAXING CHARM to this three-bedroom ranch home. Inside, the focal point is a warming fireplace with windows framing each side. The vaulted ceiling in the great room adds spaciousness to the adjoining kitchen and dining areas. A tray ceiling decorates the master suite, which also sports two walk-in closets. Two family bedrooms are located on the opposite side of the house.

THIS QUAINT FARMHOUSE LACKS NOTHING— not even a bonus room to accommodate expansion needs. With its welcoming front porch, Palladian windows, and siding, this home adds curb appeal to any streetscape. Columns and a tray ceiling define the dining room. Columns also make a grand entrance to the great room, which features built-ins, a fireplace, a kitchen pass-through, and French doors leading outside. A breakfast room off the kitchen makes the perfect place to enjoy early morning coffee. Located for privacy, the master suite has a tray ceiling in the bedroom, a spacious walk-in closet, and a master bath equipped with a double vanity, private toilet, large shower, and garden tub. The utility/mudroom is complete with a sink.

DECK
18-8 x 8-0

GREAT RM.
18-0 x 17-4
(cathedral ceiling)

fireplace

shelves

KITCHEN
13-0 x 10-0

BRKFST.
9-0 x 10-0

PORCH

MASTER BED RM.
13-0 x 17-4

BED RM.
12-0 x 11-0

lin.

walk-in closet

master bath

FOYER
6-0 x 12-8

DINING
13-0 x 12-8

bath

UTILITY
6-0 x 11-0

lin. cl

BED RM.
12-0 x 11-0

up

d w

sto.

PORCH

GARAGE
22-0 x 21-0

© 2002 DONALD A. GARDNER
All rights reserved

sto.

down

attic storage

attic storage

BONUS RM.
14-4 x 23-4

HOME PLAN

HPK1600137

Style: Country

Square Footage: 1,827

Bonus Space: 384 sq. ft.

Bedrooms: 3

Bathrooms: 2

Width: 61' - 8"

Depth: 62' - 8"

eplans.com

© 2002 Donald A. Gardner, Inc.

HOME PLAN

HPK1600138

Style: Bungalow

Square Footage: 1,922

Bedrooms: 3

Bathrooms: 2 ½

Width: 79' - 3"

Depth: 40' - 0"

Foundation: Slab

eplans.com

IN THE CRAFTSMAN TRADITION, THIS ONE-STORY HOME IS ENHANCED BY RUBBLEWORK MASONRY and multipaned windows. The covered porch leads into the entry, flanked by the living room and formal dining room. The hearth-warmed family room enjoys views to the rear screened porch. The island kitchen provides plenty of counter space and close proximity to the breakfast nook. All bedrooms reside on the left side of the plan. The master bedroom boasts a private covered patio and lavish full bath, and two family bedrooms share a full bath. A unique shop area attached to the two-car garage completes the plan.

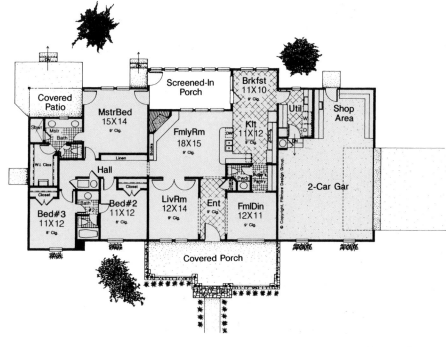

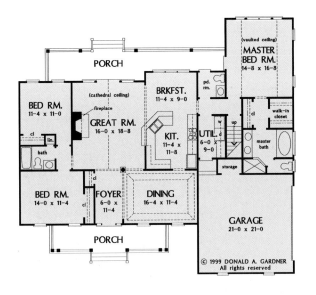

PORCH

BED RM.
11-4 x 11-0

(cathedral ceiling)
GREAT RM.
16-0 x 18-8
fireplace

BRKFST.
11-4 x 9-0

MASTER
BED RM.
14-8 x 16-8
(vaulted ceiling)

pd.
rm.

walk-in
closet

cl

KIT.
11-4 x
11-8

UTIL.
6-0 x
9-0

w
d

up

master
bath

storage

bath
cl
lin.

BED RM.
14-0 x 11-4
cl

FOYER
6-0 x
11-4

DINING
16-4 x 11-4

GARAGE
21-0 x 21-0

PORCH

© 1999 DONALD A. GARDNER
All rights reserved

BONUS RM.
14-0 x 21-0
down
attic storage   attic storage

AN ARCHED WINDOW IN A CENTER FRONT-FACING GABLE lends style and beauty to the facade of this three-bedroom home. An open common area features a great room with a cathedral ceiling, a formal dining room with a tray ceiling, a functional kitchen, and an informal breakfast area that separates the master suite from the secondary bedrooms for privacy. The master suite provides a dramatic vaulted ceiling, access to the back porch, and abundant closet space. Access to a versatile bonus room is near the master bedroom.

HOME PLAN

HPK1600139

Style: Country
Square Footage: 1,882
Bonus Space: 363 sq. ft.
Bedrooms: 3
Bathrooms: 2 ½
Width: 61' - 4"
Depth: 55' - 0"

eplans.com

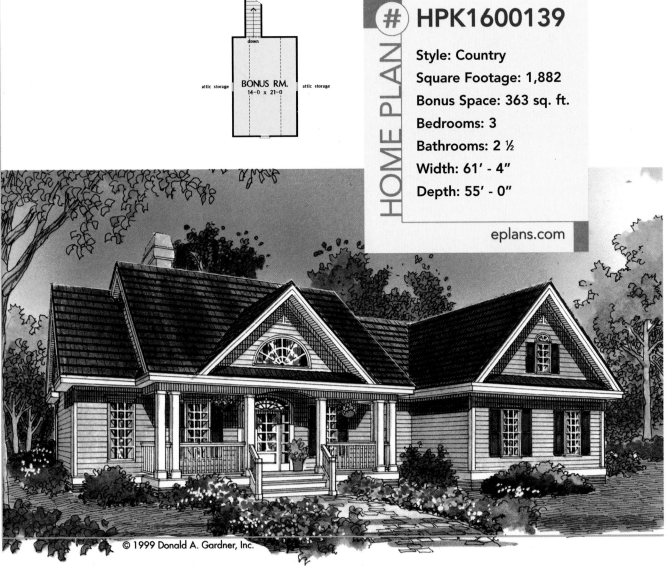

© 1999 Donald A. Gardner, Inc.

©1999 Donald A. Gardner, Inc.

THIS COUNTRY HOME FEATURES AN OPEN FLOOR PLAN that works well for today's fast-paced families. A cathedral ceiling and fireplace grace the great room. The C-shaped kitchen has a separate pantry area and enjoys a close proximity to the dining room. Two family bedrooms are split from the master suite and share a bath. The master bedroom features a large bath and a walk-in closet. A bonus room with attic storage is available for future use—perfect for the growing family. Don't miss the rear porch brightened by skylights!

HOME PLAN

HPK1600140

Style: Traditional

Square Footage: 1,540

Bonus Space: 277 sq. ft.

Bedrooms: 3

Bathrooms: 2

Width: 63' - 4"

Depth: 46' - 10"

eplans.com

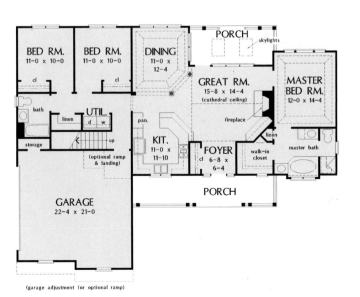

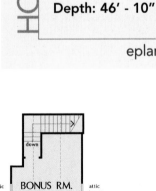

THIS PLAN'S FACADE OFFERS TRADITIONAL, HOMESPUN APPEAL, yet its interior boasts elegance and convenience. Graceful ceiling detail brings the great room, dining room, and master bedroom to new heights of style. The kitchen, just a few steps away from the dining room, flows into a windowed breakfast room that accesses the rear porch—as does the great room. Two bedrooms share a bath to the left of the plan. The spacious master suite, tucked behind the garage on the right, offers ample closet space and a deluxe bath with twin vanities and a compartmented bath and shower. Bonus space awaits expansion above the two-car garage.

HPK1600141

Style: Traditional

Square Footage: 1,955

Bonus Space: 329 sq. ft.

Bedrooms: 3

Bathrooms: 2

Width: 56' - 0"

Depth: 58' - 4"

eplans.com

© 2002 Donald A. Gardner, Inc.

HPK1600142

Style: Farmhouse

Square Footage: 1,822

Bedrooms: 3

Bathrooms: 2

Width: 58' - 0"

Depth: 67' - 2"

Foundation: Unfinished Basement, Finished Basement

eplans.com

STONE BAYS AND WOOD SIDING MAKE UP the exterior facade on this one-story home. The interior revolves around the living room with an attached dining room and the galley kitchen with a breakfast room. The master suite has a fine bath and a walk-in closet. One of three family bedrooms on the left side of the plan could be used as a home office.

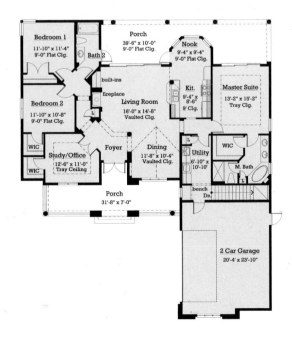

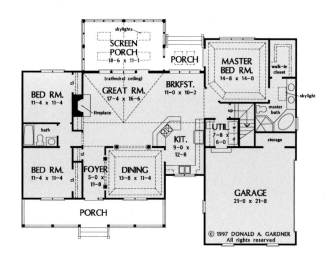

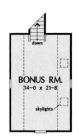

A CLASSIC COUNTRY EXTERIOR ENRICH-
ES THE APPEARANCE of this economical
home. A grand front porch and two skylit
back porches encourage weekend relaxation. The great room features a cathedral
ceiling and a fireplace with adjacent built-
ins. The master suite enjoys a double-door
entry, back-porch access, and a tray ceiling.
The master bath has a garden tub set in the
corner, a separate shower, twin vanities, and
a skylight. Loads of storage, an open floor
plan, and walls of windows make this
three-bedroom plan very livable.

HPK1600143

Style: Country Cottage

Square Footage: 1,652

Bonus Space: 367 sq. ft.

Bedrooms: 3

Bathrooms: 2

Width: 64' - 4"

Depth: 51' - 0"

HOME PLAN

eplans.com

SPECIAL ARCHITECTURAL ASPECTS turn this quaint home into much more than just another one-story ranch design. A central great room acts as the hub of the plan and is graced by a fireplace flanked on either side by windows. It is separated from the kitchen by a convenient serving bar. Formal dining is accomplished to the front of the plan in a room with a tray ceiling. Casual dining takes place in the breakfast room with its full wall of glass. Two bedrooms to the left share a full bath. The master suite and one additional bedroom are to the right.

HOME PLAN # HPK1600144

Style: Traditional

Square Footage: 1,932

Bedrooms: 4

Bathrooms: 3

Width: 63' - 0"

Depth: 45' - 0"

Foundation: Unfinished Walkout Basement, Crawlspace

eplans.com

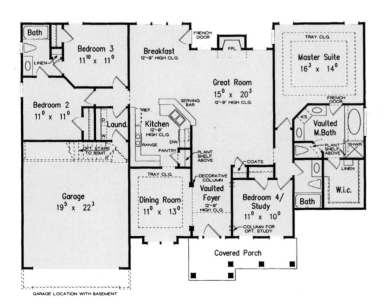

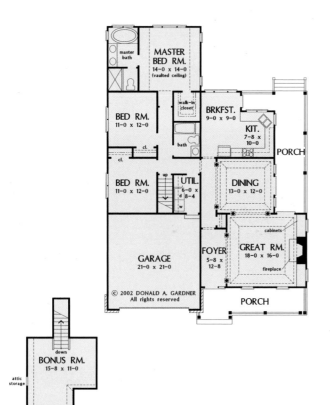

© 2002 DONALD A. GARDNER
All rights reserved

MASTER
BED RM.
14-0 x 14-0
(vaulted ceiling)

master
bath

walk-in
closet

BED RM.
11-0 x 12-0

bath

cl.

cl.

BRKFST.
9-0 x 9-0

KIT.
7-8 x
10-0

PORCH

BED RM.
11-0 x 12-0

up

UTIL.
6-0 x
8-4

DINING
13-0 x 12-0

GARAGE
21-0 x 21-0

FOYER
5-8 x
12-8

cabinets

GREAT RM.
18-0 x 16-0

fireplace

PORCH

BONUS RM.
15-8 x 11-0

down

attic
storage

10-4 x 10-0

attic
storage

THIS STRIKING NARROW-LOT BUNGALOW FEATURES an arched entrance, nostalgic front porch, and hip roof. A sidelight and fanlight over the front door usher natural light into the home and columns are used to divide space without enclosing it. Featuring a fireplace and built-in cabinetry, the great room accesses both the porch and the dining room. Columns and a tray ceiling define the dining room, which also leads to the side porch through French doors. Above the garage, there is a bonus room for expansion needs. A vaulted ceiling and spacious walk-in closet highlight the master bedroom. The master bath includes a double vanity, garden tub, and separate shower.

HPK1600145

Style: Traditional

Square Footage: 1,711

Bonus Space: 328 sq. ft.

Bedrooms: 3

Bathrooms: 2

Width: 46' - 6"

Depth: 65' - 0"

eplans.com

© 1994 Donald A. Gardner Architects, Inc.

HOME PLAN

HPK1600146

Style: Farmhouse

Square Footage: 1,807

Bonus Space: 419 sq. ft.

Bedrooms: 3

Bathrooms: 2

Width: 70' - 8"

Depth: 52' - 8"

eplans.com

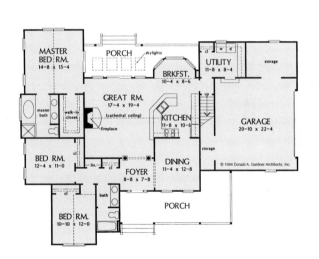

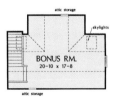

THIS COMFORTABLE COUNTRY HOME BEGINS WITH A FRONT PORCH that opens to a columned foyer. To the right, enter the formal dining room. Decorative columns define the central great room, which boasts wide views of the outdoors. A breakfast nook nearby accommodates casual dining. The master suite and the great room open to the rear porch. Family bedrooms share a full bath with dual lavatories.

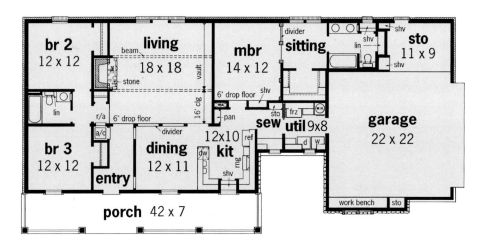

br 2
12 x 12

living
18 x 18

beam

stone

vault

16' clg

mbr
14 x 12

sitting

divider

lin

shv

sto
11 x 9

shv

shv

6' drop floor

shv

lin

6' drop floor

r/a

a/c

divider

br 3
12 x 12

entry

dining
12 x 11

pan

sto

frz

w.h.

sew

util 9x8

garage
22 x 22

12x10

kit

ref

dw

rg

shv

d

w

work bench

sto

porch 42 x 7

HOME PLAN

HPK1600147

Style: Traditional

Square Footage: 1,600

Bedrooms: 3

Bathrooms: 2

Width: 75' - 0"

Depth: 37' - 0"

Foundation: Unfinished Basement, Crawlspace, Slab

eplans.com

SOUTHERN CHARM ABOUNDS IN THIS ONE-STORY HOME with its covered porch, double dormers, and combination of stone and siding. Inside, the entry opens to the living room with its stone fireplace and beam-accented, vaulted ceiling. The U-shaped kitchen adjoins the formal dining room where dividers offer privacy between the dining and living rooms. The master suite boasts a sitting room, walk-in closet, and a private bath. On the left, two family bedrooms share a full bath.

THE ROMANCE OF A COLONIAL PLANTATION IS RESURRECTED in this charming design. Steps lead onto a covered porch and to an elegant double-door entry. The central living room, which opens to the rear porch, balances rooms on either side. Two family bedrooms share a full hall bath between them, to the right of the living room. To the left, the kitchen rests between the bayed eating area and the formal dining room. A hall at the rear of the plan leads to the master suite, which is secluded for privacy. A two-car garage, storage space, and a utility room complete this plan.

HOME PLAN

HPK1600148

Style: **Traditional**

Square Footage: **1,800**

Bedrooms: **3**

Bathrooms: **2**

Width: **66' - 0"**

Depth: **60' - 0"**

Foundation: **Crawlspace, Slab, Unfinished Basement**

eplans.com

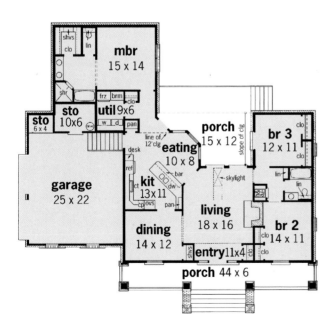

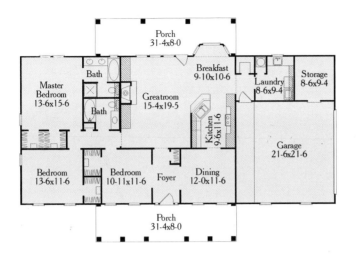

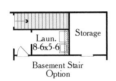

Laun.
8-6x5-6
Storage

Basement Stair
Option

DORMERS AND COLUMNS DECORATE THE EXTERIOR of this three-bedroom country home. Inside, the foyer has immediate access to one family bedroom and the formal dining area. Ahead is the great room with a warming fireplace and ribbon of windows for natural lighting. The master suite is set to the back of the plan and has a lavish bath with a garden tub, separate shower, and two vanities.

HPK1600149

Style: Southern Colonial

Square Footage: 1,688

Bedrooms: 3

Bathrooms: 2

Width: 70' - 1"

Depth: 48' - 0"

Foundation: Crawlspace, Slab, Unfinished Basement

HOME PLAN

eplans.com

THIS HOME OFFERS A BEAUTIFULLY TEXTURED FACADE.
Keystones and lintels highlight the beauty of the windows.
The vaulted great room and dining room are immersed in
light from the atrium window wall. The breakfast bay opens
to the covered porch in the backyard. A curved counter connects the kitchen to the great room. Three bedrooms, including a deluxe master suite, share the right side of the plan. All
enjoy large windows of their own. The garage is designed for
two cars, plus space for a motorcycle or yard tractor.

HOME PLAN

HPK1600150

Style: Traditional

Square Footage: 1,721

Bedrooms: 3

Bathrooms: 2

Width: 83' - 0"

Depth: 42' - 0"

**Foundation: Unfinished
Walkout Basement**

eplans.com

THIS COUNTRY HOME HAS A BIG HEART IN A COZY PACKAGE. Special touches—interior columns, a bay window, and dormers—add elegance. The central great room features a cathedral ceiling and a fireplace. A clerestory window splashes the room with natural light. The open kitchen easily services the breakfast area and the nearby dining room. The private master bedroom, with a tray ceiling and a walk-in closet, boasts amenities found in much larger homes. The bath features a skylight and a whirlpool tub. Two additional bedrooms share a bath. The front bedroom includes a walk-in closet and would make a nice study with an optional foyer entrance.

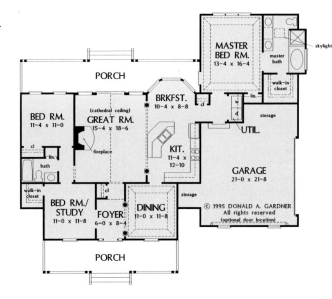

HOME PLAN

HPK1600151

Style: Country

Square Footage: 1,632

Bedrooms: 3

Bathrooms: 2

Width: 62' - 4"

Depth: 55' - 2"

eplans.com

REAR EXTERIOR

HOME PLAN

HPK1600152

Style: Farmhouse

Square Footage: 1,864

Bonus Space: 420 sq. ft.

Bedrooms: 3

Bathrooms: 2 ½

Width: 71' - 0"

Depth: 56' - 4"

eplans.com

REAR EXTERIOR

QUAINT AND COZY ON THE OUTSIDE WITH PORCHES front and back, this three-bedroom country home surprises with an open floor plan featuring a large great room with a cathedral ceiling. A central kitchen with an angled counter opens to the breakfast and great rooms for easy entertaining. The privately located master bedroom enjoys a cathedral ceiling and access to the deck. Two secondary bedrooms share a full hall bath. A bonus room makes expanding easy.

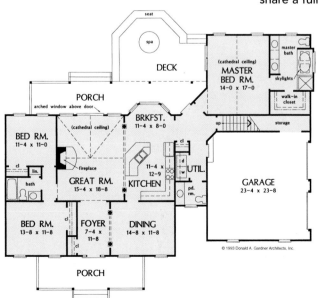

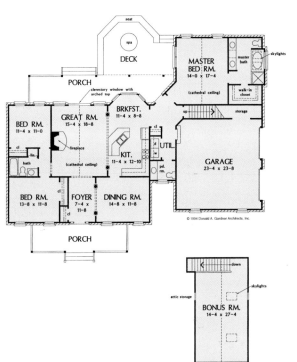

THIS BEAUTIFUL BRICK COUNTRY HOME HAS ALL THE AMENITIES needed for today's active family. Covered front and back porches, along with a rear deck, provide plenty of room for outdoor enjoyment. Inside, focus is on the large great room with its cathedral ceiling and welcoming fireplace. To the right, columns separate the kitchen and breakfast area from the great room and keep this area open. Chefs of all ages will appreciate the convenience of the kitchen with its center island and additional eating space. The master bedroom provides a splendid private retreat, featuring a cathedral ceiling and large walk-in closet. The luxurious master bath shares a double-bowl vanity, a separate shower, and a relaxing skylit whirlpool tub. At the opposite end of the plan, two additional bedrooms share a full bath. A skylit bonus room above the garage allows for additional living space.

HPK1600153

HOME PLAN

Style: Farmhouse

Square Footage: 1,954

Bonus Space: 436 sq. ft.

Bedrooms: 3

Bathrooms: 2 ½

Width: 71' - 3"

Depth: 62' - 6"

eplans.com

REAR EXTERIOR

THE COUNTRY CHARM OF THIS CAPE COD-STYLE HOME belies the elegance inside. The beautiful foyer, accented by columns that define the formal dining room, leads to the family room. Here, the vaulted space is warm and cozy, courtesy of an extended-hearth fireplace. The kitchen is open and welcoming with angled counters that offer plenty of workspace. The laundry is conveniently located near the garage entrance. In the master suite, the star is the vaulted compartmented bath. Two additional bedrooms—both with ample closets and one with a raised ceiling—complete the plan. An optional upstairs addition includes a fourth bedroom and a full bath.

HOME PLAN

HPK1600154

Style: Country Cottage

Square Footage: 1,792

Bonus Space: 255 sq. ft.

Bedrooms: 3

Bathrooms: 2

Width: 50' - 0"

Depth: 62' - 6"

Foundation: Crawlspace, Unfinished Walkout Basement

eplans.com

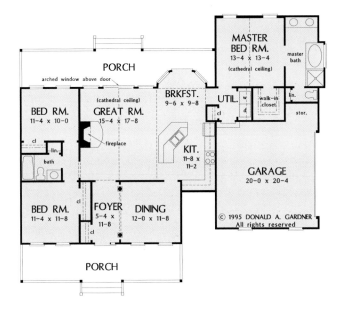

PORCH

arched window above door

BED RM.
11-4 x 10-0

GREAT RM.
15-4 x 17-8
(cathedral ceiling)

fireplace

BRKFST.
9-6 x 9-8
(cathedral ceiling)

UTIL.

KIT.
11-8 x
11-2

MASTER
BED RM.
13-4 x 13-4
(cathedral ceiling)

master bath

walk-in closet.

BED RM.
11-4 x 11-8

FOYER
5-4 x
11-8

DINING
12-0 x 11-8

GARAGE
20-0 x 20-4

PORCH

HPK1600155

HOME PLAN

Style: Farmhouse

Square Footage: 1,561

Bedrooms: 3

Bathrooms: 2

Width: 60' - 10"

Depth: 51' - 6"

eplans.com

COMBINING THE FINEST COUNTRY DETAILS WITH THE MOST MODERN LIVABILITY, this one-story home makes modest budgets really stretch. The welcoming front porch encourages you to stop and enjoy the summer breezes. The foyer leads to a formal dining room defined by columns. Beyond is the large great room with a cathedral ceiling and a fireplace. The kitchen and the breakfast room are open to the living area and include porch access. The master suite is tucked away in its own private space. It is conveniently separated from the family bedrooms, which share a full bath. The two-car garage contains extra storage space.

REAR EXTERIOR

HOME PLAN

HPK1600156

Style: Country Cottage

Square Footage: 1,933

Bonus Space: 519 sq. ft.

Bedrooms: 3

Bathrooms: 2 ½

Width: 62' - 0"

Depth: 50' - 0"

Foundation: Crawlspace, Unfinished Walkout Basement

eplans.com

TRADITIONAL IN EVERY SENSE OF THE WORD, you can't go wrong with this charming country cottage. The foyer opens on the right to a columned dining room, and ahead to the family room. Here, a raised ceiling and bright radius windows expand the space, and a warming fireplace lends a cozy touch. A sunny bayed breakfast nook flows into the angled kitchen for easy casual meals. Down the hall, two bedrooms share a full bath, tucked behind the two-car garage to protect the bedrooms from street noise. The master suite is indulgent, pampering homeowners with a bayed sitting area, tray ceiling, vaulted spa bath, and an oversized walk-in closet. A fourth bedroom and bonus space are available to grow as your family does.

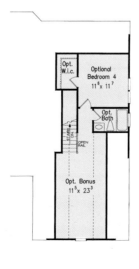

DORMERS CAST LIGHT AND INTEREST INTO THE FOYER for a grand first impression that sets the tone in this home full of today's amenities. The great room, articulated by columns, features a cathedral ceiling and is conveniently located adjacent to the breakfast room and kitchen. Tray ceilings and circle-top picture windows accent the front bedroom and dining room. A secluded master suite, highlighted by a tray ceiling in the bedroom, includes a bath with a skylight, a garden tub, a separate shower, a double-bowl vanity, and a spacious walk-in closet.

REAR EXTERIOR

HPK1600157

HOME PLAN

Style: Country Cottage

Square Footage: 1,879

Bonus Space: 360 sq. ft.

Bedrooms: 3

Bathrooms: 2

Width: 66' - 4"

Depth: 55' - 2"

eplans.com

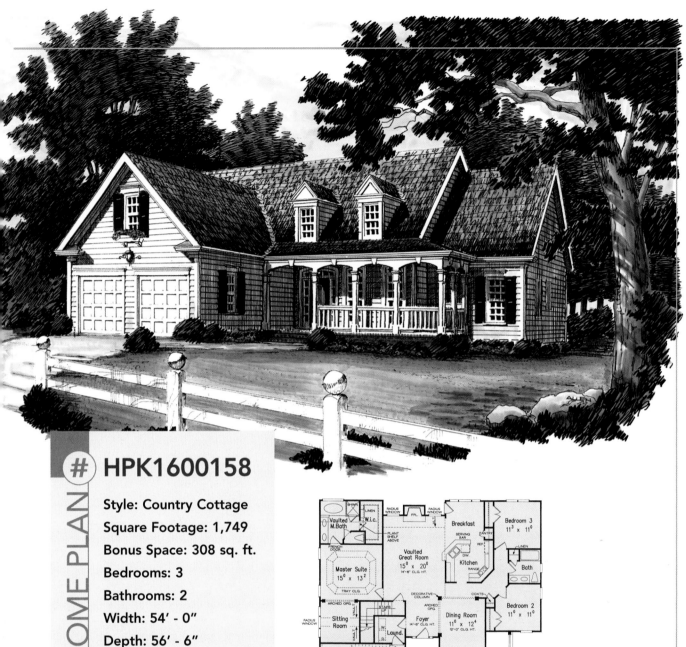

HOME PLAN

HPK1600158

Style: Country Cottage

Square Footage: 1,749

Bonus Space: 308 sq. ft.

Bedrooms: 3

Bathrooms: 2

Width: 54' - 0"

Depth: 56' - 6"

Foundation: Crawlspace, Unfinished Walkout Basement

eplans.com

OPTIONAL BONUS ROOM PLAN

THIS COZY COUNTRY COTTAGE IS ENHANCED WITH A FRONT-FACING PLANTER BOX above the garage and a charming covered porch. The foyer leads to a vaulted great room, complete with a fireplace and radius windows. Decorative columns complement the entrance to the dining room, as does a decorative arch. On the left side of the plan resides the master suite, which is resplendent with amenities including a vaulted sitting room with an arched opening, tray ceiling, and French doors to the vaulted full bath. On the right side, two additional bedrooms share a full bath.

DORMERS, ARCHED WINDOWS, AND COVERED
PORCHES lend this home its country appeal. Inside,
the foyer opens to the dining room on the right and
leads through a columned entrance to the great room.
The open kitchen easily serves the great room, the
breakfast area, and the dining room. A
cathedral ceiling graces the master
suite, which is complete with a walk-in
closet and a private bath. Two family
bedrooms share a hall bath.

REAR EXTERIOR

HOME PLAN

HPK1600159

Style: Farmhouse

Square Footage: 1,815

Bonus Space: 336 sq. ft.

Bedrooms: 3

Bathrooms: 2

Width: 70' - 8"

Depth: 70' - 2"

eplans.com

COUNTRY LIVING IN A UNIQUE FLOOR PLAN MAKES THIS DESIGN the perfect choice for just the right family. The covered front porch opens to an angled foyer that leads to a large great room with a sloped ceiling and fireplace. To the right is the formal dining room, defined by columns and plenty of windows overlooking the porch. Two secondary bedrooms share a full bath at the front of the plan. Connecting to the two-car garage via a laundry area, the kitchen provides an island cooktop and a quaint morning room. The master suite offers a retreat with a sloped ceiling, walk-in closet, and a bath with a whirlpool tub.

HOME PLAN

HPK1600160

Style: Farmhouse

Square Footage: 1,937

Bonus Space: 414 sq. ft.

Bedrooms: 3

Bathrooms: 2

Width: 76' - 4"

Depth: 73' - 4"

Foundation: Crawlspace

eplans.com

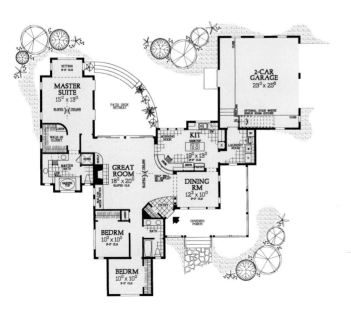

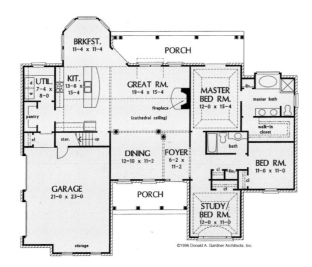

THIS DELIGHTFUL COUNTRY-COTTAGE ELEVATION GIVES WAY TO A MODERN floor plan. The formal dining room is set off from the expansive great room with decorative columns. Amenities in the nearby kitchen include an abundance of counter and cabinet space, a bi-level island with a snack bar, and a gazebo breakfast nook. The master suite is detailed with a tray ceiling and features a lush private bath with a large walk-in closet. Two additional bedrooms share a full hall bath. A bonus room over the garage can be finished as extra living space.

HOME PLAN

HPK1600161

Style: Traditional
Square Footage: 1,972
Bonus Space: 398 sq. ft.
Bedrooms: 3
Bathrooms: 2
Width: 67' - 7"
Depth: 56' - 7"

eplans.com

© 1996 Donald A. Gardner Architects, Inc.

HOME PLAN
HPK1600162

Style: Craftsman

Square Footage: 1,904

Bonus Space: 366 sq. ft.

Bedrooms: 3

Bathrooms: 2

Width: 53' - 10"

Depth: 57' - 8"

© 2002 Donald A. Gardner, Inc.

© 2002 DONALD A. GARDNER
All rights reserved

©1995 Donald A. Gardner Architects, Inc.

HOME PLAN
HPK1600163

Style: Farmhouse

Square Footage: 1,832

Bonus Space: 425 sq. ft.

Bedrooms: 3

Bathrooms: 2

Width: 65' - 4"

Depth: 62' - 0"

HOMES FROM 1,501 TO 2,000 SQUARE FEET

Complete Package—Designs with Manners and Attitude

Plans for homes between 2,001 and 2,500 square feet will appeal to homeowners who are looking to do more than shelter their family—who are seeking a design that brings distinction and excitement to their new home. Such a home may trade off economy of space or strict functionality in layout for highly specialized rooms and architectural details that express a unique vision of home living.

The concept of the pampering master suite, introduced by the family-sized home, really takes wing in the move-up home. For instance, plan HPK1600166 on page 175 devotes nearly one-third of its livable space to the master suite, including an impressive bath that features a windowed whirlpool tub, compartmented toilet, separate vanities, and an oversized stall shower. The spacious walk-in closet features a skylight, so you can distinguish your blues from your blacks. The master bedroom enjoys private access to the rear terrace.

The plan also shows how formal dining is given room in homes of this size, often yielding spectacular results. Ensure year-round use of your dining room by surrounding it with large windows that invite family and guests to linger long past the final course. Look to establish an attractive, elevated space in the home that nonetheless welcomes and comforts family and guests.

Lastly, one-story move-up homes are a great fit for empty-nesters looking to treat themselves to a new, larger home, or those

SLENDER COLUMNS elevate this dining room. But the nearby deck keeps the space friendly.

Sam Gray (2)

who need to care for elderly or special-needs family members. In the latter cases, a guest suite can serve as a second master suite—an attractive option when the guest bedroom adjoins a deck or garden. Additional bedrooms can accommodate visiting children or relatives, and serve as a study when vacant.

A RESORT-INSPIRED guest bedroom pampers visiting friends and relatives.

© 2002 Donald A. Gardner, Inc.

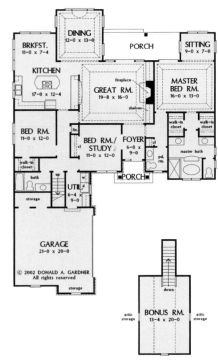

© 2002 DONALD A. GARDNER
All rights reserved

HOME PLAN

HPK1600164

Style: Craftsman

Square Footage: 2,017

Bonus Space: 319 sq. ft.

Bedrooms: 3

Bathrooms: 2 ½

Width: 54' - 0"

Depth: 74' - 0"

HOME PLAN

HPK1600165

Style: Vacation

Square Footage: 2,019

Bonus Space: 384 sq. ft.

Bedrooms: 3

Bathrooms: 2

Width: 56' - 0"

Depth: 56' - 3"

Foundation: Crawlspace

HOME PLAN

HPK1600166

Style: Bungalow

Square Footage: 2,489

Bedrooms: 3

Bathrooms: 2 ½

Width: 68' - 3"

Depth: 62' - 0"

Foundation: Finished Walkout Basement

eplans.com

THIS FINE BUNGALOW, WITH ITS MULTI-PLE GABLES, rafter tails, and pillared front porch, will be the envy of any neighborhood. A beam-ceilinged great room is further enhanced by a through-fireplace and French doors to the rear terrace. The U-shaped kitchen features a cooktop island with a snack bar and offers a beam-ceilinged break-fast/keeping room that shares the through-fireplace with the great room. Two secondary bedrooms share a full bath; the master suite is designed to pamper. Here, the homeown-er will be pleased with a walk-in closet, a separate shower, and access to the terrace. The two-car garage has a side entrance and will easily shelter the family fleet.

REAR EXTERIOR

FIRST FLOOR

BASEMENT

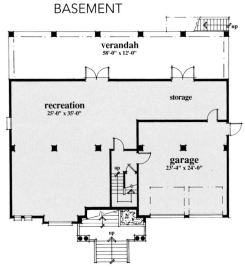

(#) HPK1600167

Style: Tidewater

Square Footage: 2,190

Bedrooms: 3

Bathrooms: 2

Width: 60' - 0"

Depth: 54' - 0"

Foundation: Island Basement

eplans.com

THE DRAMATIC ARCHED ENTRY OF THIS COTTAGE borrows freely from the Southern coastal tradition. The foyer and central hall open to the grand room. The kitchen is flanked by the dining room and the morning nook, which opens to the lanai. On the left side of the plan, the master suite also accesses the lanai. Two walk-in closets and a compartmented bath with a separate tub and shower and a double-bowl vanity complete this opulent retreat. The right side of the plan includes two secondary bedrooms and a full bath.

CRAFTSMAN-STYLE WINDOWS with a bit of Palladian flair enhance the exterior of this home. Inside, a vaulted ceiling accents the formal living room; the adjoining dining room includes columns and a built-in display cabinet. The family room and nook, also with vaulted ceilings, serve as charming informal gathering areas. Sleeping quarters, to the left of the plan, include the vaulted master suite and two additional bedrooms. All three bedrooms are conveniently close to the utility room, which offers a wash sink and counter space.

HOME PLAN

HPK1600168

Style: Craftsman

Square Footage: 2,218

Bedrooms: 3

Bathrooms: 2

Width: 50' - 0"

Depth: 70' - 0"

Foundation: Crawlspace

eplans.com

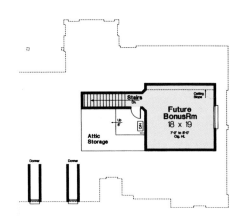

THIS CHARMER IS CONSTRUCTED WITH SHINGLE AND STONE FACADE. Fronted with rustic columns and an august Tudor-style chimney, the exterior evokes images of a country farmhouse. The dormer windows allow for a brightened entry way on sunny days. On your left lies the great room with vaulted ceiling, and the gallery, suitable for a private collection of art, faces you. The kitchen is located off to the left, joining forces with the breakfast area (the kitchen's best secret is a corner pantry). From here you can also access the covered patio. A formal dining room (also convertible to a study) opens off the gallery through an archway. After passing two hall closets and a family bedroom on your right, you will come to the bonus staircase for an upstairs attic or loft, and the master suite. A third bedroom and utility area also occupy this part of the floor.

HOME PLAN

HPK1600169

Style: Country Cottage

Square Footage: 2,439

Bonus Space: 390 sq. ft.

Bedrooms: 3

Bathrooms: 2 ½

Width: 77' - 0"

Depth: 59' - 1"

Foundation: Crawlspace, Slab

eplans.com

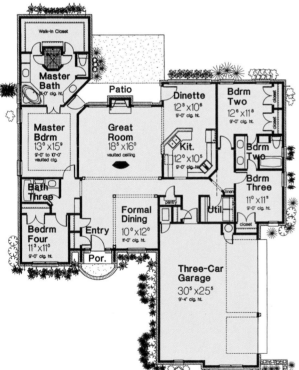

HOME PLAN

HPK1600170

Style: French

Square Footage: 2,279

Bedrooms: 4

Bathrooms: 3

Width: 60' - 0"

Depth: 78' - 0"

Foundation: Slab

eplans.com

ACCENTED BRICK AND A GOTHIC ENTRY
present a fine exterior on this Old World adaptation. Inside, the simplicity of antiquated design blends perfectly with modern efficiency for a home that lends itself to beauty and comfort. The vaulted great room will surely be the family epicenter with a warming hearth and lots of natural light. The kitchen effortlessly serves the dinette and formal dining area. Two nearby bedrooms share a Jack-and-Jill bath, as another enjoys a semiprivate bath to the left. The master suite is luxurious with a vaulted ceiling, massive walk-in closet, corner whirlpool tub, and central shower.

SPECIAL GATHERINGS AND EVENTS will take place in the heart of this splendid home. The great room, defined by columns, includes a hearth and views to the covered patio. The east wing is occupied by the sleeping quarters, with a master bedroom which features an exclusive master bath. Two family bedrooms both have walk-in closets and share a compartmented bath with twin vanities. The three-car garage opens to the hall where the utility room, the kitchen, and an additional bedroom/study can be accessed. A future bonus room is also available upstairs.

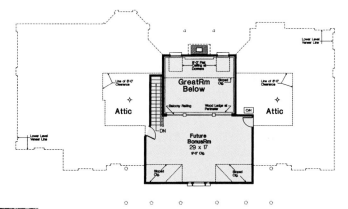

HOME PLAN

HPK1600171

Style: Farmhouse

Square Footage: 2,293

Bonus Space: 536 sq. ft.

Bedrooms: 4

Bathrooms: 3

Width: 88' - 0"

Depth: 51' - 9"

Foundation: Slab, Unfinished Basement

eplans.com

THE SIMPLICITY OF THE RANCH LIFESTYLE is indicated in every detail of this charming country design. Front and rear verandas along with earthy materials combine to give the exterior of this home a true land-lover's look. A central fireplace warms the cathedral-enhanced space of the formal great room. The casual kitchen area features an island workstation overlooking the rear veranda. The master suite is a sumptuous retreat with a sitting area, private bath, and walk-in closet. Two additional bedrooms share a full hall bath.

HOME PLAN

HPK1600172

Style: Farmhouse

Square Footage: 2,172

Bedrooms: 3

Bathrooms: 2

Width: 79' - 0"

Depth: 47' - 0"

Foundation: Crawlspace, Slab

eplans.com

HOMES FROM 2,001 TO 2,500 SQUARE FEET

STATELY COLUMNS AND BRIGHT WINDOWS grace the entry to this French farmhouse. Open rooms, French doors, and specialty ceilings add a sense of spaciousness throughout the home. Interior columns set the formal dining room apart. The great room boasts a fireplace, built-in cabinetry, and dazzling views. The master suite leads to His and Hers walk-in closets, a dual-sink vanity, a corner whirlpool tub, and an oversize corner shower. Two bedrooms with a shared bath sit in the right wing.

(#) HPK1600173

HOME PLAN

Style: Farmhouse

Square Footage: 2,329

Bedrooms: 3

Bathrooms: 2 ½

Width: 72' - 6"

Depth: 73' - 4"

Foundation: Crawlspace

eplans.com

THIS THREE-BEDROOM HOME BRINGS THE PAST to life with Tuscan columns, dormers, and fanlight windows. The entrance is flanked by the dining room and study. The great room boasts cathedral ceilings and a fireplace, with an open design that connects to the kitchen area. The spacious kitchen adjoins a breakfast nook and accesses the rear covered veranda. The master bedroom enjoys a sitting area, access to the covered veranda, and a spacious bathroom. This home is complete with two family bedrooms.

HOME PLAN

(#) HPK1600174

Style: Craftsman
Square Footage: 2,387
Bonus Space: 377 sq. ft.
Bedrooms: 3
Bathrooms: 2 ½
Width: 69' - 6"
Depth: 68' - 11"
Foundation: Slab, Crawlspace

eplans.com

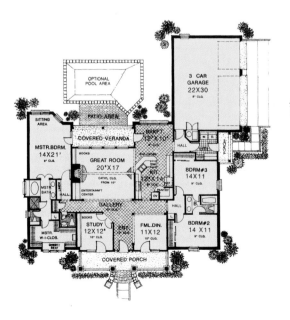

OPTIONAL LAYOUT

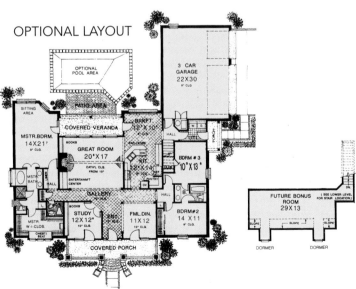

THIS GORGEOUS COUNTRY DREAM HOUSE brings down-home comfort to any neighborhood. A shaded, covered porch opens to a formal foyer with a niche, perfect for an entry table. On the left, a lovely dining room with a convenient butler's pantry overlooks the front yard. The great room is open and bright, enjoying a wall of windows, built-in media center, and cozy fireplace. The kitchen serves up delectable meals with ease. Bedrooms are situated on each side of the plan, featuring a lavish master suite with a magnificent bath. Two additional bedrooms and a den/study complete the home.

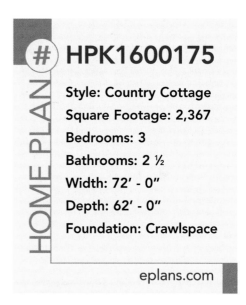

HOME PLAN

HPK1600175

Style: Country Cottage

Square Footage: 2,367

Bedrooms: 3

Bathrooms: 2 ½

Width: 72' - 0"

Depth: 62' - 0"

Foundation: Crawlspace

eplans.com

SYMMETRY AND SOUTHERN CHARM combine to make this home a family favorite. Inside, natural light is a cheerful addition. Nine-foot ceilings bring height and grandeur to every room—the living room ceiling tops off at a soaring 11 feet! The U-shaped kitchen features a bonus side counter for extra workspace, and easily serves the breakfast and dining rooms. Separated for privacy, the master suite is a joy, with a spa-style bath and His and Hers walk-in closets. Two more bedrooms are located to the far right. A bonus room would be a perfect home office, guest room, or nursery. Future space upstairs awaits your imagination.

HOME PLAN

(#) HPK1600176

Style: Traditional

Square Footage: 2,122

Bonus Space: 965 sq. ft.

Bedrooms: 3

Bathrooms: 2 ½

Width: 69' - 0"

Depth: 67' - 10"

Foundation: Slab, Unfinished Basement, Crawlspace

eplans.com

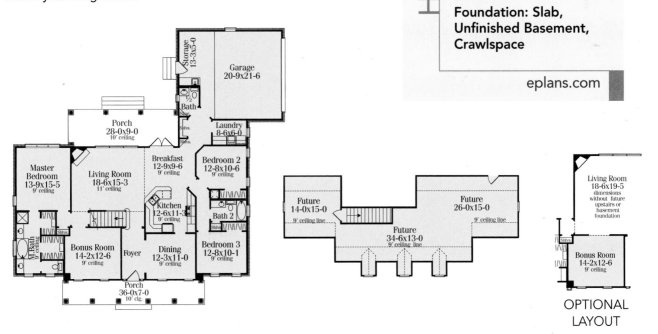

OPTIONAL LAYOUT

© 1998 Donald A Gardner, Inc.

A TRIO OF DORMERS AND A FRONT PORCH adorn the facade of this sprawling four-bedroom country home. Illuminated by the center dormer, the vaulted foyer gives way to the dining room with a tray ceiling, and the spacious great room with a cathedral ceiling, a fireplace, and built-in shelves. A split-bedroom layout provides privacy for homeowners in a generous master suite with a tray ceiling and private bath. Three additional bedrooms reside on the opposite side of the home.

HPK1600177

HOME PLAN

Style: Traditional
Square Footage: 2,487
Bedrooms: 4
Bathrooms: 3
Width: 86' - 2"
Depth: 51' - 8"

eplans.com

© 1998 Donald A. Gardner, Inc.

EXCITING VOLUMES AND NINE-FOOT CEILINGS add elegance to this comfortable, open plan. Hosts whose guests always end up in the kitchen will enjoy entertaining here, with only columns separating it from the great room. Children's bedrooms share a full bath that's complete with a linen closet. The master suite, located in a quiet wing, is highlighted by a tray ceiling and includes a skylit bath with a garden tub, private toilet, double-bowl vanity, and spacious walk-in closet.

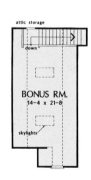

HOME PLAN

 # HPK1600178

Style: Farmhouse
Square Footage: 2,192
Bonus Space: 390 sq. ft.
Bedrooms: 4
Bathrooms: 2 ½
Width: 74' - 10"
Depth: 55' - 8"

eplans.com

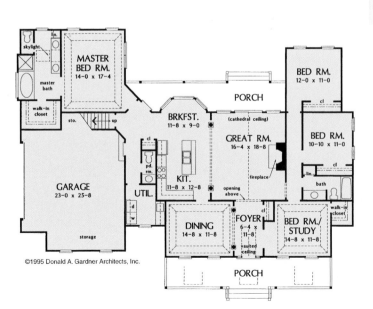

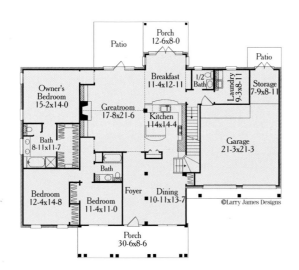

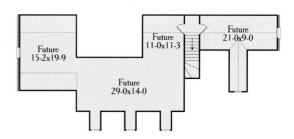

HOME PLAN

HPK1600179

Style: Traditional

Square Footage: 2,225

Bedrooms: 3

Bathrooms: 2 ½

Width: 71' - 5"

Depth: 62' - 5"

Foundation: Unfinished Basement, Crawlspace, Slab

eplans.com

AN INVITING PORCH IS ONLY A PRELUDE to the entertaining possibilities inside. Enter to find a dining room, set off by columns, to the immediate right. Ahead, the great room—with a vaulted ceiling, a fireplace, and patio access—will host many an event. The kitchen allows for guests to gather and socialize, and the breakfast nook provides a wonderful space for informal meals. The master bedroom will delight with a large walk-in closet and a bath with dual sinks and a separate tub and shower. Two more bedrooms on the first floor share a hall bath. Upstairs, future space leaves it all up to your imagination.

© William E. Poole Designs, Inc.

HOME PLAN

#HPK1600180

Style: Country Cottage

Square Footage: 2,215

Bedrooms: 3

Bathrooms: 3

Width: 69' - 10"

Depth: 62' - 6"

Foundation: Crawlspace, Unfinished Basement

eplans.com

THREE PETITE DORMERS TOP A WELCOMING COVERED PORCH and add a touch of grace to an already beautiful home. Inside, the foyer opens to the left to a formal dining room, which in turn has easy access to the efficient kitchen. Here, a pantry and a snack bar in the breakfast area make meal preparations a delight. The nearby spacious family room features a fireplace, built-in bookshelves, and outdoor access. Located away from the master suite for privacy, two family bedrooms pamper with private baths and walk-in closets. On the other end of the home, the master suite provides luxury via a huge walk-in closet, whirlpool tub, and corner shower with a seat. An optional second floor features a fourth bedroom in private splendor with its own bath and access to a recreation room complete with a second fireplace.

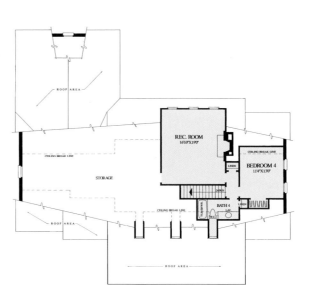

A SIMPLIFIED COUNTRY FACADE SUITS THE EASY LAYOUT
of this plan. Formal rooms flank the foyer, and the family room, kitchen, and breakfast nook will be the hub of casual living with their shared three-way fireplace. The master suite is secluded to the right, with an elegant bath and huge walk-in closet; the family bedrooms have their own space on the left.

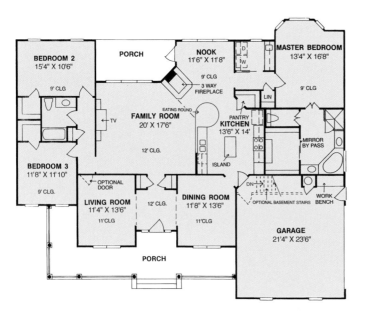

HPK1600181

Style: Farmhouse
Square Footage: 2,126
Bedrooms: 3
Bathrooms: 2
Width: 66' - 0"
Depth: 54' - 0"

HOME PLAN

eplans.com

HOME PLAN

(#) HPK1600182

Style: Country Cottage

Square Footage: 2,151

Bonus Space: 814 sq. ft.

Bedrooms: 3

Bathrooms: 2

Width: 61' - 0"

Depth: 55' - 8"

Foundation: Crawlspace, Unfinished Basement

eplans.com

COUNTRY FLAVOR IS WELL ESTABLISHED on this fine three-bedroom home. The covered front porch welcomes friends and family alike to the foyer, where the formal dining room opens off to the left. The vaulted ceiling in the great room enhances the warmth of the fireplace and the wall of windows. An efficient kitchen works well with the bayed breakfast area. The secluded master suite offers a walk-in closet and a lavish bath; on the other side of the home, two family bedrooms share a full bath. Upstairs, an optional fourth bedroom is available for guests or in-laws and provides access to a large recreation room.

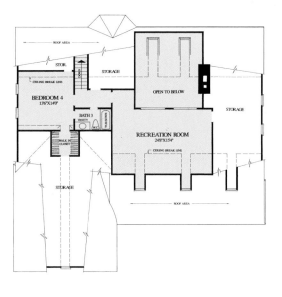

HOME PLAN

HPK1600183

Style: Farmhouse

Square Footage: 2,090

Bedrooms: 3

Bathrooms: 2 ½

Width: 84' - 6"

Depth: 64' - 0"

Foundation: Crawlspace

eplans.com

THIS CLASSIC FARMHOUSE ENJOYS A WRAPAROUND PORCH that's perfect for enjoyment of the outdoors. To the rear of the plan, a sun terrace with a spa opens from the master suite and the morning room. A grand great room offers a sloped ceiling and a corner fireplace with a raised hearth. The formal dining room is defined by a low wall and graceful archways set off by decorative columns. The tiled kitchen has a centered island counter with a snack bar and adjoins a laundry area. Two family bedrooms reside to the side of the plan, and each enjoys private access to the covered porch. A secluded master suite nestles in its own wing and features a sitting area with access to the rear terrace and spa.

© 1997 Donald A. Gardner Architects, Inc.

WITH AN EXCITING BLEND OF STYLES, this home features the wrapping porch of a country farmhouse with a brick-and-siding exterior for a uniquely pleasing effect. The great room shares its cathedral ceiling with an open kitchen, and the octagonal dining room is complemented by a tray ceiling. Built-ins flank the great room's fireplace for added convenience. The master suite features a full bath, a walk-in closet, and access to the rear porch. Two additional bedrooms share a full hall bath; a third can be converted into a study. Skylit bonus space is available above the garage, which is connected to the home by a covered breezeway.

HOME PLAN

HPK1600184

Style: Country Cottage

Square Footage: 2,273

Bonus Space: 342 sq. ft.

Bedrooms: 4

Bathrooms: 2 ½

Width: 74' - 8"

Depth: 75' - 10"

eplans.com

(#) HPK1600185

Style: Country Cottage

Square Footage: 2,069

Bonus Space: 304 sq. ft.

Bedrooms: 3

Bathrooms: 2

Width: 57' - 8"

Depth: 68' - 10"

Foundation: Crawlspace, Slab

eplans.com

READY TO LIVE IN: THIS HOME FEATURES BUILT-IN EVERYTHING! Columns burnish the inside and outside of the house for exceptional grandeur. An open floor plan situates all of your needs: a formal dining room, recreation room, kitchen with breakfast nook and snack bar, laundry, patio, and split bedrooms, featuring an incredible master suite. Perks include crafted French doors, wood fireplace, covered patio in back and a partially covered porch at the front, unusually shaped rooms, and arched windows. This design also provides for a bonus attic or loft.

THIS FLORIDA "CRACKER"-STYLE HOME IS
WARM and inviting. Inpretentious use of space is
the hallmark of the Florida Cracker. This design
shows the style at its best. Private baths for each
of the bedrooms are a fine example of this. The
huge great room, which sports a volume ceiling,
opens to the expansive rear porch for extended
entertaining. Traditional Cracker homes had sparse
master suites. Not this one! It has a lavish bed-
chamber and a luxurious bath with His and Hers
closets and a corner soaking tub. Perfect for a
sloping lot, this home can be expanded with a
lower garage and bonus space in the basement.

HOME PLAN

HPK1600186

Style: Traditional

Square Footage: 2,500

Bedrooms: 3

Bathrooms: 3

Width: 64' - 0"

Depth: 52' - 0"

Foundation: Unfinished
Basement

eplans.com

FIRST FLOOR

BASEMENT

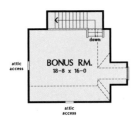

BONUS RM.
18-8 x 16-0

down

attic
access

attic
access

TURRET-STYLE BAY WINDOWS, AN ARCHED ENTRYWAY, and an elegant balustrade add timeless appeal to a remarkable facade, yet this refined exterior encompasses a very practical layout. Separated from the kitchen by an angled island, the great room features built-in shelves on both sides of the fireplace as well as French doors leading to the rear porch with a wet bar. Custom-style details include tray ceilings in the dining room and study/bedroom as well as columns in the foyer and master bath.

MASTER
BED RM.
13-4 x 18-8

master bath

SCREEN
PORCH
16-8 x 13-0

DECK

skylights

wet bar

BED RM.
13-4 x 11-4

BRKFST.
12-0 x 10-4

UTIL.
9-0 x 6-4

walk-in
closet

w d

up

(cathedral ceiling)

bath

GREAT RM.
18-8 x 19-0

fireplace

KIT.
12-0 x 14-8

BED RM.
12-0 x 12-4

GARAGE
22-8 x 21-0

pan.

walk-in
closet

FOYER
13-6 x 6-4

DINING
12-0 x 16-5

© 2001 Donald A. Gardner
All rights reserved

cl

BED RM./
STUDY
12-0 x 15-5

PORCH

storage

HPK1600187

Style: Traditional

Square Footage: 2,461

Bonus Space: 397 sq. ft.

Bedrooms: 4

Bathrooms: 2

Width: 71' - 2"

Depth: 67' - 2"

HOME PLAN

eplans.com

© 1998 Donald A. Gardner, Inc.

seat

DECK

skylights

SCREEN PORCH
16-0 x 12-0

(cathedral ceiling)

MASTER BED RM.
13-0 x 18-8

master bath

walk-in closet

skylights

BRKFST.
12-0 x 8-4

UTILITY
9-4 x 6-8

BED RM.
12-4 x 12-6

fireplace

GREAT RM.
18-0 x 19-4

(cathedral ceiling)

pd. rm.

d   w

up

walk-in closet

walk-in closet

KITCHEN
12-0 x 12-10

GARAGE
25-8 x 20-0

bath

storage

BED RM.
11-0 x 12-2

lin.

cl

FOYER
12-0 x 5-8

cl

BED RM./ STUDY
12-0 x 12-0

PORCH

DINING
12-0 x 13-8

storage

© 1998 Donald A Gardner, Inc.

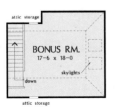

attic storage

BONUS RM.
17-6 x 18-0

skylights

down

attic storage

HOME PLAN

HPK1600188

Style: Traditional
Square Footage: 2,262
Bonus Space: 388 sq. ft.
Bedrooms: 4
Bathrooms: 2 ½
Width: 77' - 4"
Depth: 62' - 0"

eplans.com

TRUE TRADITION IS EXHIBITED IN THE BRICK-AND-SIDING facade, hipped roof, and keystone arches of this spacious four-bedroom home. Stately columns framing the front entry are repeated in the home's formal foyer. The generous great room is exemplary, boasting a fireplace with flanking built-ins. A dramatic cathedral ceiling enhances the space and is continued out into the adjoining screened porch. The nearby breakfast area is enriched by dual skylights. Three family bedrooms, two with walk-in closets, share an impressive hall bath with dual-sink vanity. Secluded on the opposite side of the home, the master suite features rear-deck access, a walk-in closet, and a private bath with corner tub and separate vanities.

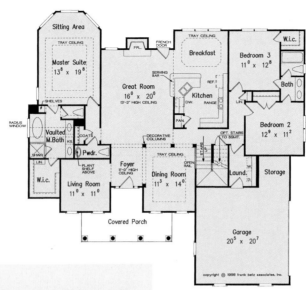

HOME PLAN

HPK1600189

Style: Country Cottage

Square Footage: 2,072

Bonus Space: 372 sq. ft.

Bedrooms: 3

Bathrooms: 2 ½

Width: 61' - 0"

Depth: 58' - 6"

Foundation: Crawlspace, Unfinished Walkout Basement

eplans.com

HORIZONTAL SIDING AND A COLUMNED PORCH indicate country flavor in this fine three-bedroom home. Inside, the foyer is flanked by a formal living room and dining room; directly ahead, the great room—with a fireplace—opens to the breakfast room and kitchen. Two family bedrooms share a full bath, and the private master suite is full of amenities. Upstairs, an optional fourth bedroom provides plenty of future expansion opportunities.

Floor plan labels:

Bedroom 2
11'-2" x 12'-9"
Tray Ceiling

Nook
13'-0" x 9'-4"
10'-0" Flat Clg.

Porch
30'-6" x 10'-0"

Master Suite
13'-0" x 20'-8"
Tray Ceiling

Kitchen
13'-0" x 12'-0"
Stepped Clg.

Dining Room
12'-8" x 16'-0"
Coffered Clg.

Living Room
17'-8" x 16'-0"
Coffered Clg.

ent.
center

Bath 2

P.

10'-0" Clg.

fireplace
art niche

WIC

WIC

art
niche

11'-0" Clg.

Foyer
18'-9" Clg.

11'-0" Clg.

L

book shelves

Entry
18'-0" x 6'-0"

M. Bath

Bedroom 1
16'-6" x 12'-3"
Tray Ceiling

Utility
7'-8" x 12'-0"
10'-0" Clg.

Study/Office
12'-0" x 13'-0"
Stepped Clg.

L

Garage
23'-6" x 23'-0"

 # HPK1600190

HOME PLAN

Style: Farmhouse

Square Footage: 2,487

Bedrooms: 3

Bathrooms: 2

Width: 70' - 0"

Depth: 72' - 0"

Foundation: Crawlspace

eplans.com

COTTAGE QUAINTNESS AND VICTORIAN ACCENTS lend a time-less style to this family design. The covered front entry porch welcomes you inside to a foyer that opens to a combined living room/dining area, defined by columns. Two sets of double doors open to the expansive rear porch. The kitchen flows into the dining room and features an island workstation and a casual breakfast nook. Two family bedrooms share a hall bath with the quiet ffice/study. The master suite provides His and Hers walk-in closets, a spacious bath, and private access to the rear porch.

SCREENED PORCH
14'-1" x 11'-6"

TRAY CEILING

MASTER BDRM
14'-2" x 15'-2"

SITTING
6'-10" x 6'-0"
9' CEILING

PATIO OR DECK
14'-3" x 15'-2"

11' HIGH CEILING

BEDROOM 3
11'-0" x 13'-6"
9' CEILING

OPTIONAL TV NICHE ABOVE FIREPLACE

COUNTRY KITCHEN
14'-3" x 22'-6"
9' CEILING

UP TO BONUS

FAMILY ROOM
14'-0" x 22'-6"
12' HIGH CEILING

LINE OF BONUS ROOM

BEDROOM 2
11'-0" x 13'-6"
9' CEILING

TRAY CEILING

PANTRY
7'-6" x 4'-6"

DESK

10'-6"

10'-6"

32'-0"

LIVING
11'-0" x 12'-0"
9' CEILING

DINING
11'-0" x 12'-0"
10' HIGH CEILING

3 CAR GARAGE
21'-4" x 33'-2"

PORCH
29'-4" x 6'-0"

ELEGANT ROUND COLUMNS "DRESS UP" this three-bedroom Southern Country design. Its classic irresistible styling makes it perfect for almost any neighborhood. The large vaulted family room, enormous country kitchen, and the bonus area create a spacious feel for the overall plan. The sumptuous master suite includes a double-tray ceiling, a sitting area, a large walk-in closet, and a luxurious bath. The country kitchen is open to the vaulted family room. A French door leads to the vaulted screened porch and master bedroom. The dining room is adorned with a decorative round column and tray ceiling. Bedrooms 2 and 3 feature walk-in closets and individual baths.

HOME PLAN

(#) HPK1600191

Style: Traditional
Square Footage: 2,097
Bonus Space: 452 sq. ft.
Bedrooms: 3
Bathrooms: 3
Width: 70' - 2"
Depth: 59' - 0"
Foundation: Slab

eplans.com

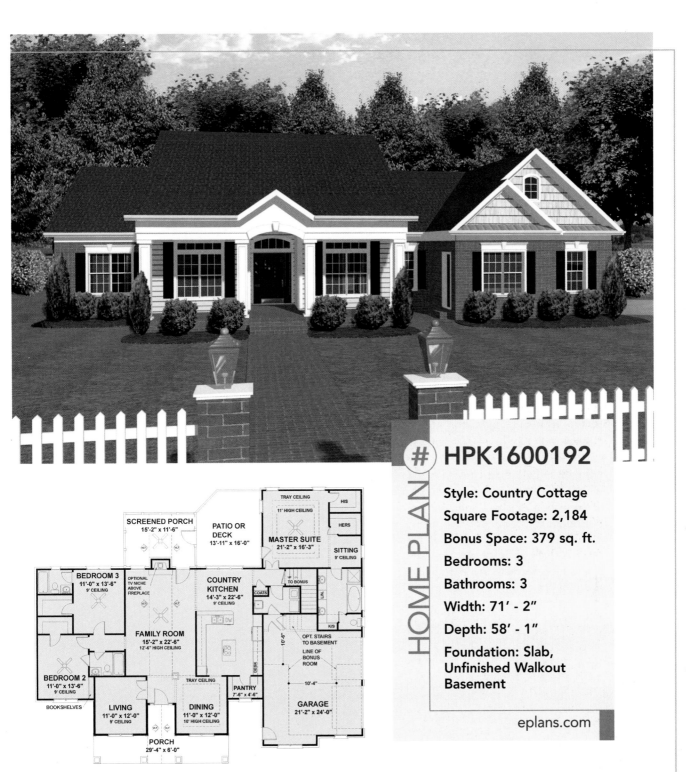

Floor Plan Labels

SCREENED PORCH
15'-2" x 11'-6"

PATIO OR DECK
13'-11" x 16'-0"

TRAY CEILING
11' HIGH CEILING

HIS

HERS

MASTER SUITE
21'-2" x 16'-3"

SITTING
9' CEILING

BEDROOM 3
11'-0" x 13'-6"
9' CEILING

OPTIONAL TV NICHE ABOVE FIREPLACE

COUNTRY KITCHEN
14'-3" x 22'-6"
9' CEILING

COATS

UP TO BONUS

LIN.

FAMILY ROOM
15'-2" x 22'-6"
12'-6" HIGH CEILING

DESK

OPT. STAIRS TO BASEMENT
LINE OF BONUS ROOM

K/S

10'-6"

BEDROOM 2
11'-0" x 13'-6"
9' CEILING

TRAY CEILING

PANTRY
7'-6" x 4'-6"

10'-4"

BOOKSHELVES

LIVING
11'-0" x 12'-0"
9' CEILING

DINING
11'-0" x 12'-0"
10' HIGH CEILING

GARAGE
21'-2" x 24'-0"

PORCH
29'-4" x 6'-0"

HOME PLAN

HPK1600192

Style: Country Cottage

Square Footage: 2,184

Bonus Space: 379 sq. ft.

Bedrooms: 3

Bathrooms: 3

Width: 71' - 2"

Depth: 58' - 1"

Foundation: Slab, Unfinished Walkout Basement

eplans.com

THIS SOPHISTICATED SOUTHERN COUNTRY HOME, with its updated classic facade and spacious interior design, is both flexible and dramatic. Three full baths, a screened porch, and bonus square footage are just a few of its irresistible features. The luxurious master suite includes a double-tray ceiling, a sitting area, His and Hers walk-in closets, and an exquisite bath. The country kitchen is open to the vaulted family room. A French door leads to the vaulted screened porch and master bedroom. A decorative square column and tray ceiling adorn the elegant dining room. Bedrooms 2 and 3 feature walk-in closets and individual baths. An optional basement foundation is available.

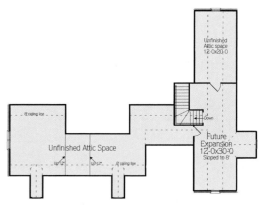

THIS UTTERLY CHARMING COUNTRY HOUSE will be a welcome sight for sore eyes come day's end. Twin chimneys bedeck the roof line of the exterior. A great room and formal dining room are immediately accessible from the foyer. Two family bedrooms open off of the great room. Speaking of the great room, note the cathedral ceiling and expansive rear view. The kitchen area features snack bar and breakfast nook, from which you can reach the rear patio. A master suite, laundry, and side-load garage occupy the remainder of the interior. Unfinished attic space provides for various possibilities; plan to expand this area with optional loft. A potential basement is also included with this design.

HOME PLAN

HPK1600193

Style: Country Cottage

Square Footage: 2,286

Bonus Space: 443 sq. ft.

Bedrooms: 3

Bathrooms: 2 ½

Width: 76' - 10"

Depth: 55' - 6"

Foundation: Crawlspace, Slab, Unfinished Basement

eplans.com

HOME PLAN

HPK1600194

Style: Traditional

Square Footage: 2,184

Bonus Space: 572 sq. ft.

Bedrooms: 3

Bathrooms: 2 ½

Width: 68' - 0"

Depth: 62' - 0"

Foundation: Crawlspace, Slab, Unfinished Basement

eplans.com

SYMMETRY AND BALANCE BEST DESCRIBE THIS BRICK home, which is accented by gabled roofs and dormers. Three sets of French doors under a covered porch provide entry to a foyer and great room, perfect for entertaining on a grand scale. A wall of windows and a set of French doors with access to the rear patio are the focal points of the great room. A cheery fire in the great room's large fireplace—with a built-in bookcase—will brighten any occasion. A rear covered porch opens to a large patio accessible from the breakfast nook. Nearby, the well-appointed kitchen includes a snack/serving bar.

IF YOU ARE LOOKING FOR A HOME THAT GROWS WITH YOUR FAMILY, THIS IS IT! Six rounded columns grace the front porch and lend a Colonial feel to this great home plan. Inside, the foyer opens to the formal dining space, which is only a few steps to the kitchen. A walk-in pantry, spacious counters and cabinets, snack bar, adjoining breakfast area, and planning desk make this kitchen efficient and gourmet. A private master suite features a sitting bay, twin walk-in closets, and an amenity-filled bath. Two oversized secondary bedrooms enjoy walk-in closets and share a corner bath. The entire second level is future space that will become exactly what you need. Plenty of storage can be found in the garage.

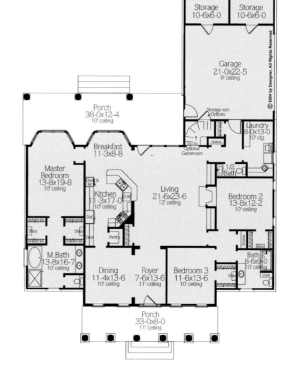

REAR EXTERIOR

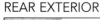

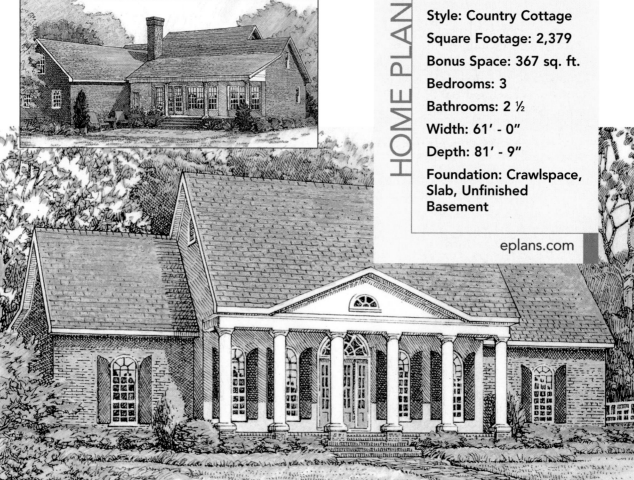

HPK1600195

Style: Country Cottage

Square Footage: 2,379

Bonus Space: 367 sq. ft.

Bedrooms: 3

Bathrooms: 2 ½

Width: 61' - 0"

Depth: 81' - 9"

Foundation: Crawlspace, Slab, Unfinished Basement

HOME PLAN

eplans.com

© William E. Poole Designs, Inc.

A LONG COVERED FRONT PORCH WELCOMES YOU to this attractive three-bedroom home. Inside, the foyer opens to the formal living room on the left and also leads back to the comfortable family room. Here, a fireplace, built-ins, and sliding glass doors to the rear deck make it a great place to gather. Two family bedrooms reside on the right side of the home, each with a private bath and a walk-in closet. The homeowner will surely love the master suite, which is full of amenities such as a huge walk-in closet, a whirlpool tub, and separate shower and two vanities.

HOME PLAN # HPK1600196

Style: Colonial
Square Footage: 2,394
Bedrooms: 3
Bathrooms: 3
Width: 82' - 6"
Depth: 52' - 8"
Foundation: Crawlspace

eplans.com

© William E. Poole Designs

PILLARS AND SHUTTERED WINDOWS GRACE THE FACADE of this handsome home. Space is well organized for casual and comfortable family living and for memorable social events. The formal dining room is just to the left as guests enter and is served from the kitchen through a butler's pantry. Straight ahead from the foyer the spacious great room enjoys a fireplace at one end and is connected to the kitchen by a counter/bar at the opposite end. The stylish breakfast bay projects out over the covered rear porch. Four bedrooms, including an unforgettable master suite, are also located on the first level.

HPK1600197

HOME PLAN

Style: Gothic Revival

Square Footage: 2,402

Bonus Space: 294 sq. ft.

Bedrooms: 4

Bathrooms: 2 ½

Width: 56' - 6"

Depth: 82' - 0"

Foundation: Crawlspace, Slab, Unfinished Basement

eplans.com

REAR EXTERIOR

YOUR TOUR OF THIS HOUSE BEGINS with an impressive entrance formed by twin columns, elevated porch, double doors, and vaulted ceilings. You'll also find here built-in twin closets and bookcases, lending a cerebral quality. The dining room is located off the right of the entry, and the master suite is to the left. Proceed straight ahead to the family room with fireplace and rear view. A columned archway separates the family room and kitchen. The latter features a pantry, preparation island and breakfast area. The remainder of the floor plan holds two family bedrooms with shared bath, a laundry, storage area, and access to the garage. There is also an optional staircase leading to a basement included.

(#) HPK1600198

HOME PLAN

Style: Traditional

Square Footage: 2,339

Bedrooms: 3

Bathrooms: 2

Width: 72' - 8"

Depth: 61' - 4"

Foundation: Crawlspace, Slab, Unfinished Basement

eplans.com

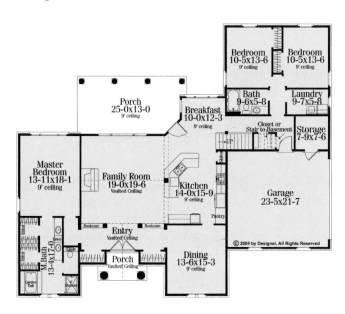

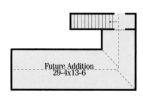

CIRCULAR BRICK STAIRS LEADING TO A COLUMNED, covered porch with arched center grace your entrance to this dream home. The foyer leads immediately through archways to a dining room on the right and family room straight ahead. The foyer and family rooms provide 11 feet of vertical clearance for an aura of added majesty. The master suite is located to the left of the family room. The kitchen will furnish all of your preparatory needs, with curved counter area, pantry, and breakfast room for quick, informal eating. There is even a handy half bath tucked away at the far end. The family bedrooms cozy up to one another just beyond the eating area—brook no excuses not to come to breakfast! Laundry, storage area, additional bath, indoor garage access, and expansion capacity for a basement or attic round out what you'll find inside.

HOME PLAN

HPK1600199

Style: Traditional

Square Footage: 2,373

Bonus Space: 1,178 sq. ft.

Bedrooms: 3

Bathrooms: 2 ½

Width: 73' - 1"

Depth: 58' - 6"

Foundation: Crawlspace, Slab, Unfinished Basement

eplans.com

REAR EXTERIOR

THE LARGE FRONT WINDOW HIGHLIGHTS THE ELE-GANCE of this home's exterior. The windows pour natural light into the cheery and spacious home office, which includes a private entrance, guest bath, two closets, and vaulted ceiling. The delightful great room features a vaulted ceiling, a fireplace, extra storage closets, and patio doors to the sun deck. An extra-large kitchen contains a walk-in pantry, cooktop island, and bay window. The vaulted master suite includes transomed windows, a walk-in closet, and a luxurious bath.

HOME PLAN

HPK1600200

Style: Traditional

Square Footage: 2,452

Bedrooms: 3

Bathrooms: 2 ½

Width: 70' - 8"

Depth: 70' - 0"

Foundation: Unfinished Basement

eplans.com

SIX COLUMNS AND A STEEPLY PITCHED ROOF lend elegance to this four-bedroom home. To the right of the foyer, the dining area sits conveniently near the efficient island kitchen that enjoys plenty of work space. Natural light will flood the breakfast nook through a ribbon of windows facing the rear yard. Escape to the relaxing master bedroom, with its luxurious bath set between His and Hers walk-in closets. The great room is complete with a warming fireplace and built-ins. Three family bedrooms enjoy private walk-in closets and share a fully appointed bath.

Basement Stair Location

HOME PLAN

HPK1600201

Style: Country Cottage

Square Footage: 2,267

Bedrooms: 4

Bathrooms: 2 ½

Width: 71' - 2"

Depth: 62' - 0"

Foundation: Unfinished Basement, Crawlspace, Slab

eplans.com

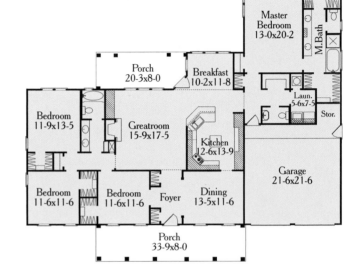

HOME PLAN

HPK1600202

Style: Traditional

Square Footage: 2,398

Bonus Space: 302 sq. ft.

Bedrooms: 3

Bathrooms: 2 ½

Width: 69' - 0"

Depth: 60' - 4"

Foundation: Unfinished Basement

eplans.com

A LUXURIOUS DUAL MASTER SUITE IS THE HIGHLIGHT of this exquisite brick ranch design. Details including a double-course brick water table, finely crafted window and eve trim, and a stately front porch create a truly elegant facade. For those seeking a classic traditional home offering posh appointments, spacious rooms, and carefully planned livability, this is the perfect home plan. Protected by the lovely front porch, the entry features high ceilings and leads directly to the family room with its 14-foot ceiling and fireplace. Just off the entry, stairs lead to the bonus room. Each of the secondary bedrooms provides direct access to the shared bath. The master suite is truly a luxurious escape, with its study, spacious dual bed areas, fireplace, and sumptuous bath.

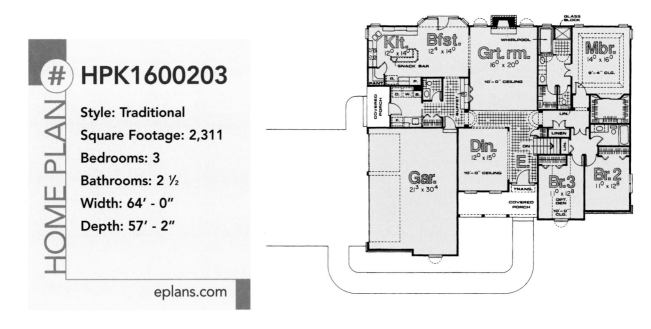

HPK1600203

Style: Traditional

Square Footage: 2,311

Bedrooms: 3

Bathrooms: 2 ½

Width: 64' - 0"

Depth: 57' - 2"

eplans.com

INTERESTING DETAILS ON THE FRONT PORCH add to the appeal of this ranch home. The great room is highlighted by a pass-through wet bar/buffet and sits just across the hall from the formal dining room. The bedrooms are found in a cluster to the right of the home: a master suite, and two family bedrooms sharing a full bath. The private master suite contains a shower with glass-block detailing, a whirlpool tub, and dual vanities.

HOME PLAN

#HPK1600204

Style: Traditional

Square Footage: 2,001

Bedrooms: 3

Bathrooms: 2

Width: 60' - 0"

Depth: 50' - 0"

Foundation: Crawlspace

eplans.com

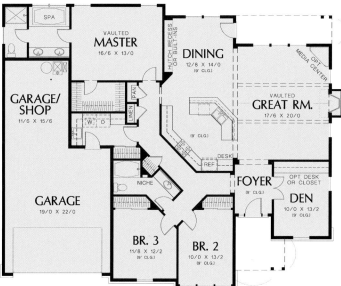

REMINISCENT OF THE SECURITY and comfort found in traditional American homes, this lovely design combines fresh country style with old-fashioned values. From the arched entry, the foyer leads inside to a sprawling great room, aptly named, with vaulted ceilings, a fireplace, and an optional media center. The open, unique kitchen easily serves the dining area, complete with a hutch area (or choose built-ins). Looking out over the rear property, the master suite enjoys a vaulted ceiling, pampering spa bath, and abundant closet space. Two bedrooms at the front of the home share an angled bath; a nearby den may also be used as a fourth bedroom. A two- or three-car garage accommodates a shop area for the do-it-yourselfer.

(#) HPK1600205

Style: Transitional

Square Footage: 2,145

Bedrooms: 3

Bathrooms: 2

Width: 71' - 2"

Depth: 51' - 0"

Foundation: Unfinished Basement

eplans.com

FINISHED IN ENDURING BRICK, THIS ONE-STORY home possesses appeal that stands the test of time. Its floor plan is also a classic, with a central great room, formal dining room, and breakfast room with sun-room access. The kitchen sits between the dining room and breakfast room and leads to the laundry room and a service entry to the two-car garage. Bedrooms are more privately located on the left side of the plan. The master bedroom features a tray ceiling and has a bath with a corner whirlpool tub and walk-in closet.

HOME PLAN

HPK1600206

Style: Traditional

Square Footage: 2,018

Bedrooms: 3

Bathrooms: 2

Width: 74' - 11"

Depth: 49' - 2"

Foundation: Crawlspace, Slab, Unfinished Basement

eplans.com

A PALLADIAN WINDOW SET INTO A FRONT-FACING gable highlights this country home. The dining room, on the right, includes accent columns and convenient kitchen service. The great room offers twin sets of French doors that access the rear porch. Meal preparation will be easy in the kitchen with a work island and cheerful light streaming in from the bay-windowed breakfast nook. The master suite is set to the rear and features a walk-in closet made for two, dual vanities, and a compartmented toilet. Two family bedrooms near the front of the plan share a full bath.

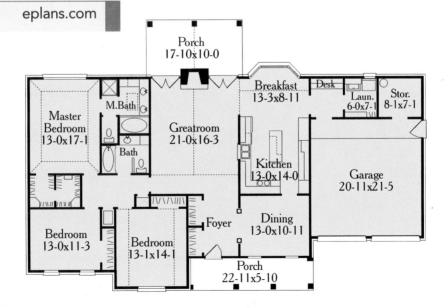

Porch
17-10x10-0

Master
Bedroom
13-0x17-1

M.Bath

Bath

Greatroom
21-0x16-3

Breakfast
13-3x8-11

Desk

Laun.
6-0x7-1

Stor.
8-1x7-1

Kitchen
13-0x14-0

Garage
20-11x21-5

Bedroom
13-0x11-3

Bedroom
13-1x14-1

Foyer

Dining
13-0x10-11

Porch
22-11x5-10

PREPARE FOR INSTANT ENAMORATION! A friendly veranda is first to greet those who venture within. A cheerful foyer points the way to the common living area on the right, or to the master suite on the left (a hall closet is cleverly hidden from view). The family room and kitchen, with space for food storage and preparation, as well as informal dining, comprise one open area. The nook lets out onto a lovely outdoor area with space for a hot tub and home-grown flora. One enters the garage in back via the patio, or directly off the laundry room. Two family bedrooms with shared bath nestle at the other end of this wing. Provisions for a bonus room are included in this plan.

HOME PLAN

(#) HPK1600207

Style: Country Cottage

Square Footage: 2,034

Bonus Space: 370 sq. ft.

Bedrooms: 3

Bathrooms: 2 ½

Width: 76' - 0"

Depth: 63' - 6"

Foundation: Crawlspace, Slab, Unfinished Basement

eplans.com

REAR EXTERIOR

MULTIPANE WINDOWS, MOCK SHUTTERS, and a covered front porch exhibit the charm of this home's facade. Inside, the foyer is flanked by a spacious, efficient kitchen to the right and a large, convenient laundry room to the left. The living room features a warming fireplace. To the right of the living room is the formal dining room; both rooms share a snack bar and direct access to the kitchen. Sleeping quarters are split, with two family bedrooms and a full bath on the right side of the plan and the deluxe master suite on the left. The private master bath offers such luxuries as a walk-in closet, a twin-sink vanity, a garden tub, and a separate shower.

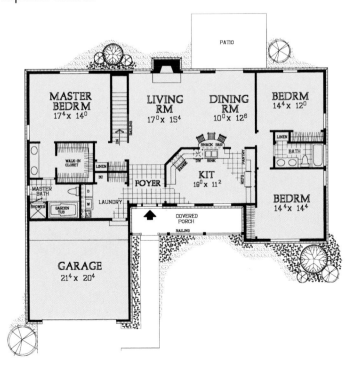

HOME PLAN

HPK1600208

Style: Farmhouse

Square Footage: 2,076

Bedrooms: 3

Bathrooms: 2

Width: 64' - 8"

Depth: 54' - 7"

Foundation: Unfinished Basement

eplans.com

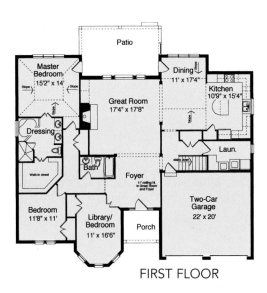

FIRST FLOOR

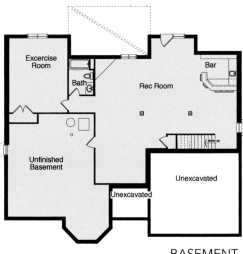

BASEMENT

HOME PLAN

HPK1600209

Style: Transitional

Square Footage: 2,098

Bedrooms: 2

Bathrooms: 2

Width: 58' - 10"

Depth: 50' - 4"

Foundation: Finished Walkout Basement

eplans.com

A SOLID BRICK EXTERIOR WITH WOOD TRIM and angles gives a strong appearance to this delightful one-story home. A large foyer introduces the open great room, decorated with high windows and a warm fireplace. A grand opening into the dining area visually expands the great room, while a sloped ceiling adds a dramatic effect. A circular island with seating adds a stylish element to the gourmet kitchen. An abundance of counter space, cabinets and a pantry make working in this kitchen a pleasure. A sloped ceiling tops the master bedroom suite, while a whirlpool tub, double-bowl vanity, shower, and large walk-in closet provide luxury and comfort for the homeowner. A door to the patio from the master suite is a pleasant surprise. The option of creating a library in the third bedroom and accessing additional square footage in the walkout basement offer flexibility to this exciting home.

FEATURES THAT MAKE THIS HOUSE A SPECTACULAR HOME
include a wraparound porch, stone and siding exterior, and a garage that is set to the rear. The beauty continues to the interior with a large great room that boasts a sloped ceiling, gas fireplace, and a series of windows that offer a view to the rear porch. A spacious breakfast area becomes a great place to start the day with the surround of windows and sloped ceiling. A snack bar and an abundance of counter space create a delightful kitchen. A room set to the front of the kitchen can function as a formal dining room or private study. A bath with shower is convenient to the garage entry. The master bedroom suite is designed to pamper the homeowner with comfort. Plant ledges and built-in shelves add decorative touches. A bonus space overlooks the great room adding additional living square footage for your family's enjoyment.

 # HOME PLAN HPK1600210

Style: Farmhouse

Square Footage: 2,183

Bonus Space: 241 sq. ft.

Bedrooms: 3

Bathrooms: 3

Width: 80' - 0"

Depth: 74' - 0"

Foundation: Unfinished Basement

eplans.com

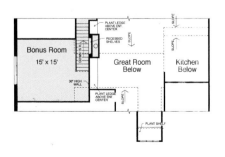

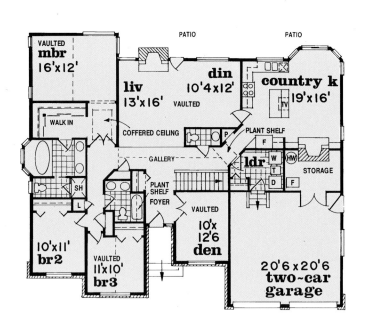

HPK1600211

Style: Traditional
Square Footage: 2,058
Bonus Space: 82 sq. ft.
Bedrooms: 3
Bathrooms: 2 ½
Width: 61' - 10"
Depth: 50' - 4"
Foundation: Crawlspace, Unfinished Basement

eplans.com

THIS FLOOR PLAN IS DESIGNED TO MAXIMIZE THE VIEW to the rear of the lot. Double doors off the foyer open to a vaulted den or study. The gallery hall introduces the vaulted living and dining rooms. The country kitchen offers a masonry fireplace, breakfast bay, and preparation island with television nook. A spacious master bedroom features both coffered and vaulted ceilings. The walk-in wardrobe opens to a lavish ensuite with His and Hers vanity and whirlpool spa. Two additional bedrooms, one with a vaulted ceiling, share a main bathroom with twin vanities and a soaking tub.

HORIZONTAL SIDING, MULTIPANE WINDOWS, and a spindled railing lend a prairies-and-plains flavor to this traditional home. A roomy foyer with a sloped ceiling and built-in shelves leads through a tiled vestibule with built-in shelves to the spacious gathering room, complete with a warming fireplace. An angled kitchen with a snack bar easily serves the formal dining room, which leads outdoors to the rear entertainment terrace. The luxurious master suite has its own door to the terrace as well as a fabulous private bath with a windowed whirlpool tub. Two additional bedrooms share a full bath and a hall that offers more wardrobe space. One of the family bedrooms could serve as a study or home office.

HOME PLAN

HPK1600212

Style: Traditional

Square Footage: 2,034

Bedrooms: 3

Bathrooms: 2

Width: 75' - 0"

Depth: 47' - 5"

Foundation: Unfinished Basement

eplans.com

MULTIPLE GABLES, A STONE-AND-SIDING EXTERIOR, and a covered entry create a beautiful facade on this one-level home. The great room, dining area, and spacious kitchen combine to offer a large family gathering place. The placement of the entertainment alcove and fireplace provide a view from all three locations. An 11-foot ceiling tops the great room and dining area. Generous counter space, cabinetry, an island, and pantry in the kitchen, in addition to the adjacent laundry room and a small home office, form an efficient work area. For privacy, the master suite is separated from the secondary bedrooms. A spectacular covered rear porch with fireplace extends the outdoor enjoyment to cooler weather. Split stairs lead to a full basement for storage or additional square footage.

HOME PLAN

HPK1600213

Style: Craftsman

Square Footage: 2,199

Bedrooms: 3

Bathrooms: 2 ½

Width: 74' - 8"

Depth: 60' - 7"

Foundation: Unfinished Basement

eplans.com

HOME PLAN

(#) HPK1600214

Style: Country Cottage

Square Footage: 2,170

Bedrooms: 4

Bathrooms: 3

Width: 62' - 0"

Depth: 61' - 6"

Foundation: Finished Walkout Basement

eplans.com

Floor plan labels:

BEDROOM NO. 3
11'-6" X 11'-0"

BATH

BEDROOM NO. 2
11'-4" X 11'-0"

SUN ROOM
12'-0" X 13'-8"

PORCH

MASTER BATH

W.I.C.

MASTER BEDROOM
13'-4" X 15'-6"

PORCH

BREAKFAST
10'-0" X 9'-0"

FAMILY ROOM
18'-0" X 14'-0"

KITCHEN
12'-0" X 13'-2"

LAUNDRY

DN

BATH

STORAGE

DINING ROOM
11'-4" X 11'-4"

FOYER
6'-8" X 11'-10"

DEN/GUEST BEDROOM
11'-4" X 14'-0"

TWO CAR GARAGE
20'-4" X 19'-8"

PORCH

THIS CLASSIC COTTAGE BOASTS A STONE-AND-WOOD EXTERIOR with a welcoming arch-top entry that leads to a columned foyer. An extended-hearth fireplace is the focal point of the family room, and a nearby sunroom with covered porch access opens up the living area to the outdoors. The gourmet island kitchen opens through double doors from the living area; the breakfast area looks out to a porch. Sleeping quarters include a master wing with a spacious, angled bath and a sitting room or den that has its own full bath—perfect for a guest suite. On the opposite side of the plan, two family bedrooms share a full bath.

THIS HOME'S EUROPEAN STYLING will work well in a variety of environments. When it comes down to the details, this plan has it all. Begin with the front door, which opens into the dining and great rooms—the latter complete with fireplace and doors that open onto the back porch. The kitchen combines with the breakfast nook to create ample space for meals. This plan incorporates four bedrooms; you may want to use one as an office and another as a study. The master bedroom houses a fabulous bath with twin walk-in closets and a spa tub.

Copyright 1992 Stephen S. Fuller, Inc.

HOME PLAN

HPK1600216

Style: Traditional

Square Footage: 2,120

Bedrooms: 3

Bathrooms: 3

Width: 62' - 0"

Depth: 62' - 6"

Foundation: Unfinished Walkout Basement

eplans.com

ARCHED-TOP WINDOWS ACT AS GRACEFUL ACCENTS for this wonderful design. Inside, the floor plan is compact but commodious. The family room serves as the center of activity. It has a fireplace and connects to a lovely sunroom with rear-porch access. The formal dining room to the front of the plan is open to the entry foyer. A private den also opens off the foyer with double doors. It has its own private, cozy fireplace. The kitchen area opens to the sunroom, and it contains an island work counter. Bedrooms are split, with the master suite to the right side of the design and family bedrooms to the left. There are three full baths in this plan.

QUOINS, ARCHED LINTELS, AND TWIN pedimented dormers lend this house a sweet country feel. Columns and a vaulted ceiling make the interior elegant. French doors lead to a living room found at the left of the entrance, and decorative columns adorn the elegant dining room. The spacious family room is enhanced by the vaulted ceiling and cozy fireplace. Two lovely bay windows embellish the rear of the house. The island kitchen features a roomy pantry, a serving bar, and a breakfast area with a French door that opens to the outside through a transom. The master suite boasts a tray ceiling, sitting area, a deluxe bath with built-in plant shelves, a radius window, dual vanities, and a large walk-in closet.

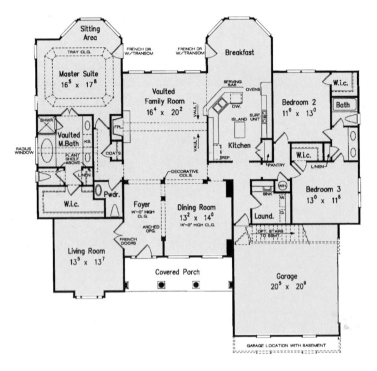

HOME PLAN

HPK1600217

Style: European Cottage

Square Footage: 2,388

Bedrooms: 3

Bathrooms: 2 ½

Width: 63' - 0"

Depth: 60' - 0"

Foundation: Crawlspace, Unfinished Walkout Basement, Slab

eplans.com

ONE-STORY LIVING TAKES A LOVELY TRADITIONAL TURN in this brick home. The entry foyer opens to the formal dining room and the great room through graceful columned archways. The open gourmet kitchen, bayed breakfast nook, and keeping room with a fireplace will be a magnet for family activity. Sleeping quarters offer two family bedrooms, a hall bath, and a rambling master suite with a bayed sitting area and a sensuous bath.

HOME PLAN

HPK1600218

Style: Traditional

Square Footage: 2,377

Bedrooms: 3

Bathrooms: 2

Width: 69' - 0"

Depth: 49' - 6"

Foundation: Finished Walkout Basement

eplans.com

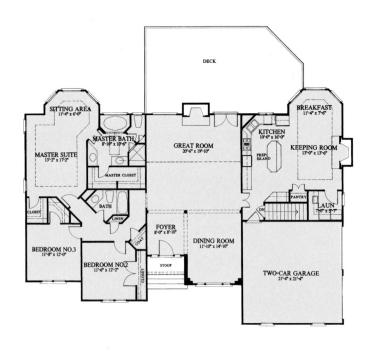

THE ABUNDANCE OF DETAILS IN THIS PLAN makes it the finest in one-story living. The great room and formal dining room are loosely defined by a simple column at the entry foyer, allowing for an open, dramatic sense of space. The kitchen with a prep island shares the right side of the plan with a bayed breakfast area and a keeping room with a fireplace. Sleeping accommodations to the left of the plan include a master suite with a sitting area, two closets, and a separate tub and shower. Two family bedrooms share a full bath. Additional living and sleeping space can be developed in the walkout basement.

HOME PLAN

HPK1600219

Style: French

Square Footage: 2,295

Bedrooms: 3

Bathrooms: 2

Width: 69' - 0"

Depth: 49' - 6"

Foundation: Unfinished Walkout Basement

eplans.com

© 1998 AMERICAN HOME GALLERY, LTD.

THIS ATTRACTIVE BRICK COTTAGE HOME with an arched covered entry gives family and friends a warm welcome. The jack-arch window detailing adds intrigue to the exterior. The foyer, dining room, and great room are brought together, defined by decorative columns. To the right of the foyer, a bedroom with a complete bath could double as a home office or children's den. The spacious kitchen has a centered work island and an adjacent keeping room with a fireplace—ideal for families that like to congregate at mealtimes. The abundance of windows throughout the back of the home provides a grand view of the back property. The master suite enjoys privacy to the rear of the home. A garden tub, large walk-in closet, and two vanities make a perfect homeowner retreat.

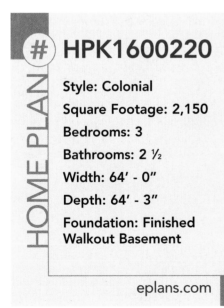

HOME PLAN

HPK1600220

Style: Colonial

Square Footage: 2,150

Bedrooms: 3

Bathrooms: 2 ½

Width: 64' - 0"

Depth: 64' - 3"

Foundation: Finished Walkout Basement

eplans.com

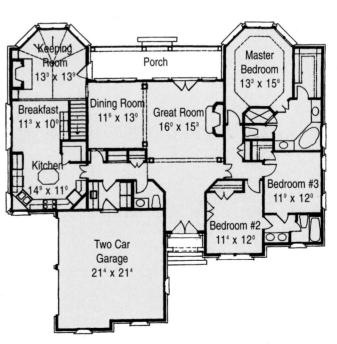

FIRST FLOOR

BASEMENT

LIFTED FROM THE FRENCH COUNTRYSIDE! Arched windows with wooden shutters meet stucco and stone masonry with wood framing to immerse you in your European Country cottage. Enter and discover a library with tray ceiling to house your treasured collection. Entertain in the great room on the main level or upstairs in your home theater, where you will also find the family room, kitchenette, third bedroom with full bath and walk-in closet, and extra storage. The master suite features His and Her matching walk-in closets, and an enormous bathroom. The family bedroom on the main level has an extra-high ceiling. Off of the great room, there's a kitchen with center island, pantry and bar with an eating area leading directly onto a rear covered porch. The only thing missing is a vineyard, and a view of the Alps!

HOME PLAN

HPK1600221

Style: French Country
Square Footage: 2,255
Bedrooms: 2
Bathrooms: 2
Width: 53' - 0"
Depth: 78' - 0"

eplans.com

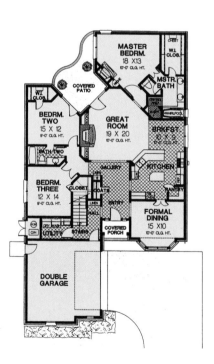

A TOUCH OF TUDOR AND A TOUCH OF THE ENGLISH cottage—this home is designed for comfort. A tiled entry, gallery, kitchen, and breakfast nook give a sense of casual space. The formal dining area is set to the right and enjoys a bumped-out bay window. Two bedrooms share a hall bath on the right of the plan. The master suite looks out to the rear covered patio and is pampered by a full bath and walk-in closet. The great room is the hub of this plan, featuring a warm fireplace and patio access. A bonus room is perfect for a guest bedroom or recreation room.

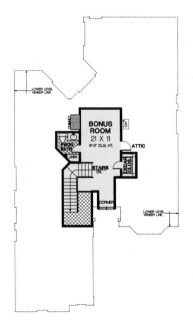

HPK1600222

Style: European Cottage

Square Footage: 2,168

Bonus Space: 308 sq. ft.

Bedrooms: 3

Bathrooms: 2

Width: 44' - 10"

Depth: 79' - 10"

Foundation: Slab

eplans.com

HOME PLAN

HOMES FROM 2,001 TO 2,500 SQUARE FEET

THE STONE ENTRYWAY AND STEEP ROOFLINES accent the rustic nature of this home's facade. French doors lead guests and homeowners into an elegant entry and gallery. This home offers plenty of living space throughout. The large angled kitchen, featuring an island, extends to the open breakfast nook. A fireplace warms the family room in the winter and offers access to the covered rear patio for convenient summer outdoor entertaining. Another covered patio can be privately accessed through the master suite and the breakfast nook. Three family bedrooms and one master bedroom complete this plan.

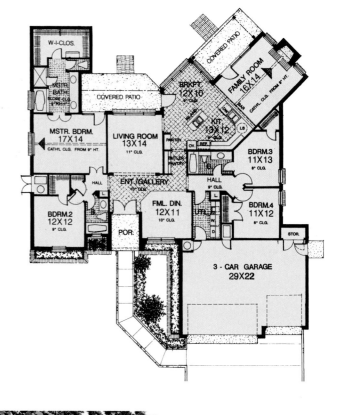

(#) HOME PLAN

HPK1600223

Style: French

Square Footage: 2,282

Bedrooms: 4

Bathrooms: 3

Width: 63' - 10"

Depth: 71' - 1"

Foundation: Crawlspace, Slab

eplans.com

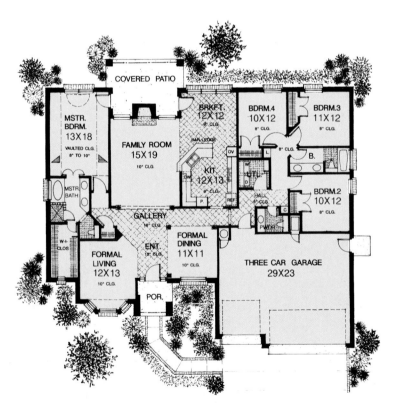

HOME PLAN

HPK1600224

Style: Traditional

Square Footage: 2,333

Bedrooms: 4

Bathrooms: 2 ½

Width: 65' - 0"

Depth: 54' - 1"

Foundation: Slab

eplans.com

THE COPPER-TOPPED BAY WINDOW
flashes magnificently against the stone-and-brick facade of this elegant home. Inside, a sunburst transom and sidelights pour natural light into the entry and gallery. A bayed living room resides to the left of the entry and the dining room to the right, making entertaining a breeze. The hearth-warmed family room is open to the breakfast nook and the kitchen with a serving bar. Three family bedrooms share access to a full bath to the right of the plan, while a luxurious master suite sits to the left.

HOME PLAN

HPK1600225

Style: European Cottage

Square Footage: 2,163

Bedrooms: 3

Bathrooms: 2

Width: 44' - 0"

Depth: 83' - 0"

Foundation: Slab

eplans.com

THIS COZY STUCCO DESIGN FITS A SHADY LANE IN TOWN or takes advantage of the views in the country. French doors open from an arched entryway with a transom window to the foyer. Two family bedrooms flank the foyer, and a hallway opens to the dining room. Across the hall, the kitchen and breakfast room serve up casual and formal meals. A loggia, just before the family room, accesses a garden courtyard. The family room sports a fireplace, built-ins, and French doors to the rear yard. The master suite features a spacious walk-in closet and an amenity-filled bath.

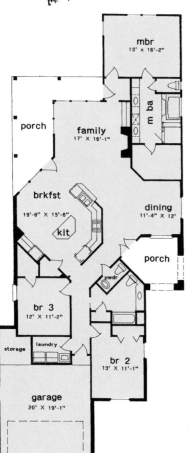

AN ORNATE STUCCO FACADE WITH BRICK highlights refines this charming French cottage. The double-door entrance sits to the side—perfect for a courtyard welcome. A dining and family room utilize an open layout for easy traffic flow. The circular kitchen space features an island and complementary breakfast bay. Bedrooms 2 and 3 share a hall bath. The master suite, apart from the main living areas, enjoys privacy and a full bath with a spacious walk-in closet. The rear porch encourages outdoor relaxation.

HOME PLAN

HPK1600226

Style: European Cottage

Square Footage: 2,007

Bedrooms: 3

Bathrooms: 2 ½

Width: 40' - 0"

Depth: 94' - 10"

Foundation: Slab

eplans.com

STEEPLY PITCHED GABLES on this home's facade bring to mind quaint country churches, but this home takes quaint and pushes it to comfortable luxury. The formal dining room sits across the tiled gallery from the spacious great room. Plenty of natural light filters in from the wall of windows in the great room. To the right, two family bedrooms share a Jack-and-Jill bath and feature walk-in closets. A large kitchen, breakfast area, and utility room serve both casual and formal areas. The master suite enjoys a roomy bath and walk-in closet. An extra bedroom or study is just down the hall, close to a full bath.

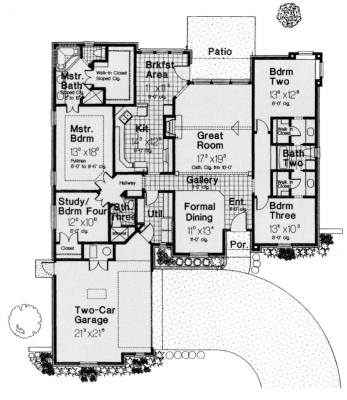

HOME PLAN

HPK1600227

Style: European Cottage

Square Footage: 2,288

Bedrooms: 4

Bathrooms: 3

Width: 57' - 5"

Depth: 57' - 10"

Foundation: Slab

eplans.com

STONE MASONRY, COLUMNS, AND INTRICATE WINDOW glazing mark this exterior, with further surprises in store inside. An arched entry gives way to a planning area on the right, or to the family room straight ahead. A snack bar separates the family room from the kitchen, and the latter from the dining area. A wonderful covered porch is accessible directly from the dining room. The master and family bedrooms exist at opposite ends of the main level. The master suite boasts a tray ceiling in the bedroom, and a sloped ceiling, double vanity, compartmented toilet and shower, and walk-in closet grace the bath. But wait until you see the up stairs: there's a patio, study, game room, exercise room and theater, plus a bar, and storage space galore.

HOME PLAN

(#) HPK1600228

Style: Traditional

Square Footage: 2,038

Bedrooms: 3

Bathrooms: 2

Width: 59' - 0"

Depth: 58' - 0"

eplans.com

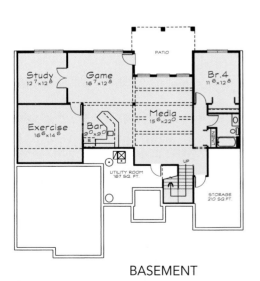

BASEMENT

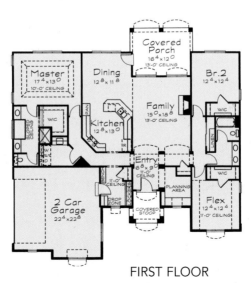

FIRST FLOOR

OPTIONAL LAYOUTS

HPK1600229

Style: Transitional

Square Footage: 2,224

Bedrooms: 4

Bathrooms: 3

Width: 58' - 6"

Depth: 74' - 0"

Foundation: Slab

eplans.com

ARCHES CROWNED BY GENTLE, HIPPED ROOFLINES provide an Italianate charm in this bright and spacious family-oriented plan. A covered entry leads to the foyer that presents the angular, vaulted living and dining rooms. A kitchen with a V-shaped counter includes a walk-in pantry and looks out over the breakfast nook and family room with a fireplace. The master suite features a sitting room, two walk-in closets, and a full bath with a garden tub. Two additional bedrooms share a full bath located between them. A fourth bedroom, with its own bath, opens off the family room, and works perfectly as a guest room.

THE ELEGANCE AND GRACE OF THIS SPLIT-LEVEL
plan are apparent at first sight. Impressive arches open into the foyer, with the wide-open great room beyond, opening to a covered porch through French doors. Enter both the master suite and the adjacent den/study through French doors. A private courtyard keeps the master bath shielded from the front yard. From the nook, near two good-sized bedrooms with a shared bathroom, stairs lead up to a bonus room that includes a large balcony to take advantage of your lot with a view.

 # HPK1600230

HOME PLAN

Style: Contemporary
Square Footage: 2,237
Bonus Space: 397 sq. ft.
Bedrooms: 3
Bathrooms: 2
Width: 60' - 0"
Depth: 70' - 0"
Foundation: Slab

eplans.com

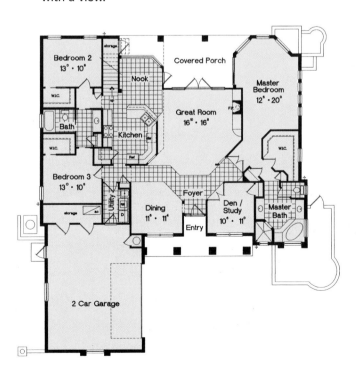

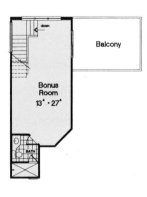

THE IMPRESSIVE FACADE of this home—brick quoins, sunburst and muntin windows, and stately pillars—is complemented by the beauty and elegance found within. A raised ceiling in the foyer and living room is only one of the unique features of this plan. The huge family gathering space boasts a magnificent media/fireplace wall. There is a mitered glass nook off the kitchen which has a walk-in pantry. The master suite is remarkable with its arched entry, tray ceiling, His and Hers vanities, compartmented toilet, and a huge walk-in dressing salon. Two additional bedrooms share a full bath.

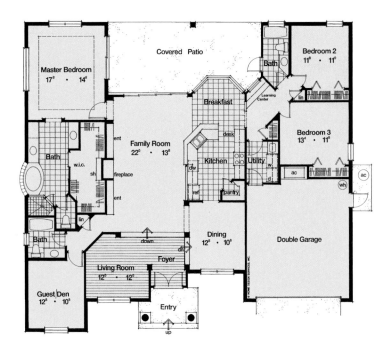

HOME PLAN

(#) **HPK1600231**

Style: **Mediterranean**

Square Footage: **2,456**

Bedrooms: **3**

Bathrooms: **3**

Width: **63' - 8"**

Depth: **58' - 0"**

Foundation: **Slab**

eplans.com

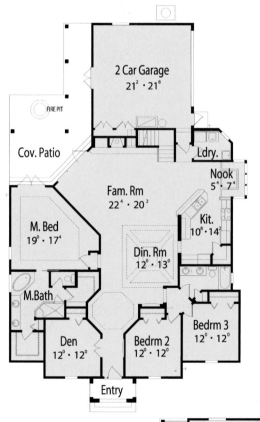

HOME PLAN

(#) HPK1600232

Style: International
Square Footage: 2,293
Bonus Space: 509 sq. ft.
Bedrooms: 3
Bathrooms: 2
Width: 51' - 0"
Depth: 79' - 4"
Foundation: Slab

eplans.com

MULTIPLE ROOFLINES, SHUTTERS, and a charming vaulted entry lend interest and depth to the exterior of this well-designed three-bedroom home. Inside, double doors to the left open to a cozy den. The dining room, open to the family room and foyer, features a stunning ceiling design. A fireplace and patio access and view adorn the family room. Two family bedrooms share a double-sink bathroom to the right, and the master bedroom resides to the left. Note the private patio access, two walk-in closets, and luxurious bath that ensure a restful retreat for the homeowner.

THIS HOME BOASTS GREAT CURB APPEAL with its Mediterranean influences— glass block and muntin windows, decorative oval window, impressive pillars, and a stucco facade. The family side of this home abounds with thoughtful design features, like the island in the kitchen, the media/fireplace wall in the family room, and the mitered glass breakfast nook. A dramatic arched entry into the master suite leads to a gently curving wall of glass block, a double vanity, extra large shower, compartmented toilet, and large walk-in closet. Also special is the design of the three secondary bedrooms, which share private bath facilities.

HOME PLAN

HPK1600233

Style: Mediterranean

Square Footage: 2,348

Bedrooms: 4

Bathrooms: 3

Width: 61' - 4"

Depth: 65' - 0"

Foundation: Slab

eplans.com

from the actual blueprints. For more detailed information, please check the floor plans carefully.

HOME PLAN

(#) HPK1600234

Style: Italianate

Square Footage: 2,385

Bedrooms: 3

Bathrooms: 3

Width: 60' - 0"

Depth: 52' - 0"

Foundation: Slab

eplans.com

THIS ENTICING EUROPEAN VILLA BOASTS AN ITALIAN CHARM and a distinct Mediterranean feel. The foyer steps lead up to the formal living areas. To the left, a study is expanded by a vaulted ceiling and double doors that open to the front balcony. The island kitchen is conveniently open to a breakfast nook. The guest quarters reside on the right side of the plan—one suite boasts a private bath; the other uses a full hall bath. The secluded master suite features two walk-in closets and a pampering whirlpool master bath. The home is completed by a basement-level garage.

BASEMENT

FIRST FLOOR

HOME PLAN

HPK1600235

Style: Contemporary

Square Footage: 2,258

Bedrooms: 4

Bathrooms: 3

Width: 66' - 0"

Depth: 73' - 4"

Foundation: Slab

eplans.com

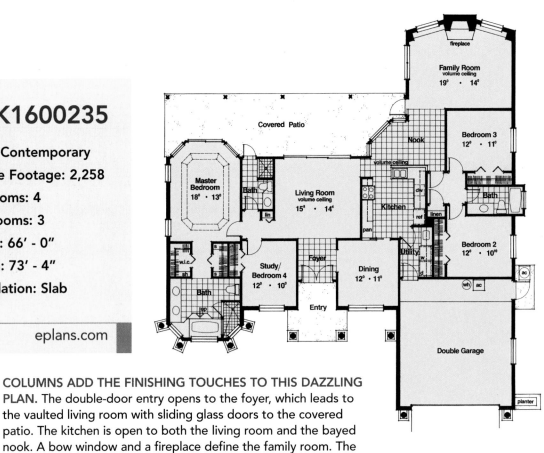

COLUMNS ADD THE FINISHING TOUCHES TO THIS DAZZLING PLAN. The double-door entry opens to the foyer, which leads to the vaulted living room with sliding glass doors to the covered patio. The kitchen is open to both the living room and the bayed nook. A bow window and a fireplace define the family room. The master bedroom features access to the covered patio and provides dual walk-in closets and a spa tub. Two additional bedrooms share a full bath.

HOME PLAN

(#) HPK1600236

Style: Mediterranean

Square Footage: 2,259

Bedrooms: 4

Bathrooms: 3

Width: 59' - 8"

Depth: 54' - 4"

Foundation: Slab

eplans.com

AN EXQUISITE VILLA AWAITS! SPANISH
INFLUENCE abounds in this home design:
tray ceilings and an open floor plan create
Mediterranean character throughout the interior of this home. French doors guard the
entrance to the foyer—with extra ceiling
height—which provides an immediate view of the common area of the house.
Four bedrooms are located on either wing of the floor plan, with one and a half
baths on the family side, and a double vanity bath with spa tub in the master
suite. A formal dining area is immediately to your left. The great room occupies
the center of the floor, with approximately 19 square feet of space, and offers a
view of the comparably expansive patio, accessible via sliding doors directly
behind the snack bar. The kitchen is built for convenience, sporting a curving
preparation island cleverly contoured to match the rest of the common area.

LOW-PITCHED ROOFS AND A GRAND columned entry introduce a floor plan that's designed for the 21st Century. Ceramic tiles lead from the foyer to the breakfast area and roomy kitchen, which offers an angled wrapping counter and overlooks the family room. French doors open off the foyer to a secluded den or guest suite, which complements the near-by master suite. A gallery hall off the breakfast nook leads to family sleeping quarters, which share a full bath.

HOME PLAN

#) HPK1600237

Style: Contemporary

Square Footage: 2,287

Bedrooms: 4

Bathrooms: 2 ½

Width: 63' - 4"

Depth: 62' - 4"

Foundation: Slab

eplans.com

HOME PLAN

HPK1600238

Style: NW Contemporary

Square Footage: 2,412

Bedrooms: 3

Bathrooms: 2 ½

Width: 60' - 0"

Depth: 59' - 0"

Foundation: Slab

eplans.com

THIS GORGEOUS DESIGN WOULD EASILY ACCOMMODATE a sloping lot. With windows and glass panels to take in the view, this design would make an exquisite seaside resort. A grand great room sets the tone inside, with an elegant tray ceiling and French doors to a private front balcony. The formal dining room is off the center of the plan for quiet elegance and is served by a nearby gourmet kitchen. Three steps up from the foyer, the sleeping level includes a spacious master suite with a sizable private bath. The two additional bedrooms access a shared bath with two vanities.

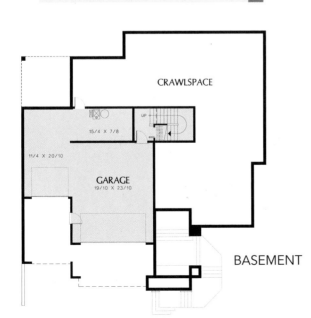

BASEMENT

FIRST FLOOR

THE IMPRESSIVE, DOU-BLE-DOOR ENTRY to the walled courtyard sets the tone for this Santa Fe masterpiece home. The expansive great room shows off its casual style with a centerpiece fireplace and abundant windows overlooking the patio. Joining the great room is the formal dining room, again graced with windows and patio doors. The large gourmet kitchen has an eat-in snack bar and joins the family room to create a warm atmosphere for casual entertaining. Family-room extras include a fireplace, entertainment built-ins, and double doors to the front courtyard. Just off the family room are the two large family bedrooms, which share a private bath. The relaxing master suite is located off the great room and has double doors to the back patio.

HOME PLAN # HPK1600239

Style: Contemporary
Square Footage: 2,226
Bedrooms: 3
Bathrooms: 2 ½
Width: 103' - 1"
Depth: 71' - 11"
Foundation: Slab

eplans.com

THIS SANTA FE-STYLE HOME IS AS WARM as a desert breeze and just as comfortable. Outside details are reminiscent of old-style adobe homes, and the interior caters to convenient living. The front covered porch leads to an open foyer. Columns define the formal dining room and the giant great room. The kitchen has an enormous pantry and a snack bar and is connected to a breakfast nook with rear-patio access. Two family bedrooms on the right side of the plan share a full bathroom that includes twin vanities. The master suite on the left side of the plan has a monstrous walk-in closet and a bath with a spa-style tub and a separate shower.

HOME PLAN

 # HPK1600240

Style: SW Contemporary
Square Footage: 2,015
Bedrooms: 3
Bathrooms: 2 ½
Width: 96' - 5"
Depth: 54' - 9"
Foundation: Slab

eplans.com

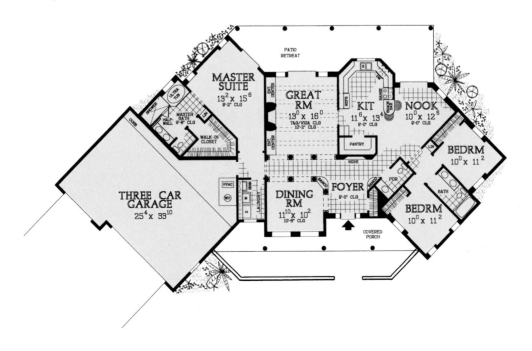

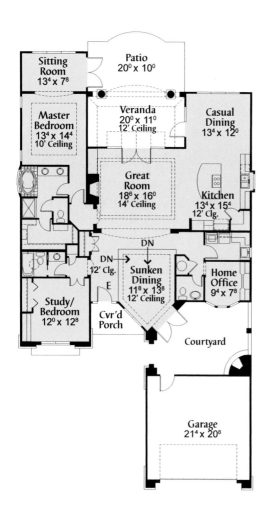

Sitting Room 13⁴ x 7⁸

Patio 20⁰ x 10⁰

Master Bedroom 13⁴ x 14⁴ 10' Ceiling

Veranda 20⁰ x 11⁰ 12' Ceiling

Casual Dining 13⁴ x 12⁰

Great Room 18⁶ x 16⁰ 14' Ceiling

Kitchen 13⁴ x 15⁴ 12' Clg.

DN

DN 12' Clg.

Sunken Dining 11⁸ x 13⁸ 12' Ceiling

Home Office 9⁴ x 7⁸

E

Study/ Bedroom 12⁰ x 12⁸

Cvr'd Porch

Courtyard

Garage 21⁴ x 20⁸

TWO BEDROOMS AND TWO BATHS make this contemporary design the perfect starter or empty-nest home. The sunken dining room, with a soaring 12-foot ceiling, includes French doors that open to the courtyard. Nearby, the kitchen includes a walk-in pantry and an island cooktop, which adjoins a casual dining area with veranda access. The central great room, which also opens to the veranda, includes a fireplace. Sleeping quarters—the master suite and one secondary bedroom that can double as a study—reside to the left of the plan; the master suite includes a private sitting area with entry to a rear patio. A home office, brightened by a bay window, completes the plan.

HOME PLAN

HPK1600241

Style: SW Contemporary

Square Footage: 2,097

Bedrooms: 2

Bathrooms: 2 ½

Width: 49' - 4"

Depth: 79' - 2"

Foundation: Slab

eplans.com

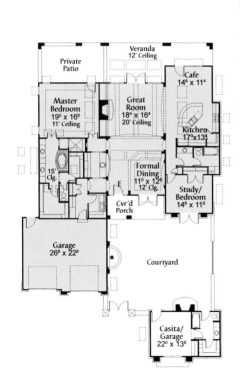

HOME PLAN
HPK1600242

Style: SW Contemporary

Square Footage: 2,430

Bedrooms: 3

Bathrooms: 2

Width: 64' - 4"

Depth: 74' - 6"

Foundation: Slab

HOME PLAN
HPK1600243

Style: SW Contemporary

Square Footage: 2,331

Bedrooms: 3

Bathrooms: 3

Width: 63' - 8"

Depth: 100' - 4"

Foundation: Slab

This Bold House—Big Plans for Big Dreamers

Luxury homes are for those looking to spare no expense when it comes to style and comfort. Not only impressive for their size, these homes feature the best in materials, upgrades, and design. Every room delivers a home that deeply satisfies.

These plans also showcase the industry's best solutions for integrating indoor and outdoor living. Luxury homes—particularly in the Mediterranean styles—offer elaborate covered courtyards called lanais, which often include landscaping, water features, wet bars, and outdoor kitchens. Owners will find that a well-conceived lanai allows the home to open up the rear of the plan in spectacular ways without sacrificing privacy or security. The same strategy is used in the master suites of some homes to hide a bayed soaking tub—with a walled privacy garden placed just outside the window.

The cost-cutting method of building interior walls at right angles with as few corners as possible is abandoned for layouts that favor eye-catching forms and gorgeously detailed ceilings. Window walls and pocket doors allow the entire rear of the plan to feel and function as if they are even larger.

The master suite attains the highest comforts of the modern home. The bedrooms often include sitting areas and private porches; the baths are spacious and exquisitely detailed. Exercise rooms or dressing rooms may complement de rigueur walk-ins. In short, the homes collected in this section demonstrate the very best that our designers have to offer.

Kohler

DELICATE DETAILING and highest-end materials justify large spaces. Choose furnishings and finishes—such as the art sconce (right) and beautiful color palette—that make enough impact, or risk turning a big room into a big bore.

HOME PLAN #

HPK1600244

Style: Santa Fe
Square Footage: 3,144
Bedrooms: 4
Bathrooms: 3
Width: 139' - 10"
Depth: 63' - 8"
Foundation: Slab

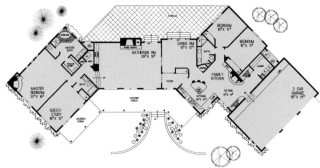

HOME PLAN #

HPK1600245

Style: Santa Fe
Square Footage: 2,792
Bedrooms: 3
Bathrooms: 2 ½
Width: 89' - 2"
Depth: 88' - 9"

© 2002 Donald A. Gardner, Inc.

HPK1600246

Style: Ranch

Square Footage: 3,061

Bedrooms: 3

Bathrooms: 3 ½

Width: 86' - 1"

Depth: 84' - 8"

eplans.com

THIS UPDATED HACIENDA OFFERS THE UTMOST IN LIVABILITY. Enter through a rugged stone lanai to an elegant gallery hall, which accesses the combined great room/dining area. A double-sided fireplace warms this space as well as the courtyard to the right. The adjacent master suite features a curved wall of windows and a deluxe bath with a huge walk-in closet. On the opposite side of the plan, the kitchen's serving-bar island looks into the bay-windowed breakfast nook. A roomy pantry will delight the family cook. A utility room and half-bath are convenient to both the kitchen and the two-car garage. Opening from the other side of the kitchen is a hearth-warmed family room that accesses the rear lanai. At the right front of the plan reside two additional bedrooms—each with its own bath.

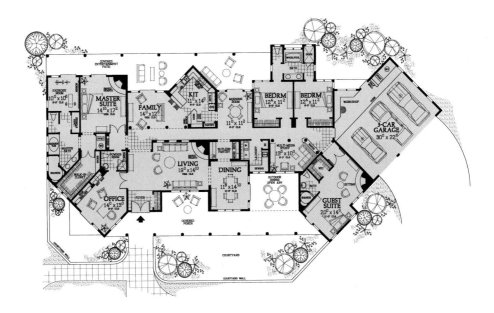

HPK1600247

Style: SW Contemporary

Square Footage: 3,838

Bedrooms: 4

Bathrooms: 3 ½

Width: 127' - 6"

Depth: 60' - 10"

Foundation: Slab

eplans.com

THIS DIAMOND IN THE DESERT gives new meaning to old style. A courtyard leads to a covered porch with nooks for sitting and open-air dining. The gracious living room is highlighted by a corner fireplace; the formal dining room comes with an adjacent butler's pantry and access to the porch dining area. Two sleeping zones are luxurious with whirlpool tubs and separate showers. The master suite also boasts an exercise room and a nearby private office. A guest suite includes a private entrance and another corner fireplace.

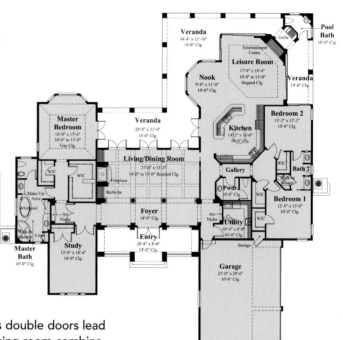

HOME PLAN

HPK1600248

Style: Mission

Square Footage: 3,343

Bedrooms: 3

Bathrooms: 2 ½ + ½

Width: 84' - 0"

Depth: 92' - 0"

Foundation: Slab

eplans.com

THIS DISTINCTIVE STUCCO HOME IS REMINISCENT OF EARLY MISSION-STYLE

architecture. Decorative vigas line the entry as double doors lead into an elongated columned foyer. A living/dining room combination ahead enjoys abundant light from three French doors, and the warmth of a Southwestern fireplace. An abbreviated hall leads either to the bedroom gallery or to the gourmet kitchen. A sunny nook and leisure room just beyond are bathed in natural light. A veranda grill is perfect in any season. Separated from the rest of the home for complete privacy, the master suite relishes a bay window, veranda access, and a lavish bath.

ENJOY THIS BEAUTIFUL WESTERN VACATION HOME!

Exposed rafter tails, arched porch detailing, massive paneled front doors, and stucco exterior walls enhance the Western character of this U-shaped ranch house. Double doors open to a spacious, slope-ceilinged art gallery. The quiet sleeping zone is comprised of an entire wing. The extra room at the front of this wing may be used for a den or an office. The family dining and kitchen activities are located at the opposite end of the plan. Indoor-outdoor living relationships are outstanding. The large, open courtyard is akin to the fabled Greek atrium. It is accessible from each of the zones and functions with a covered arbor, which looks out over the rear landscape. The master suite has a generous sitting area, a walk-in closet, twin lavatories, a whirlpool tub, and a stall shower.

HOME PLAN

HPK1600249

Style: Mediterranean

Square Footage: 2,539

Bedrooms: 3

Bathrooms: 2 ½

Width: 75' - 2"

Depth: 68' - 8"

Foundation: Slab

eplans.com

AN OPEN COURTYARD TAKES CENTER STAGE in this home, providing a happy marriage of indoor/outdoor relationships. Art collectors will appreciate the gallery that enhances the entry and showcases their favorite works. The centrally located great room supplies the nucleus for formal and informal entertaining. A raised-hearth fireplace flanked by built-in media centers adds a special touch. The master suite provides a private retreat where you may relax—try the sitting room or retire to the private bath for a pampering soak in the corner whirlpool tub.

HOME PLAN

 # HPK1600250

Style: SW Contemporary
Square Footage: 3,163
Bedrooms: 4
Bathrooms: 3 ½
Width: 75' - 2"
Depth: 68' - 8"
Foundation: Slab

eplans.com

HOMES OVER 2,501 SQUARE FEET

BESIDES GREAT CURB APPEAL, this home has a wonderful floor plan. The foyer features a fountain that greets visitors and leads to a formal dining room on the right and a living room on the left. A large family room at the rear has a built-in entertainment center and a fireplace. The U-shaped kitchen is perfectly located for servicing all living and dining areas. To the right of the plan, away from the central entertaining spaces, are three family bedrooms sharing a full bath. On the left side, with solitude and comfort for the master suite, are a large sitting area, an office, and an amenity-filled bath. A deck with a spa sits outside the master suite.

HOME PLAN

(#) HPK1600251

Style: Mediterranean

Square Footage: 2,831

Bedrooms: 4

Bathrooms: 3

Width: 84' - 0"

Depth: 77' - 0"

Foundation: Slab

eplans.com

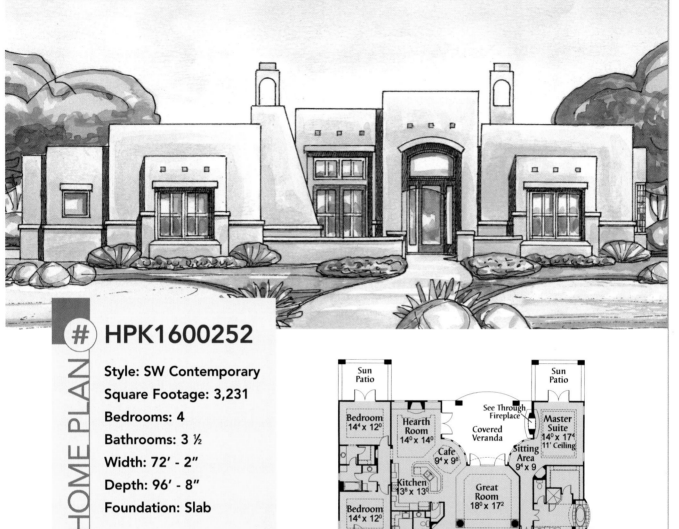

HPK1600252

Style: SW Contemporary

Square Footage: 3,231

Bedrooms: 4

Bathrooms: 3 ½

Width: 72' - 2"

Depth: 96' - 8"

Foundation: Slab

HOME PLAN

eplans.com

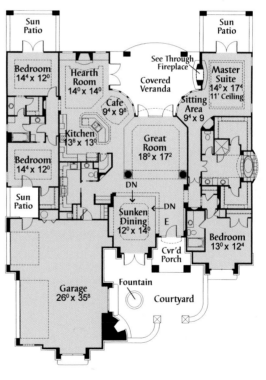

COME HOME TO LUXURY LIVING IN FRESH SOUTHWESTERN STYLE. The enchantment begins with a gracious front courtyard, enhanced by a fountain. A covered porch invites you inside, where a sunken dining room—with double-door access to the courtyard—awaits to the left of the foyer. Kitchen space in this home goes on and on, making it open to any activity or occasion. The kitchen proper features ample pantry space and a curved sinktop-island bar. This bar serves the unique 'cafe' space, enhanced by a ribbon of windows. Amplifying the kitchen area is the hearth room, a comfy setting for casual dining or family time. At the center of the plan is the uniquely-shaped great room, defined by columns and featuring access to the rear veranda. The deluxe master suite, on the right of the home, enjoys a sumptuous bath and shares a see-through fireplace with the covered veranda. This suite and the two left bedrooms enjoy private sun patios. An additional bedroom at the right front has its own bath, making it an ideal guest suite.

HOMES OVER 2,501 SQUARE FEET

THIS LOVELY FIVE-BEDROOM HOME EXUDES THE BEAUTY AND WARMTH of a Mediterranean villa. The foyer views explode in all directions with the dominant use of octagonal shapes throughout. Double doors lead to the master wing, which abounds with niches. The sitting area of the master bedroom has a commanding view of the rear gardens. A bedroom just off the master suite is perfect for a guest room or office. The formal living and dining rooms share expansive glass walls and marble or tile pathways. The mitered glass wall of the breakfast nook can be viewed from the huge island kitchen. Two secondary bedrooms share the convenience of a Pullman-style bath. An additional rear bedroom completes this design.

HOME PLAN

HPK1600253

Style: Mediterranean

Square Footage: 3,424

Bonus Space: 507 sq. ft.

Bedrooms: 5

Bathrooms: 4

Width: 82' - 4"

Depth: 83' - 8"

Foundation: Slab

eplans.com

The Sater Design Collection, Inc.

HOME PLAN

HPK1600254

Style: Italianate

Square Footage: 3,993

Bedrooms: 5

Bathrooms: 3 ½

Width: 80' - 0"

Depth: 104' - 0"

Foundation: Slab

eplans.com

THE TEODORA REDEFINES THE INTERPLAY between indoor and outdoor spaces, creating a wonderfully livable Floridian home with elegant touches at every turn. Doors open to two verandas, and windows bring light into the home from a variety of locations. In the gallery, for example, high transom windows introduce light from above, and the breakfast nook is bathed in light from from its fixed glass window. In every room, the relationship to the outdoors takes center stage, whether through French doors, as in the bedroom, or the sliding glass door in the guest room. Special touches on the verandas, like the fireplace outside the master suite or the grill outside the leisure room, create destinations outdoors, as well.

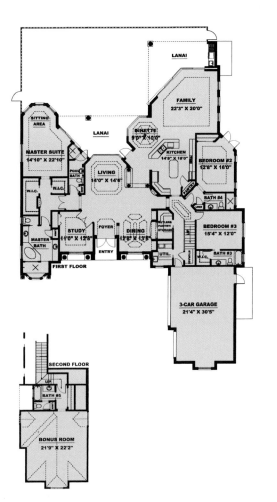

THIS STUNNING HOME WON THE PARADE OF HOMES AWARD for Best Architectural Design. It features a unique balance of coziness and elegance. The floor plan flows flawlessly without compromising privacy or style. Natural views and outdoor living spaces enhance the open, spacious feeling inside this home. The overall layout and flow of the house and coffered ceilings maximize daylight while reflecting grandeur and richness. A pass-through wet bar may also be used as a butler's pantry. The loft above the garage is a fun and logical use of space for a second-floor game room or media room. The gourmet kitchen is superior in design and convenience. The dropped coffered ceiling in the kitchen provides intimate recessed lighting and a wonderful place to display art and kitchen decor.

(#) HPK1600255

HOME PLAN

Style: Mediterranean

Square Footage: 3,370

Bonus Space: 630 sq. ft.

Bedrooms: 3

Bathrooms: 3 ½

Width: 74' - 6"

Depth: 109' - 6"

Foundation: Slab

eplans.com

Photography courtesy of Jim Freeman Commercial Photography.

HPK1600256

Style: Mediterranean

Square Footage: 3,508

Bedrooms: 3

Bathrooms: 4

Width: 75' - 0"

Depth: 104' - 10"

Foundation: Slab

HOME PLAN

eplans.com

ONCE YOU VENTURE WITHIN THIS EUROPEAN HIDEAWAY, you'll never wish to return state side! Palladian and box windows, stucco and tiled roof highlight the exterior of this stunner. Coffered and sloped ceilings proliferate inside. A decorative window facing the front of the house camouflages the three-car garage. French doors garnish the foyer, study and master suite with sitting area. A patio with optional pool and spa is directly across from the foyer through sliding doors in the living room. To the right of the living room lie three additional bedrooms with two baths, utility and storage areas, breakfast room and kitchen, and the formal dining room with butler's pantry immediately to the right of the foyer. Did we mention the 20' x 30' family room and the summer kitchen?

THE ELEGANT ENTRY OF THIS COLONIAL HOME gives it a stately appearance with its columns and pediment. Inside, the entry opens to the living room where the first of two fireplaces is found. The formal dining room adjoins both the living room and the kitchen. The spacious breakfast area looks out onto the patio. The master suite is found on the right with two additional bedrooms, and a fourth bedroom is on the left, giving privacy for overnight guests.

HOME PLAN

HPK1600004

Style: Georgian

Square Footage: 3,136

Bedrooms: 4

Bathrooms: 3 ½

Width: 80' - 6"

Depth: 72' - 4"

Foundation: Crawlspace

eplans.com

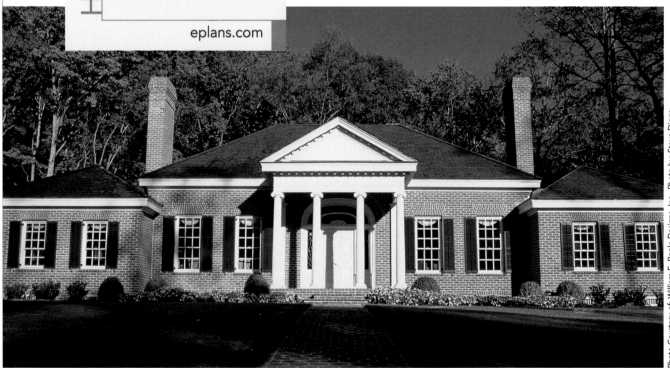

HPK1600258

HOME PLAN #

Style: Mediterranean

Square Footage: 2,537

Bedrooms: 3

Bathrooms: 3

Width: 46' - 10"

Depth: 98' - 0"

Foundation: Slab

eplans.com

A SOARING GREAT ROOM ANCHORS THE INTERIOR in this narrow lot, Mediterranean style that accommodates an entire household on one level. One's first impression from the foyer, the 20-foot square great room, forms a larger space with the dining room, kitchen, and breakfast room on the right. A spectacular covered lanai, suitable for an optional pool bath, lies beyond, with the master suite and study to the left. Each wing of the floor extends past the entrance, housing the fourth bedroom and shared bath on the left, and two more bedrooms with shared bath, utility room, and two-car garage on the right.

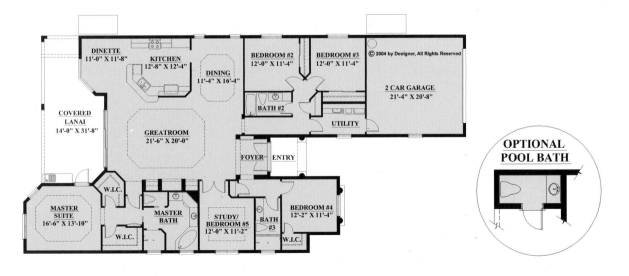

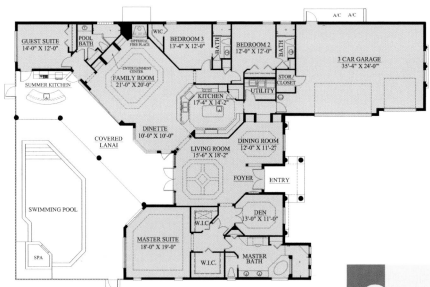

THIS PARADE OF HOMES AWARD WINNER has striking curb appeal with its well-balanced and detailed Mediterranean facade. The floor plan offers open, formal, and casual living areas. Plenty of natural light and views to spacious outdoor areas are provided by the use of pocketing sliding-glass doors, French doors, windows, and mitered glass. This design offers four full bedrooms with four full baths. The family room features a built-in entertainment center with fireplace and is easily furnished. The functional and spacious kitchen is open to the family room and dinette.

HOME PLAN

HPK1600259

Style: Mediterranean

Square Footage: 3,490

Bedrooms: 4

Bathrooms: 4

Width: 69' - 8"

Depth: 115' - 0"

Foundation: Slab

eplans.com

HOME PLAN

HPK1600260

Style: Floridian
Square Footage: 2,998
Bedrooms: 3
Bathrooms: 2 ½
Width: 64' - 8"
Depth: 84' - 0"
Foundation: Slab

eplans.com

TRADITIONAL STYLE ABOUNDS in this single-level home. Its graciously columned entry and hipped roof with deep overhangs prevent overheating but allow abundant natural light to stream inside and are in keeping with some of the best features of a Mediterranean home that suits any setting. The expansive master bedroom suite provides both easy access and privacy, and is set in the home's right wing along with a separate bedroom and bath that are just perfect for a study. An open plan graced with arches plus a seamless transition to the outdoor living space on the veranda adds up to a home designed for easy entertaining.

HOMES OVER 2,501 SQUARE FEET

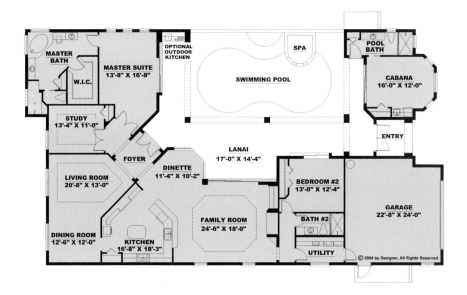

HOME PLAN

#HPK1600261

Style: Mediterranean

Square Footage: 2,948

Bedrooms: 3

Bathrooms: 3

Width: 54' - 8"

Depth: 99' - 8"

Foundation: Slab

eplans.com

THIS IS DEFINITELY SUN COUNTRY—with an expansive lanai garnished with your private pool! Venture beneath the historic red-tiled roof, stucco, and arched, Palladian windows to glimpse how they really live in the Sunshine State. If you can tear yourself away from the central attraction, view the family room with tray ceilings on your left, and take a peak into the guest suite with its private bath. We've also secreted here a utility room for wet bathing suits. Visit the kitchen area, with 100% functional wrap-around counter and dinette. Access the dining room, which forms a larger room with the conventional living room. A foyer off this area opens onto the lanai through French doors directly across, and gives way to the master suite—with study and private access to the lanai—on the left. This plan also provides for an optional outdoor kitchen on the lanai, a pool bath, spa, and cabana.

© The Sater Design Collection, Inc.

WITH CALIFORNIA STYLE AND MEDITERRANEAN GOOD LOOKS, this striking stucco manor is sure to delight. The portico and foyer open to reveal a smart plan with convenience and flexibility in mind. The columned living room has a warming fireplace and access to the rear property. In the gourmet kitchen, an open design with an island and walk-in pantry will please any chef. From here, the elegant dining room and sunny nook are easily served. The leisure room is separated from the game room by a built-in entertainment center. The game area can also be finished off as a bedroom. To the rear, a guest room is perfect for frequent visitors or as an in-law suite. The master suite features a bright sitting area, oversized walk-in closets, and a pampering bath with a whirlpool tub. Extra features not to be missed: the outdoor grill, game-room storage, and gallery window seat.

HOME PLAN

HPK1600262

Style: Italianate

Square Footage: 3,743

Bedrooms: 4

Bathrooms: 3 ½

Width: 80' - 0"

Depth: 103' - 8"

Foundation: Slab

eplans.com

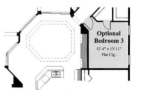

OPTIONAL LAYOUT

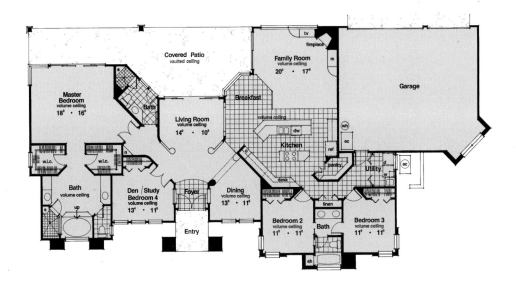

THE ANGLES IN THIS HOME CREATE UNLIMITED VIEWS and space. Majestic columns of brick add warmth to a striking elevation. Inside, the foyer commands a special perspective on living areas including the living room, dining room, and den. The island kitchen serves the breakfast nook and the family room. A large pantry provides ample space for food storage. Nearby, in the master suite, mitered glass and a private bath set the tone for simple luxury. Two secondary bedrooms share privacy and quiet at the front of the house. The den may also convert to a fourth bedroom, if desired.

HOME PLAN

 # HPK1600263

Style: Traditional
Square Footage: 2,597
Bedrooms: 4
Bathrooms: 3
Width: 96' - 6"
Depth: 50' - 0"
Foundation: Slab

eplans.com

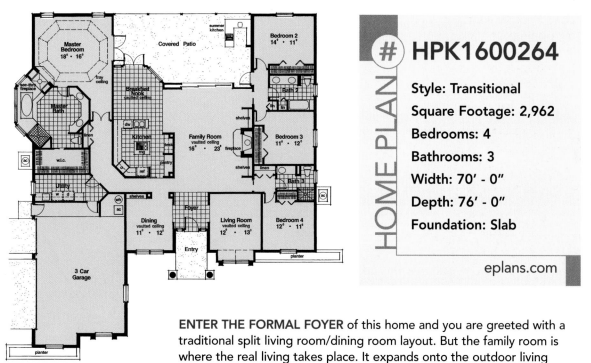

HOME PLAN

HPK1600264

Style: Transitional

Square Footage: 2,962

Bedrooms: 4

Bathrooms: 3

Width: 70' - 0"

Depth: 76' - 0"

Foundation: Slab

eplans.com

ENTER THE FORMAL FOYER of this home and you are greeted with a traditional split living room/dining room layout. But the family room is where the real living takes place. It expands onto the outdoor living space, which features a summer kitchen. The ultimate master suite contains coffered ceilings, a "boomerang" vanity, and angular mirrors that reflect the bayed soaking tub and shower. Efficient use of space creates a huge closet with little center space.

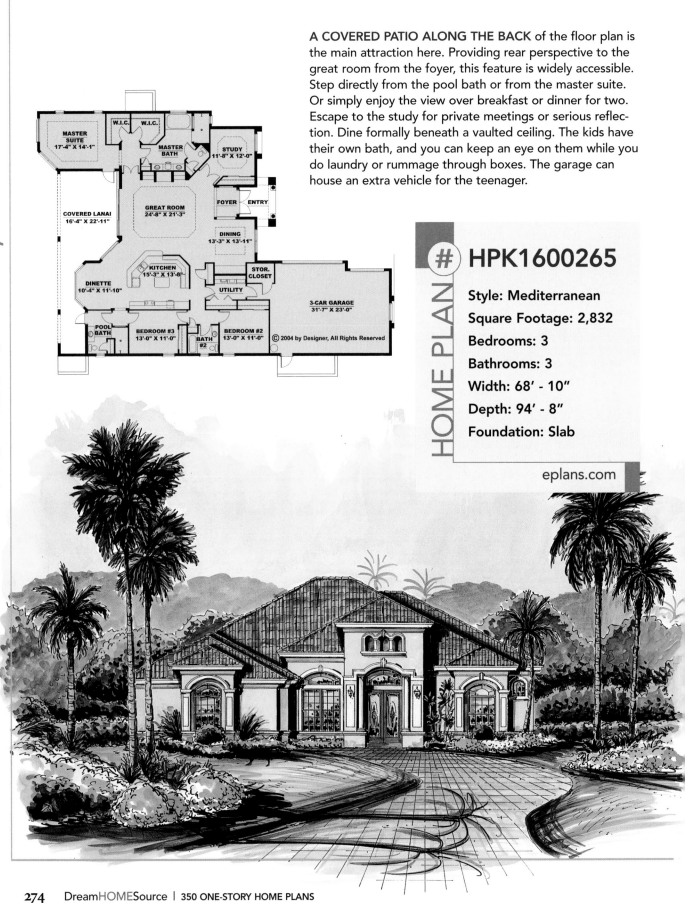

A COVERED PATIO ALONG THE BACK of the floor plan is the main attraction here. Providing rear perspective to the great room from the foyer, this feature is widely accessible. Step directly from the pool bath or from the master suite. Or simply enjoy the view over breakfast or dinner for two. Escape to the study for private meetings or serious reflection. Dine formally beneath a vaulted ceiling. The kids have their own bath, and you can keep an eye on them while you do laundry or rummage through boxes. The garage can house an extra vehicle for the teenager.

HOME PLAN

HPK1600265

Style: Mediterranean

Square Footage: 2,832

Bedrooms: 3

Bathrooms: 3

Width: 68' - 10"

Depth: 94' - 8"

Foundation: Slab

eplans.com

HOME PLAN

HPK1600266

Style: Floridian

Square Footage: 2,794

Bedrooms: 3

Bathrooms: 3

Width: 70' - 0"

Depth: 98' - 0"

Foundation: Slab

eplans.com

CLASSIC COLUMNS, CIRCLE-HEAD WINDOWS, and a bay-windowed study give this stucco home a wonderful street presence. The foyer leads to the formal living and dining areas. An arched buffet server separates these rooms and contributes an open feeling. The kitchen, nook, and leisure room are grouped for informal living. A desk/message center in the island kitchen, art niches in the nook, and a fireplace with an entertainment center and shelves add custom touches. Two secondary suites have guest baths and offer full privacy from the master wing. The master suite hosts a private garden area; the bath features a walk-in shower that overlooks the garden and a water closet room with space for books or a television. Large His and Hers walk-in closets complete these private quarters.

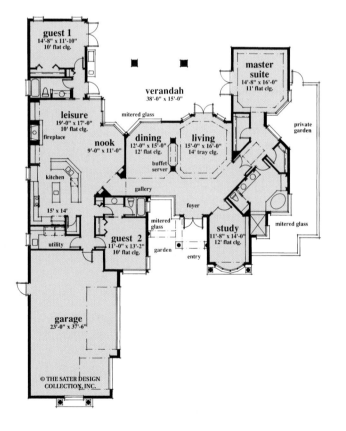

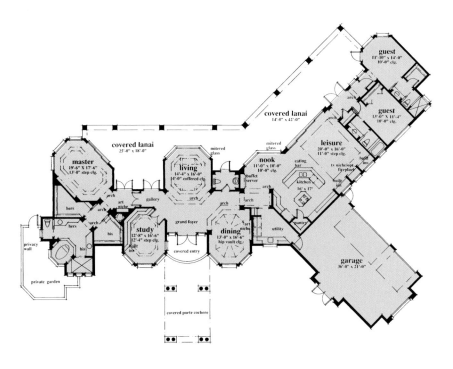

HPK1600267

Style: Mediterranean

Square Footage: 3,398

Bedrooms: 3

Bathrooms: 3 ½

Width: 121' - 5"

Depth: 96' - 2"

Foundation: Slab

eplans.com

BRINGING THE OUTDOORS IN THROUGH A MULTI-TUDE OF BAY WINDOWS is what this design is all about. The grand foyer opens to the living room with a magnificent view to the covered lanai. The study and dining room flank the foyer. The master suite is found on the left with an opulent private bath and views of the private garden. To the right, the kitchen adjoins the nook that boasts a mitered-glass bay window overlooking the lanai. Beyond the leisure room are two guest rooms, each with private baths.

Photo courtesy of Sater Design Collection. This home, as shown in photographs, may differ from

(#) HPK1600268

Style: Mediterranean

Square Footage: 3,725

Bonus Space: 595 sq. ft.

Bedrooms: 3

Bathrooms: 3 ½

Width: 84' - 3"

Depth: 115' - 2"

Foundation: Slab

eplans.com

HOME PLAN

THIS AIRY BUNGALOW belongs on the coastline among palm trees. The smoothly glazed, elongated windows and intricately ornamented openings give the exterior a modern but classy flair. Inside exists a maze of brightly lit, uniquely patterned rooms for entertaining or relaxing. Stunning details include arched and alcove entrances, His and Hers closets, and a wet bar.

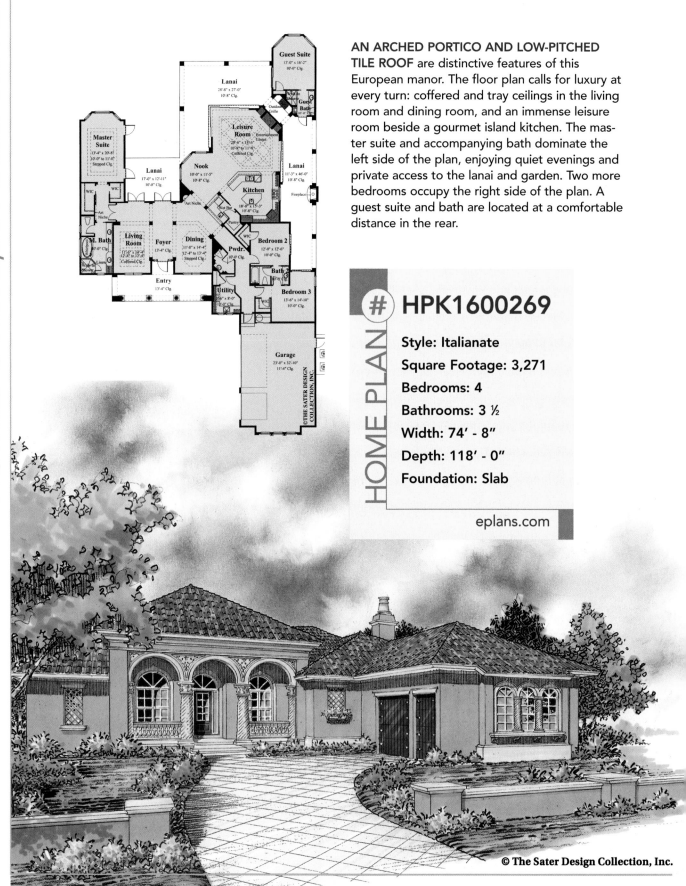

AN ARCHED PORTICO AND LOW-PITCHED
TILE ROOF are distinctive features of this
European manor. The floor plan calls for luxury at
every turn: coffered and tray ceilings in the living
room and dining room, and an immense leisure
room beside a gourmet island kitchen. The master suite and accompanying bath dominate the
left side of the plan, enjoying quiet evenings and
private access to the lanai and garden. Two more
bedrooms occupy the right side of the plan. A
guest suite and bath are located at a comfortable
distance in the rear.

HPK1600269

HOME PLAN

Style: Italianate

Square Footage: 3,271

Bedrooms: 4

Bathrooms: 3 ½

Width: 74' - 8"

Depth: 118' - 0"

Foundation: Slab

eplans.com

© The Sater Design Collection, Inc.

SIMPLE, YET STUNNING, this home proves that you can have it all: beauty and elegance in an at-home environment. At the entry, arched transoms allow sunlight into the foyer and the living room. To the left of the living room is the dining area with a tray ceiling and French doors that open to the veranda. To the right, a see-through fireplace is shared with the study. Wrapping counters, a corner pantry, and an island in the gourmet kitchen allow stress-free meal preparation. The leisure room opens to the spacious morning nook, displays a pyramid ceiling, and includes a warming fireplace. The master suite greets homeowners with lovely French doors and provides access to a master bath with a whirlpool tub, separate shower, two vanities, and a walk-in closet.

the actual blueprints. For more detailed information, please check the floor plans carefully.

 # HPK1600270

HOME PLAN

Style: Mediterranean

Square Footage: 3,877

Bedrooms: 3

Bathrooms: 3 ½

Width: 102' - 4"

Depth: 98' - 10"

Foundation: Slab

eplans.com

DON'T BE FOOLED BY APPEARANCES!
Although this Southwestern-inspired home looks like a traditional family design, the floor plan is anything but ordinary. Raised ceilings in nearly every room create a feeling of spaciousness, and personal touches abound. The entry gives way to a formal dining room. Located for convenience, a china hutch and buffet niche are just ahead. The wet bar and island kitchen will entertain guests, as the great room invites gatherings by the fireplace. Each of the four bedrooms has private outdoor access; the master suite enjoys an exclusive patio (with a fireplace) and a lavish private bath.

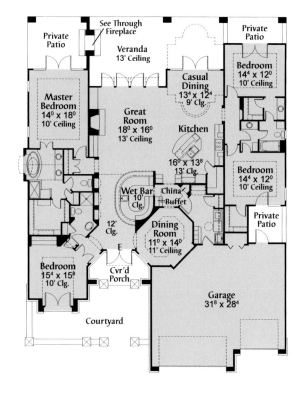

(#) HPK1600271

HOME PLAN

Style: SW Contemporary

Square Footage: 2,715

Bedrooms: 4

Bathrooms: 3

Width: 62' - 4"

Depth: 81' - 8"

Foundation: Slab

eplans.com

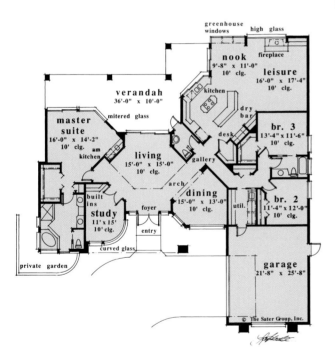

Floor plan labels:

- greenhouse windows
- high glass
- nook 9'-8" x 11'-0" 10' clg.
- fireplace
- leisure 16'-0" x 17'-4" 10' clg.
- verandah 36'-0" x 10'-0"
- kitchen
- dry bar
- mitered glass
- master suite 16'-0" x 14'-2" 10' clg.
- am kitchen
- living 15'-4" x 15'-0" 10' clg.
- desk
- gallery
- br. 3 13'-4" x 11'-6" 10' clg.
- arch
- built ins
- study 11' x 15' 10' clg.
- foyer
- dining 15'-0" x 13'-0" 10' clg.
- util.
- br. 2 11'-4" x 12'-0" 10' clg.
- entry
- curved glass
- private garden
- garage 21'-8" x 25'-8"
- © The Sater Group, Inc.

HOME PLAN

HPK1600272

Style: Floridian

Square Footage: 2,762

Bedrooms: 3

Bathrooms: 2 ½

Width: 74' - 0"

Depth: 77' - 0"

Foundation: Slab

eplans.com

A DIFFERENT AND EXCITING FLOOR PLAN defines this three-bedroom home. Clear and simple rooflines and a large welcoming entryway make it unique. A large archway frames the dining-room entry to the gallery hall. The hall leads past the kitchen toward the informal leisure and nook areas. High glass above the built-in fireplace allows for natural light and rear views. Greenhouse-style garden windows light the nook. The large master suite contains a morning kitchen and a sitting area. The bath features a make-up space, walk-in shower, and private garden tub. The two-car garage enters the home through a vast utility room that provides a large folding table.

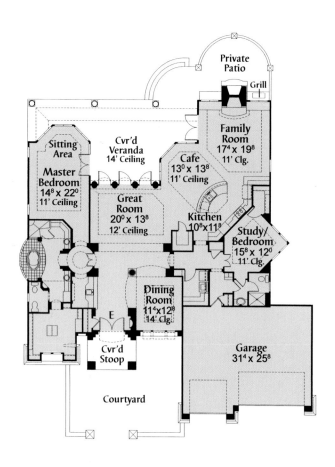

THIS LOVELY SOUTHWESTERN ADAPTATION blends the best of traditional family style with the open planning of Santa Fe. Glass double doors lead to a formal entry; the dining room is on the right, set off by a column and elegant ceiling treatment. Ahead, the great room boasts three doors to the rear veranda. The kitchen is designed to please, incorporating a bowed island and lots of workspace. A sun-lit cafe accommodates casual meals. The family room delights in a two-way fireplace, shared with the rear private patio. A built-in grill is a fun addition. The master suite has a circular foyer, yielding a lavish bath, bayed bedroom, and wet bar.

HPK1600273

HOME PLAN

Style: SW Contemporary
Square Footage: 2,720
Bedrooms: 2
Bathrooms: 2
Width: 72' - 10"
Depth: 79' - 10"
Foundation: Slab

eplans.com

HOME PLAN

(#) HPK1600274

Style: Mediterranean

Square Footage: 2,565

Bedrooms: 3

Bathrooms: 3

Width: 51' - 0"

Depth: 97' - 6"

Foundation: Slab

eplans.com

IMAGINE A CURVING DRIVEWAY AND PALM TREES fronting this villa. An arched portico of stucco and tile, and arched, Palladian windows greet you and visitors through double doors. You can survey from the columned foyer the covered patio, stretching the width of the interior. The patio affords access to the family room, breakfast nook, and living room, as well as to the master suite through another set of French doors. At the end of this suite lies the study, with tray ceilings for hushed erudition. The opposite wing is given over to family needs: two bedrooms with shared bath, a grandiose family room, utility room, and two-car garage.

A GRAND COLUMNED ENTRY ADORNS THE FACADE of this contemporary Southwestern home. Tall windows, skylights, and abundant French doors allow floods of natural light inside. The plan begins with a sunken dining room, topped by a 15-foot tray ceiling. Columns are echoed in the great room, where rear-veranda access invites the outdoors in. In the kitchen, a boomerang-shaped island overlooks the quaint "cafe" and cozy hearth room. Bedrooms on the far left share a Jack-and-Jill bath and access private patios. The master suite enjoys privacy, enhanced by a bowed sitting room and sumptuous spa bath. A nearby secondary bedroom has a private bath and is perfect as a guest suite, home office, or nursery.

HPK1600275

Style: SW Contemporary

Square Footage: 3,052

Bedrooms: 4

Bathrooms: 3 ½

Width: 73' - 0"

Depth: 87' - 8"

Foundation: Slab

HOME PLAN

eplans.com

HPK1600276

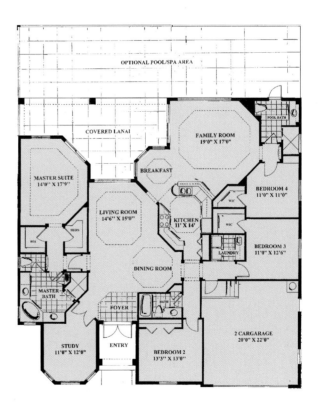

 # HOME PLAN

Style: Mediterranean

Square Footage: 2,581

Bedrooms: 4

Bathrooms: 3

Width: 60' - 0"

Depth: 75' - 0"

Foundation: Slab

eplans.com

FOUR BEDROOMS AND THREE FULL BATHS are included in this economical floor plan. Enjoy open views to the outdoors from the master suite, living room, breakfast area, and family room. In addition to a private study, there is a separate dining area adjacent to the living room creating a great entertainment space. The pool bath is accessible from the interior and exterior of the house. Another full bath is located next to the larger bedroom. The master suite offers access to the lanai and the luxurious master bath has dual sinks, a huge corner shower, and corner garden tub. Carefree, easy living is the standard in this delightful Mediterranean style home.

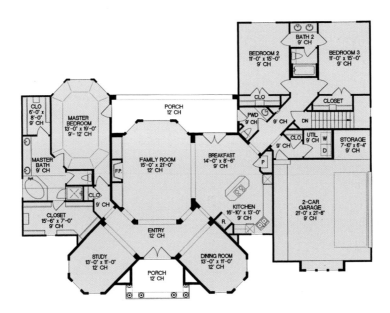

THIS EUROPEAN STUCCO HOME is a well-designed one-story villa. Turrets top identical bayed rooms that are enclosed behind double doors just off the entry. The formal dining room and study are situated in the window-filled turrets. The family room is a spacious entertaining area with a fireplace and built-ins. An efficient kitchen is uniquely designed with its island and angular shape. The split-bedroom floor plan places the master suite away from the two family bedrooms.

HPK1600277

Style: Traditional
Square Footage: 2,517
Bedrooms: 3
Bathrooms: 2 ½
Width: 77' - 0"
Depth: 59' - 0"

HOME PLAN

eplans.com

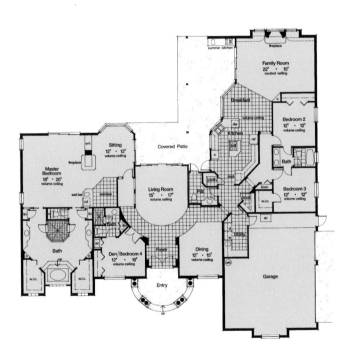

HPK1600278

Style: Contemporary

Square Footage: 3,556

Bedrooms: 4

Bathrooms: 3 ½

Width: 85' - 0"

Depth: 85' - 0"

Foundation: Slab

eplans.com

A BEAUTIFUL CURVED PORTICO PROVIDES A MAJESTIC ENTRANCE to this one-story home. To the left of the foyer is a den/bedroom with a private bath, ideal for use as a guest suite. The exquisite master suite features a see-through fireplace and an exercise area with a wet bar. The family wing is geared for casual living with a powder room/patio bath, a huge island kitchen with a walk-in pantry, a glass-walled breakfast nook, and a grand family room with a fireplace and media wall. Two family bedrooms share a private bath.

STEP OUT ON THE LANAI OF THIS ELEGANT FLORIDIAN and enjoy the cooling breezes from the formal living area, the private master suite, or the cheerful breakfast nook. The spacious kitchen is a cook's delight with its large pantry, an island cooktop, and garden greenhouse window. The leisure room hosts a fireplace with built-in shelves and convenient access to an outdoor patio and grill. The sumptuous master wing features a bayed study, a huge walk-in closet, plenty of space for a sitting area, and a relaxing master bath with private garden view.

HPK1600279

Style: Floridian

Square Footage: 3,104

Bedrooms: 3

Bathrooms: 3 ½ + ½

Width: 73' - 0"

Depth: 108' - 0"

Foundation: Slab

eplans.com

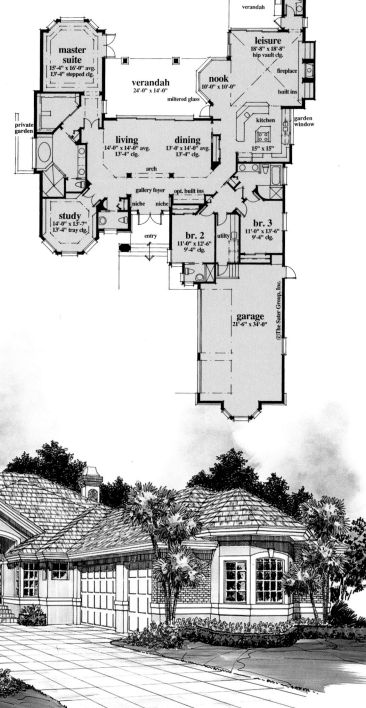

© The Sater Group, Inc.

HOME PLAN

(#) HPK1600280

Style: French

Square Footage: 2,775

Bedrooms: 3

Bathrooms: 2 ½

Width: 74' - 0"

Depth: 59' - 0"

Foundation: Crawlspace

eplans.com

A QUAINT DINING GAZEBO adds a delightful touch to the facade of this lovely home. It complements the formal living room, with a fireplace, found just to the right of the entry foyer (be sure to notice the elegant guest bath to the left). Family living takes place at the rear of the plan in a large family room with a through-fireplace to the study. A breakfast nook enhances the well-appointed kitchen. The master suite has a vaulted ceiling and boasts a huge walk-in closet and a pampering bath. Two family bedrooms share a full bath.

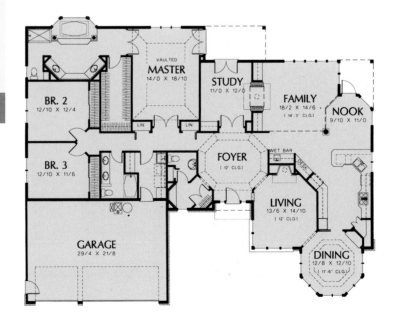

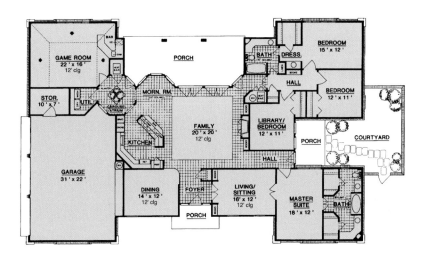

THIS STATELY COUNTRY HOME is a quaint mix of Colonial style and romantic French flavor. Inside, formal living and dining rooms flank the entry foyer. Two sets of double doors open from the family room onto the rear patio. A romantic courtyard is placed to the far right of the plan, just beyond the family bedrooms. A three-car garage with an extra storage room offers plenty of space. The family game room is reserved for recreational fun.

HOME PLAN

HPK1600281

Style: Traditional

Square Footage: 2,791

Bedrooms: 3

Bathrooms: 2

Width: 84' - 0"

Depth: 54' - 0"

Foundation: Crawlspace, Slab

eplans.com

Mark Englund. This home, as shown in photographs, may differ from the actual

REMINISCENT OF THE OLD NEWPORT MANSIONS, this luxury house has volume ceilings, a glamorous master suite with a hearth-warmed sitting area, a glassed-in sunroom, a home office, three porches with a deck, and a gourmet kitchen with a pantry. Graceful French doors are used for all the entrances and in the formal living and dining rooms. The magnificent kitchen boasts a large pantry. A centrally positioned family room is graced with a large fireplace and is accessed by the rear porch, living room, and dining room.

**HPK1600282**

Style: Farmhouse

Square Footage: 4,038

Bedrooms: 4

Bathrooms: 4 ½

Width: 98' - 0"

Depth: 90' - 0"

Foundation: Unfinished Basement, Crawlspace, Slab

eplans.com

THOUGH DESIGNED AS A GRAND ESTATE, this home retains the warmth of a country manor with intimate details on the inside and out. A one-of-a-kind drive court leads to private parking and ends in a two-car garage; a separate guest house is replete with angled walls and sculptured ceilings. A continuous vault follows from the family room through the kitchen and nook. The vault soars even higher in the bonus room with a sundeck upstairs. Two exquisitely appointed family bedrooms with window seats and walk-in closets share a full bath. The master suite has pampering details such as a juice bar and media wall, walk-in closets, and covered patio access.

HOME PLAN

HPK1600283

Style: European Cottage

Square Footage: 2,816

Bonus Space: 290 sq. ft.

Bedrooms: 4

Bathrooms: 3 ½ + ½

Width: 94' - 0"

Depth: 70' - 5"

Foundation: Slab

eplans.com

Mark Englund. This home, as shown in photographs, may differ from the actual

HOME PLAN

(#) HPK1600284

Style: European Cottage

Square Footage: 2,816

Bonus Space: 290 sq. ft.

Bedrooms: 3

Bathrooms: 3 ½

Width: 94' - 0"

Depth: 114' - 0"

Foundation: Slab

eplans.com

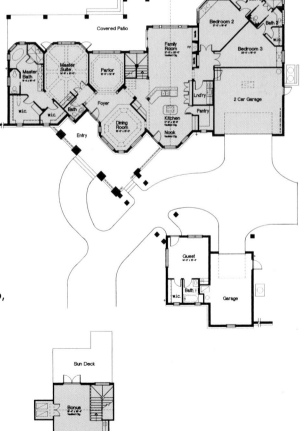

A STRIKING FRONT-FACING PEDIMENT, BOLD COLUMNS, and varying rooflines set this design apart from the rest. An angled entry leads to the foyer, flanked on one side by the dining room with a tray ceiling and on the other by a lavish master suite. This suite is enhanced with a private bath, two large walk-in closets, a garden tub, a compartmented toilet and bidet, and access to the covered patio. The parlor also enjoys rear-yard views. The vaulted ceilings provide a sense of spaciousness from the breakfast nook and kitchen to the family room. A laundry room and roomy pantry are accessible from the kitchen area. Two family bedrooms reside on the right side of the plan; each has its own full bath and both are built at interesting angles. An upstairs, vaulted bonus room includes French doors opening to a second-floor sundeck.

THIS COUNTRY ESTATE IS BEDECKED WITH ALL THE DETAILS THAT PRONOUNCE ITS FRENCH origins. They include the study, family room, and keeping room. Dine in one of two areas—the formal dining room or the casual breakfast room. A large porch to the rear can be reached through the breakfast room or the master suite's sitting area. All three bedrooms in the plan have walk-in closets. Bedrooms 2 and 3 share a full bath that includes private vanities.

HOME PLAN

HPK1600285

Style: French
Square Footage: 3,032
Bedrooms: 3
Bathrooms: 3
Width: 73' - 0"
Depth: 87' - 8"
Foundation: Slab

eplans.com

© The Sater Design Collection, Inc.

HOME PLAN

HPK1600286

Style: Italianate

Square Footage: 3,942

Bedrooms: 3

Bathrooms: 4

Width: 83' - 10"

Depth: 106' - 0"

Foundation: Slab

eplans.com

WELCOME HOME TO A COUNTRY MANOR WITH RENAISSANCE FLAIR. Full-length, squint-style windows and brick accents bring Old World charm to a modern plan. Designed for flexibility, the open foyer, living room, and dining room have infinite decor options. Down a gallery (with art niches), two bedroom suites enjoy private baths. The bon-vivant island kitchen is introduced with a wet bar and pool bath. In the leisure room, family and friends will revel in expansive views of the rear property. An outdoor kitchen on the lanai invites alfresco dining. Separated for ultimate privacy, the master suite is an exercise in luxurious living. Past the morning kitchen and into the grand bedroom, an octagonal sitting area is bathed in light. The bath is gracefully set in the turret, with a whirlpool tub and views of the master garden.

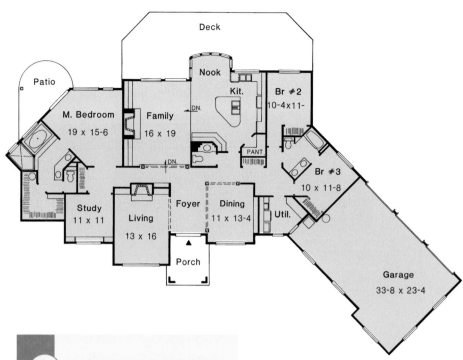

(#) HPK1600287

Style: NW Contemporary

Square Footage: 2,744

Bedrooms: 3

Bathrooms: 2 ½

Width: 110' - 0"

Depth: 70' - 0"

Foundation: Crawlspace

eplans.com

LOOKING A BIT LIKE A SINGLE-STORY CASTLE, this impressive design will stand out in any neighborhood. Enter under a brick arch to the foyer; on the right, a dining room is defined by columns, and on the left, a living room greets guests with a warming fireplace. A sunken family room lies ahead, complete with a fireplace framed by built-ins. The kitchen employs a unique use of space, with a cooktop island, side counter/snack bar, and an attached sun-filled nook. Two bedrooms are located nearby and share a full bath between them. Situated for privacy, the master suite takes advantage of natural light and creature comforts like a spa tub and private patio access. A study completes the plan.

HOME PLAN

HPK1600288

Style: Contemporary

Square Footage: 3,312

Bedrooms: 3

Bathrooms: 3 ½

Width: 90' - 11"

Depth: 81' - 3"

eplans.com

OPTIONAL LAYOUT

REAR EXTERIOR

A FRENCH FACADE EXPOSES A FLOOR PLAN WITH LUXURY. The oval entry is an appropriate beginning to the formal living room and open dining room, private study, and gallery hall. The kitchen features an island for the household gourmet and is located conveniently to the dining room, breakfast bay, and family room. The master suite is a secluded paradise of amenities. Included are an oversized walk-in closet, His and Hers vanities, separate shower and tub, compartmented toilet, and another walk-in closet. At the far left of the plan, two secondary bedrooms share a full bath, and both feature walk-in closets.

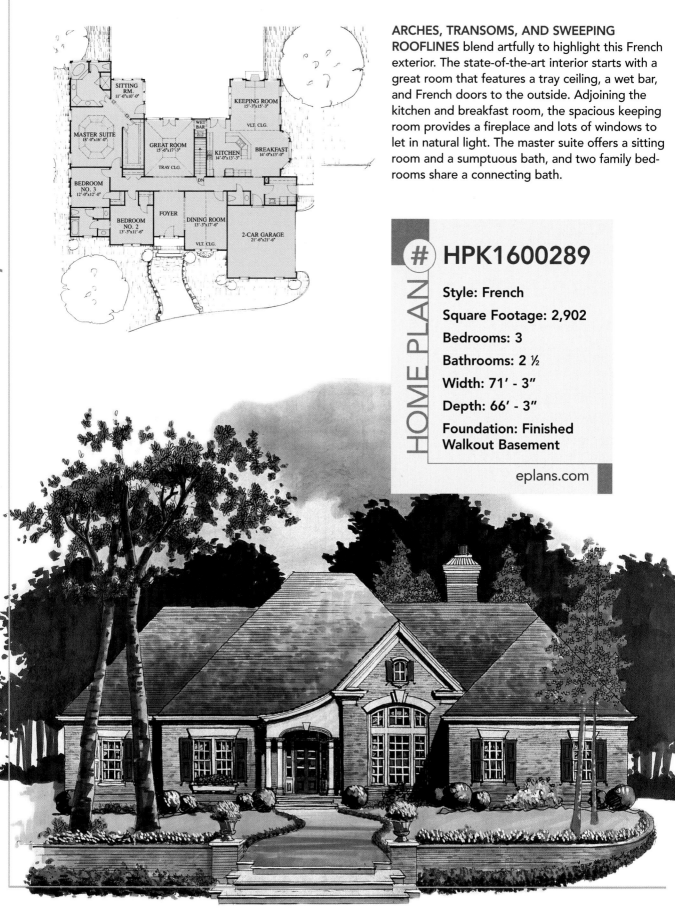

ARCHES, TRANSOMS, AND SWEEPING ROOFLINES blend artfully to highlight this French exterior. The state-of-the-art interior starts with a great room that features a tray ceiling, a wet bar, and French doors to the outside. Adjoining the kitchen and breakfast room, the spacious keeping room provides a fireplace and lots of windows to let in natural light. The master suite offers a sitting room and a sumptuous bath, and two family bedrooms share a connecting bath.

HPK1600289

HOME PLAN

Style: French

Square Footage: 2,902

Bedrooms: 3

Bathrooms: 2 ½

Width: 71' - 3"

Depth: 66' - 3"

Foundation: Finished Walkout Basement

eplans.com

HPK1600290

Style: Craftsman

Square Footage: 3,615

Basement: 2,803 sq. ft.

Bedrooms: 4

Bathrooms: 3 ½ + ½

Width: 98' - 0"

Depth: 94' - 0"

Foundation: Finished Basement

eplans.com

HOME PLAN

A COMBINATION OF STONE, SIDING, AND MULTIPLE ROOFLINES creates a cottage feel to this large home. Inside, the master suite opens from a short hallway and enjoys a private fireplace, access to the rear covered porch, a spacious walk-in closet, compartmented toilet, separate shower, garden tub, and dual vanities. The gourmet kitchen enjoys an island cooktop, snack bar, access to the covered porch, and conveniently serves the adjoining dining room and lodge room. Two additional family bedrooms share a full bath in the basement and a guest suite is located upstairs near the front door.

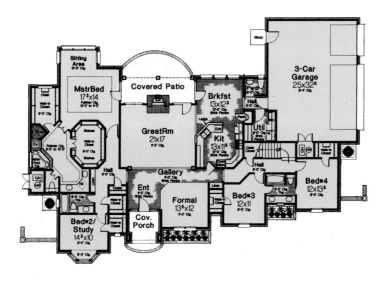

HPK1600291

Style: Traditional

Square Footage: 2,941

Bonus Space: 342 sq. ft.

Bedrooms: 4

Bathrooms: 3 ½

Width: 91' - 0"

Depth: 64' - 7"

Foundation: Slab

eplans.com

WITH ALL THE CHARM AND DISTINGUISHED BEAUTY of a French Country home, this elegant estate is designed for luxury and convenience. Brick-paver flooring flows from the entry into the gourmet kitchen and through to the bright breakfast area for continental flair. Continuing this motif, the great room boasts an extended brick-hearth fireplace. On the far right, two bedrooms share a Jack-and-Jill tiled bath. A third bedroom/study, with a sunny bay window and an adjacent bath, makes a fine nursery or guest suite. The awe-inspiring master suite resides to the left rear, a quiet and luxurious haven. A sitting area, filled with natural light, joins a pampering spa bath with an angled whirlpool tub, and two enormous walk-in closets, to provide a soothing retreat from the world. Extra storage space abounds; future space above the garage awaits your imagination.

HOME PLAN

HPK1600292

Style: Country Cottage

Square Footage: 2,888

Bedrooms: 4

Bathrooms: 3

Width: 68' - 6"

Depth: 78' - 1"

Foundation: Slab

eplans.com

ALTERNATE EXTERIORS—BOTH EUROPEAN STYLE! Stone quoins and shutters give one facade the appearance of a French Country cottage. The other, with keystone window treatment and a copper roof over the bay window, creates the impression of a stately French chateau. From the entry, formal living areas are entered through graceful columned openings—living room to the left and dining room to the right. Straight ahead, the comfortable family room awaits with its warming fireplace and cathedral ceiling, offering room to relax and enjoy casual gatherings. The private master suite features a Pullman ceiling, a luxurious bath, and twin walk-in closets. A private lanai is accessed from the master bath. Located nearby, Bedroom 2 serves nicely as a guest room or easily converts to a nursery or study. Two family bedrooms, a connecting bath, handy kitchen, breakfast room, and utility room complete the floor plan.

ALTERNATE EXTERIOR

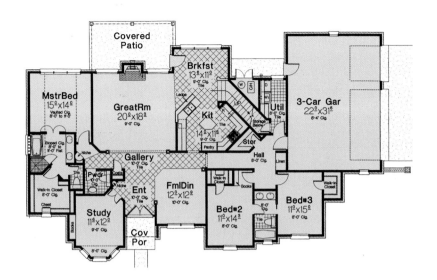

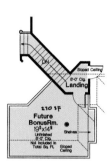

THE SIDE-LOADING THREE-CAR GARAGE is set back and hidden from view, keeping this home's facade clean and fresh. The family room and entry flank the study where it widens into the gallery. From here you enter the magnificent great room with its fireplace and patio beyond, or turn left to reach the lavish master suite. To the right, find the two family bedrooms with the shared full bath, or the diamond-shaped kitchen with the adjoining breakfast nook. The utility room is tucked behind the staircase that rises to the future bonus room.

HPK1600293

HOME PLAN

Style: European Cottage

Square Footage: 2,530

Bonus Space: 270 sq. ft.

Bedrooms: 3

Bathrooms: 2 ½

Width: 83' - 10"

Depth: 51' - 10"

Foundation: Slab

eplans.com

WITH A SOLID EXTERIOR OF ROUGH CEDAR AND STONE, this new French Country design will stand the test of time. A wood-paneled study in the front features a large bay window. The heart of the house is found in a large open great room with a built-in entertainment center. The spacious master bedroom features a corner reading area and access to an adjacent covered patio. A three-car garage and three additional bedrooms complete this generous family home.

HPK1600294

Style: French
Square Footage: 2,590
Bedrooms: 4
Bathrooms: 3 ½
Width: 73' - 6"
Depth: 64' - 10"
Foundation: Slab

eplans.com

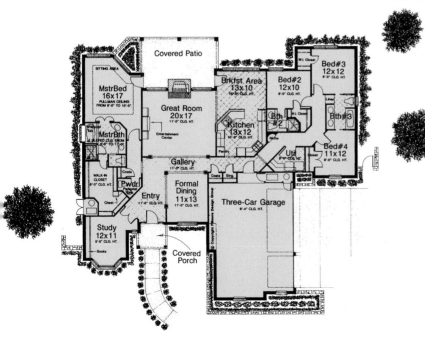

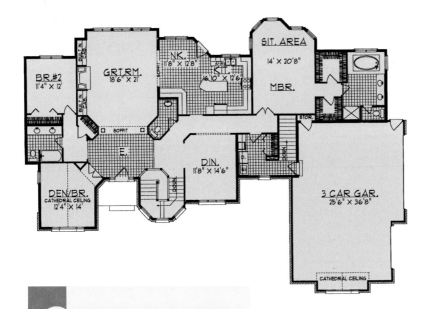

HPK1600295

Style: Ranch

Square Footage: 2,600

Bedrooms: 3

Bathrooms: 2 ½

Width: 87' - 0"

Depth: 60' - 0"

Foundation: Unfinished Basement

eplans.com

VARIED ROOFLINES, SHUTTERS, AND MULTI-PANE WINDOWS combine to make this one-story home a neighborhood showpiece. A tiled entry presents a grand view of the spacious great room, which is complete with a warming fireplace and built-in cabinets. A den opens off the foyer through double doors and can be used as a guest bedroom when needed. The island in the kitchen provides extra work-space to an already well-equipped area. With direct access to both the formal dining room and breakfast nook, the kitchen is a warm and bright place to share morning coffee and after-school snacks. A sumptuous master suite features a sitting bay, two walk-in closets, and a lavish bath. The three-car garage is reached through the laundry room.

HOME PLAN

(#) HPK1600296

Style: French Country

Square Footage: 3,064

Bonus Space: 366 sq. ft.

Bedrooms: 4

Bathrooms: 4

Width: 79' - 6"

Depth: 91' - 0"

Foundation: Slab

eplans.com

THIS OPULENT FRENCH CHATEAU ESTATE UNFOLDS a dramatic interior with two layout choices. A formal entry is flanked by the beautiful dining room and a private den with coffered ceiling, built-ins, and double doors. The living room is an ideal space for after-dinner entertaining. A wet bar and corner fireplace warm up the space and the view of the pool adds light and color. Family spaces are not overlooked and the kitchen, eating nook, family room, and lanai are great recreation areas. The lanai provides an outdoor kitchen, convenient for snacks after a swim. Two secondary bedrooms share a Jack-and-Jill bath. An entire wing is dedicated to the master suite. Secluded luxury, the master bath includes an oversized walk-in closet, shower enclosure, soaking tub, dual-sink vanity, and a private garden courtyard.

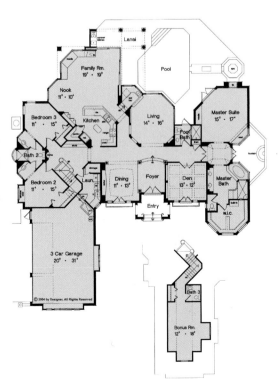

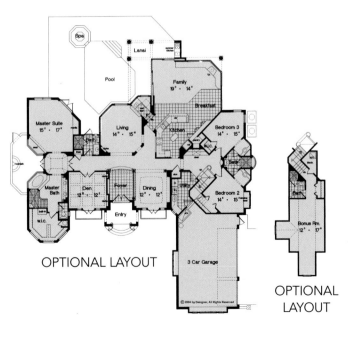

OPTIONAL LAYOUT

OPTIONAL LAYOUT

STATELY IN BRICK, WITH A CHIMNEY IN BACK, this transitional beckons you across its portico to stand on the foyer. The formal dining room to the right is sectioned by columns to maintain openness with the gathering room, yet preserve a measure of privacy. A study lies around the corner, bringing you full center into the gathering room. Enjoy great views from here across an attached deck, or go on out through the sliding doors through the kitchen or breakfast nook. Also access the deck privately from the master bedroom. Laundry, storage, pantry, and two more suites with shared bath round out the main floor. Upstairs, step onto the covered veranda to relish fresh air after working out in your private fitness room, or before retiring downstairs. With another kitchen for quick snacks and beverages, your recreation area will be the talk of the neighborhood.

HOME PLAN

HPK1600297

Style: Transitional

Square Footage: 3,153

Basement: 1,837 sq. ft.

Bedrooms: 3

Bathrooms: 2 ½

Width: 78' - 2"

Depth: 86' - 6"

Foundation: Finished Walkout Basement

eplans.com

HOME PLAN

HPK1600298

Style: European Cottage

Square Footage: 3,185

Bedrooms: 3

Bathrooms: 3 ½

Width: 65' - 0"

Depth: 90' - 0"

Foundation: Slab

eplans.com

Floor plan labels:

entertainment center

leisure
17'-4" x 21'-0"
step clg.

built ins

nook
10'-0" x 11'-0"
10'-0" clg.

covered lanai
22'-0" x 12'-0"

master
14'-6" x 20'-0"
step clg.

eating bar

kitchen

12' x 17'

butlers pantry

server

butt joint glass

dining
11'-8" x 16'-0"
step clg.

buffet server

living
14'-8" x 16'-0"
step clg.

arch

dressing

walk in wardrobe

arch

art niche

gallery

arch

his

hers

guest
11'-6" x 12'-0"
10'-0" clg.

arch

butt joint glass

foyer

arch

guest
11'-4" x 13'-0"
10'-0" clg.

covered entry

study
10'-0" x 14'-0"
14'-0" clg.

private garden

books

utility

workbench

garage
22'-0" x 21'-0"

©THE SATER DESIGN COLLECTION, INC.

THE QUIET ELEGANCE OF THIS HOME'S EXTERIOR speaks volumes about the way it lives inside. From its grand entrance into an open dining area and living room with tray ceilings and expansive views out through a covered lanai in back, the public spaces of this home were made for entertaining. And there is plenty of space for overnight guests in a separate wing to the left, close to the kitchen and leisure room, but set far enough apart for privacy. Rather than one undifferentiated space, the master bedroom suite has a unique bath angled off to the side.

WITH ENORMOUS WINDOWS FRONTING THE DINING ROOM AND STUDY, this home projects an aura that is at once imposing and elegant. With a roof-top dormer providing ambient light in the foyer, you'll enter through French doors to a study on your left, dining room on the right, or straight ahead into the great room with added ceiling height. The kitchen and breakfast area are just to your left, with laundry room and two bedrooms occupying the left side of the house. The sunroom contains three sets of French doors, from the breakfast nook, master bedroom, or porch. The master suite, to the right of the great room, contains everything a couple needs, and a guest suite is discretely located at the other end of the hall. A three-car garage has one exterior and two interior entrances. Plan has provision for basement stairs from the conjunction of the nook and garage.

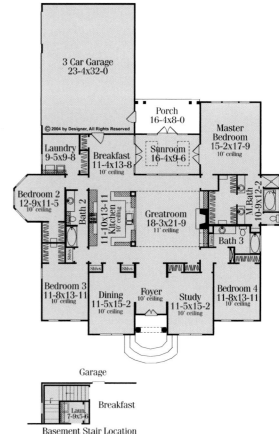

HOME PLAN

HPK1600299

Style: French

Square Footage: 2,962

Bedrooms: 4

Bathrooms: 3

Width: 68' - 0"

Depth: 88' - 3"

Foundation: Crawlspace, Slab, Unfinished Basement

eplans.com

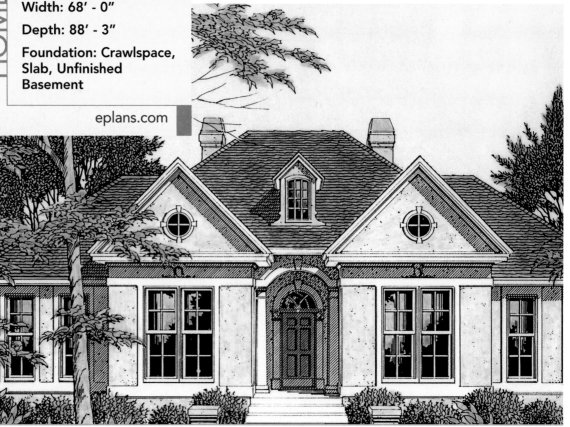

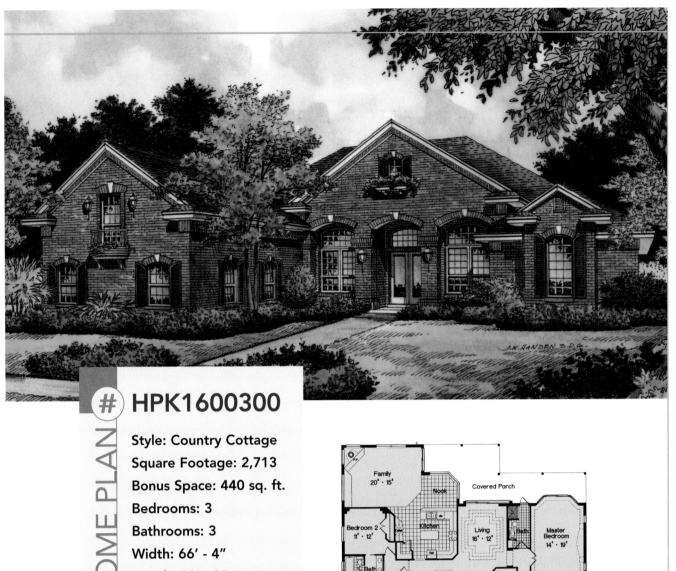

HOME PLAN

HPK1600300

Style: Country Cottage

Square Footage: 2,713

Bonus Space: 440 sq. ft.

Bedrooms: 3

Bathrooms: 3

Width: 66' - 4"

Depth: 80' - 8"

Foundation: Slab

eplans.com

INTERESTING ARCHES, COLUMNS, AND CAN-TILEVERS ADORN this elegant home. A dining room with a tray ceiling flanks the foyer to the left, and a den/study is to the right. The large living room enjoys rear views and a covered porch. The island kitchen has an abundance of counter space and flows directly into a bayed breakfast nook. The hearth-warmed family room boasts easy access to the kitchen. The master bedroom resides on the right side of the plan; amenities include His and Hers walk-in closets and sinks, a garden tub, separate shower, compartmented toilet, and a sitting bay that looks to the rear porch.

THIS HOME'S VARYING HIPPED-ROOF PLANES make a strong statement. Exquisite classical detailing includes delightfully proportioned columns below a modified pedimented gable and masses of brick punctuated by corner quoins. The central foyer, with its high ceiling, leads to interesting traffic patterns. This extremely functional floor plan fosters flexible living patterns. There are formal and informal living areas, which are well defined by the living and family rooms. The sunken family room, wonderfully spacious with its high, sloping ceiling, contains a complete media-center wall and a fireplace flanked by doors to the entertainment patio. Occupying the isolated end of the floor plan, the master suite includes an adjacent office/den with a private porch.

HPK1600301

HOME PLAN

Style: Plantation
Square Footage: 2,946
Bedrooms: 4
Bathrooms: 3
Width: 94' - 1"
Depth: 67' - 4"
Foundation: Slab

eplans.com

THIS NEOCLASSICAL HOME has plenty to offer! The elegant entrance is flanked by a formal dining room on the left and a beam-ceilinged study—complete with a fireplace—on the right. An angled kitchen is sure to please with a work island, plenty of counter and cabinet space, and a snack counter that it shares with the sunny breakfast room. A family room with a second fireplace is nearby. The lavish master suite features many amenities, including a huge walk-in closet, a three-sided fireplace, and a lavish bath. Two secondary bedrooms have private baths. Finish the second-floor bonus space to create an office, a play room, and a full bath. A three-car garage easily shelters the family fleet.

HOME PLAN

HPK1600302

Style: Neoclassic

Square Footage: 3,828

Bonus Space: 1,018 sq. ft.

Bedrooms: 3

Bathrooms: 3 ½ + ½

Width: 80' - 6"

Depth: 70' - 8"

Foundation: Crawlspace

eplans.com

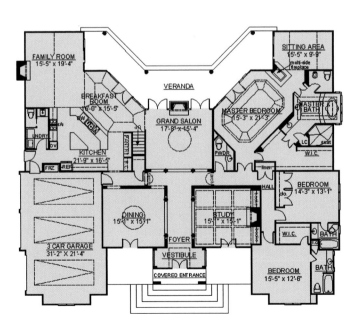

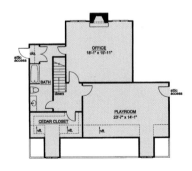

HOMES OVER 2,501 SQUARE FEET

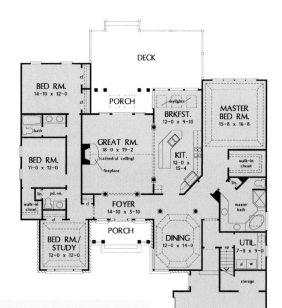

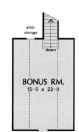

HOME PLAN

HPK1600303

Style: Traditional

Square Footage: 2,544

Bonus Space: 394 sq. ft.

Bedrooms: 4

Bathrooms: 2 ½

Width: 62' - 8"

Depth: 82' - 1"

eplans.com

REFINED ELEGANCE CHARACTERIZES THIS STUNNING HOME with dynamic open floor plan. Elegant columns separate the large great room with cathedral ceiling from the smart, angled kitchen with skylit breakfast area. Tucked away for privacy, the master suite is a grand getaway with a well-appointed bath that includes a corner tub, separate shower, and spacious vanity. The semi-private privy is also a plus. Stunning tray ceilings enhance the bedroom/study and the dining room. The dining room is also distinguished by two stately columns gracing the hallway to the kitchen and foyer. As for plenty of closet and storage space, this home has it, even an additional bonus room above the garage.

REAR EXTERIOR

COLUMNS INTRODUCE A WELCOMING COVERED PORCH that leads into the foyer. Here, still more columns define the formal dining room. The nearby family room is complete with a fireplace and built-ins and offers access to the sunroom/breakfast area. The lavish master suite is designed to pamper and will be a pleasant retreat for the homeowner. Two secondary bedrooms—or make one an office—share a full bath.

HOME PLAN

(#) **HPK1600001**

Style: Traditional

Square Footage: 2,752

Bedrooms: 3

Bathrooms: 2 1/2

Width: 90' - 0"

Depth: 72' - 10"

Foundation: Unfinished Basement

eplans.com

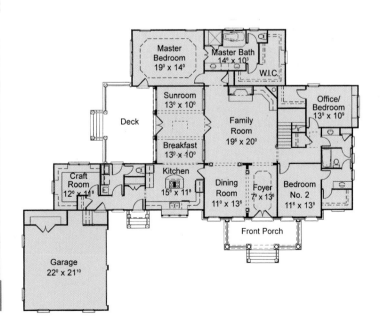

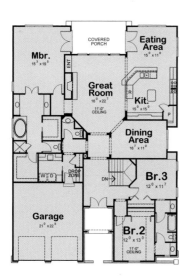

ESCAPE TO THE FRENCH COUNTRYSIDE IN YOUR PRIVATE COTTAGE. A hipped dormer anchoring a pitched roof announces this house of distinction. Sunlight graces the entryway, courtesy of the dormer window, upon which you enter through French doors and are rewarded with a view to the gathering room with fireplace down the main hallway. A split staircase leads to the combination game/rec room with bar, exercise room, an extra bedroom with attached bath, and plentiful storage space. Bedrooms 2 and 3 are tucked away to the right of the entry on the main floor. Upon touring the kitchen—complete with separate dining and eating areas, and pantry—you'll be surprised at all the room. Be sure not to miss the master suite with dual vanity, spa tub, separately compartmented shower and toilet, and two closets. You'll never want to emerge from the forest as long as you have this haven!

HOME PLAN

HPK1600305

Style: French Country
Square Footage: 2,640
Bedrooms: 3
Bathrooms: 2 ½
Width: 50' - 0"
Depth: 70' - 4"

eplans.com

HOME PLAN

(#) HPK1600306

Style: Traditional

Square Footage: 2,625

Bonus Space: 447 sq. ft.

Bedrooms: 4

Bathrooms: 2 ½

Width: 63' - 1"

Depth: 90' - 2"

eplans.com

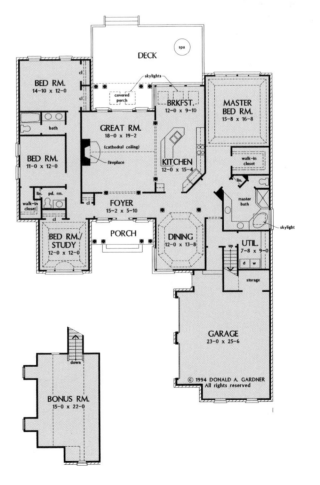

THIS STATELY BRICK FACADE features a columned, covered porch that ushers visitors into the large foyer. An expansive great room with a fireplace and access to a covered rear porch awaits. The centrally located kitchen is within easy reach of the great room, formal dining room, and skylit breakfast area. Split-bedroom planning places the master bedroom and elegant master bath to the right of the home. Two bedrooms with abundant closet space are placed to the left; an optional bedroom or study with a Palladian window faces the front. A large bonus room is located above the garage.

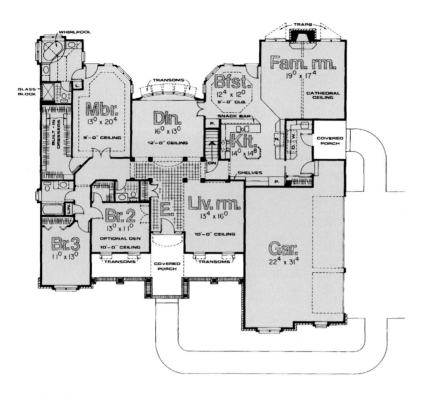

HPK1600307

Style: Traditional

Square Footage: 2,538

Bedrooms: 3

Bathrooms: 2 ½

Width: 68' - 8"

Depth: 64' - 8"

eplans.com

THE GRAND FRONT PORCH GIVES THIS HOME UNIQUE STYLE and majestic curb appeal. Inside, the entry centers on the stately dining room with its bowed window. Both the living room and the second bedroom—which can be converted into a den—have 10-foot ceilings. The island kitchen features abundant storage space, a lazy Susan, and a snack bar. A sun-filled breakfast area opens to the large family room with its cathedral ceiling and central fireplace. The private bedroom wing offers two secondary bedrooms and a luxurious master suite featuring a spacious walk-in closet with built-in dressers, and private access to the backyard. The master bath includes a vaulted ceiling, a corner whirlpool tub, and His and Hers vanities.

HOME PLAN

HPK1600308

Style: Craftsman

Square Footage: 2,818

Bedrooms: 4

Bathrooms: 3

Width: 70' - 0"

Depth: 69' - 10"

eplans.com

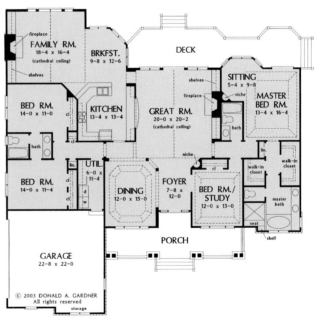

PROMOTING EASY LIVING, this home has plenty of Craftsman character with a low-maintenance exterior. Doubled columns and stone accents create architectural interest. Inside, columns and a tray ceiling distinguish the dining room, and beautiful double doors open into the study/bedroom. Art niches, fireplaces, and built-in cabinetry add beauty and convenience. The kitchen has a handy pass-through to the great room. The spacious deck accommodates outdoor living. The master suite has a bayed sitting area and French doors that lead to the deck. The master bath is equipped with a double vanity, garden tub, and shower with a shelf and seat.

THIS TRADITIONAL HOME, WITH ELEGANT ARCHED WINDOWS and hipped rooflines, offers both outdoor and indoor spaces for making family life and entertaining a delight. From either the lavish master suite or the breakfast alcove, enter a covered patio where you can enjoy early morning coffee or a quiet evening reading. From here, a larger patio extends outward, perfect for barbecues. It conveniently connects to a pool area. The formal living and dining rooms, connected by a gallery hall, are congenial for social get-togethers. The well-equipped kitchen easily serves the dining room, breakfast area, and family room. Four bedrooms and a study all enjoy nine-foot ceilings. A three-car garage completes the plan.

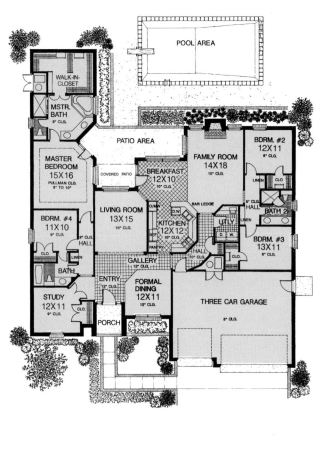

HPK1600309

HOME PLAN

Style: Traditional

Square Footage: 2,590

Bedrooms: 4

Bathrooms: 3

Width: 64' - 0"

Depth: 74' - 4"

Foundation: Slab

eplans.com

A BRICK ARCHWAY COVERS THE FRONT PORCH of this European-style home, creating a truly grand entrance. Situated beyond the entry, the living room takes center stage with a fireplace flanked by tall windows. To the right is a bayed eating area and an efficient kitchen. Steps away is the formal dining room. Skillful planning creates flexibility for the master suite. If you wish, use Bedroom 2 as a secondary bedroom or guest room, with the adjacent study accessible to everyone. Or, if you prefer, combine the master suite with the study and use it as a private retreat with Bedroom 2 as a nursery, creating a wing that provides complete privacy. Completing this clever plan are two family bedrooms, a powder room, and a utility room.

HOME PLAN

 # HPK1600310

Style: Traditional
Square Footage: 2,696
Bedrooms: 4
Bathrooms: 3 ½
Width: 80' - 0"
Depth: 64' - 1"
Foundation: Slab

eplans.com

HOMES OVER 2,501 SQUARE FEET

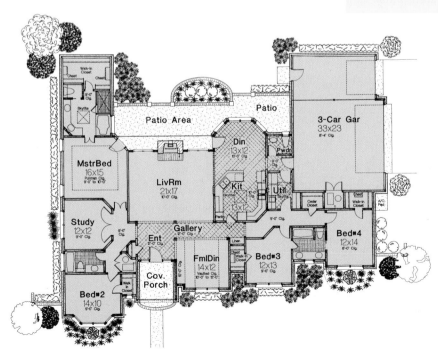

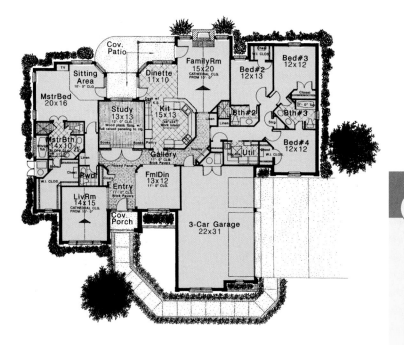

HPK1600311

Style: Traditional

Square Footage: 2,990

Bedrooms: 4

Bathrooms: 3 ½

Width: 80' - 0"

Depth: 68' - 0"

Foundation: Slab

eplans.com

A BRICK EXTERIOR, CAST-STONE TRIM, AND CORNER QUOINS make up this attractive single-living-area design. The entry introduces a formal dining room to the right and a living room with a wall of windows to the left. The hearth-warmed family room opens to the kitchen/dinette, both with 10-foot ceilings. A large bay window enhances the dinette with a full glass door to the covered patio. A large master suite with vaulted ceilings features a bayed sitting area, a luxurious bath with double sinks, and an oversize walk-in closet.

ALTERNATE EXTERIOR

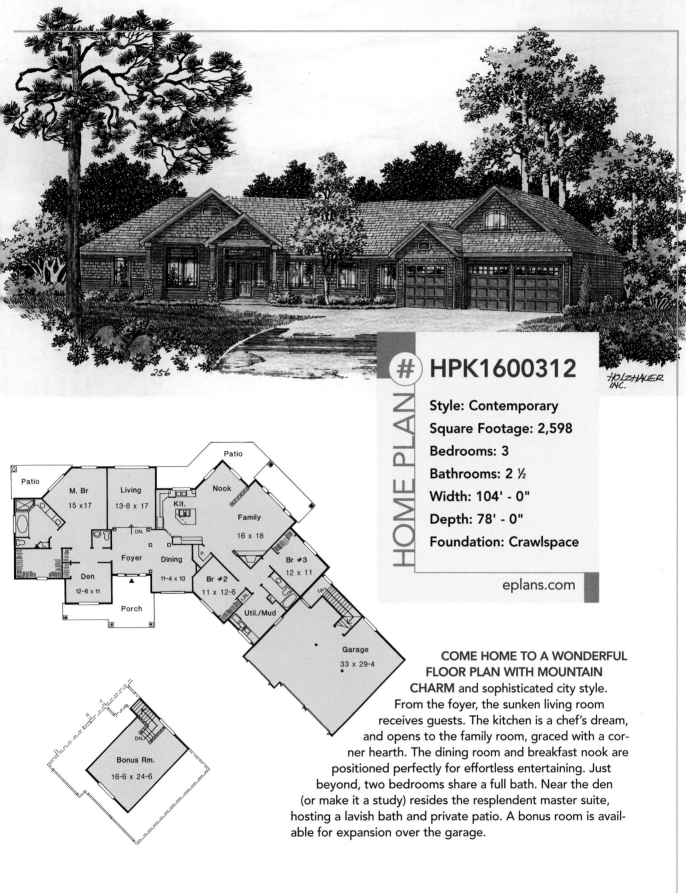

HPK1600312

HOLZHAUER INC.

Style: Contemporary

Square Footage: 2,598

Bedrooms: 3

Bathrooms: 2 ½

Width: 104' - 0"

Depth: 78' - 0"

Foundation: Crawlspace

eplans.com

COME HOME TO A WONDERFUL FLOOR PLAN WITH MOUNTAIN CHARM and sophisticated city style. From the foyer, the sunken living room receives guests. The kitchen is a chef's dream, and opens to the family room, graced with a corner hearth. The dining room and breakfast nook are positioned perfectly for effortless entertaining. Just beyond, two bedrooms share a full bath. Near the den (or make it a study) resides the resplendent master suite, hosting a lavish bath and private patio. A bonus room is available for expansion over the garage.

RUSTIC ELEGANCE IS THE THEME OF THIS COUNTRY MARVEL. An inviting country covered porch wraps around the front. To the right of the foyer, a quaint music room is open to the vaulted gathering room. Through three double doors, a pampering parlor awaits. The central splendor of this design is the family pool and indulging spa. To the right of the pool room, the master suite is secluded for privacy and includes a luxury-style master bath. Next to the master bedroom, a private theater is a quiet and relaxing retreat. A fireside library creates a romantic allure and is an appropriate addition to this heavenly plan.

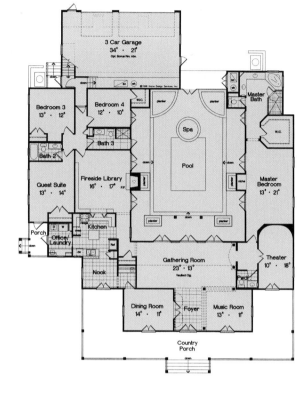

HOME PLAN

**HPK1600313**

Style: Farmhouse

Square Footage: 3,886

Bonus Space: 444 sq. ft.

Bedrooms: 4

Bathrooms: 3 ½

Width: 77' - 4"

Depth: 99' - 0"

Foundation: Slab

eplans.com

HPK1600314

Style: Craftsman

Square Footage: 3,278

Bedrooms: 4

Bathrooms: 3 ½

Width: 75' - 10"

Depth: 69' - 4"

Foundation: Crawlspace

eplans.com

FORM FOLLOWS FUNCTION AS DUAL GALLERY HALLS lead from formal areas to split sleeping quarters in this Prairie adaptation. At the heart of the plan, the grand-scale great room offers a raised-hearth fireplace framed by built-in cabinetry and plant shelves. Open planning combines the country kitchen with an informal dining space and adds an island counter with a snack bar. A lavish master suite harbors a sitting area with private access to the covered pergola. The secondary sleeping wing includes a spacious guest suite. A fifth bedroom or home office offers its own door to the wraparound porch.

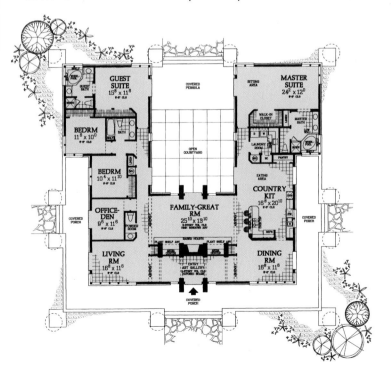

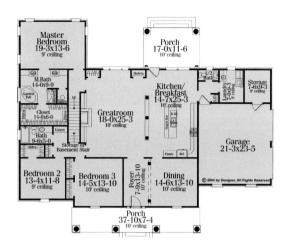

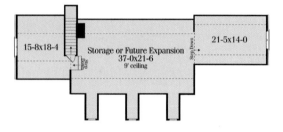

REAR EXTERIOR

THREE DORMERS SIT ATOP A WIDE, FRIENDLY PORCH that welcomes visitors to this attractive stucco and brick home. Inside, well-defined spaces use half-walls and columns to keep the layout open. A lovely dining room sits off the open island kitchen. A halfwall accented with columns creates a transition to the greatroom. A beautiful fireplace and flanking built-ins complete the space. Two family bedrooms offer plenty of closet space and share a full bath. The master suite enjoys nine-foot ceilings, a massive walk-in closet, and a super bath made for two. The second level is a great space for storage, media room, or future expansion space.

HOME PLAN

HPK1600315

Style: Traditional

Square Footage: 2,561

Bonus Space: 1,494 sq. ft.

Bedrooms: 3

Bathrooms: 2 ½

Width: 76' - 8"

Depth: 62' - 0"

Foundation: Crawlspace, Slab, Unfinished Basement

eplans.com

STATELY WHITE COLUMNS ADORN AN ARCHED PORTICO

in between red brick and dark-colored shingles and shutters on this All-American. The foyer contains a 13-foot ceiling, and provides direct access to the formal dining room on the left. A handy double coat closet follows, whereupon one enters the living room, with a wonderful vaulted ceiling. A fireplace and view across the porch is immediately noticeable. The master suite and built-in bookcase and linen closet are to the right. The kitchen leads off the left of the living room, and features a curved preparation island, restaurant-style, and reinforcing the feeling of expansiveness. A convenient pantry stands immediately to the left. Breakfast is served in the nook, alongside the porch window. A half bath and access to the garage are accessible here. A utility area and two bedrooms with shared bath are off of the other end of the kitchen, with optional staircase.

HOME PLAN

HPK1600316

Style: Traditional

Square Footage: 4,658

Bonus Space: 1,008 sq. ft.

Bedrooms: 3

Bathrooms: 2 ½

Width: 68' - 1"

Depth: 66' - 0"

Foundation: Crawlspace, Slab, Unfinished Basement

eplans.com

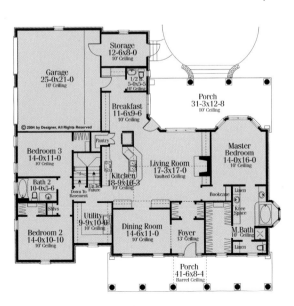

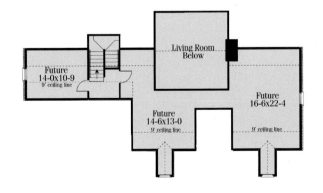

HOMES OVER 2,501 SQUARE FEET

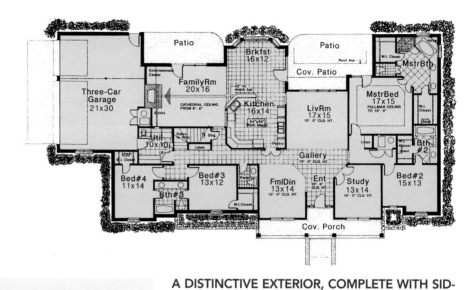

HPK1600317

Style: Traditional

Square Footage: 3,270

Bedrooms: 4

Bathrooms: 3 ½

Width: 101' - 0"

Depth: 48' - 1"

Foundation: Crawlspace, Slab

eplans.com

A DISTINCTIVE EXTERIOR, COMPLETE WITH SIDING, STONE, AND BRICK, presents a welcoming facade on this four-bedroom home. The large family room includes a cathedral ceiling, a fireplace, and built-ins. The island kitchen has plenty of work space and direct access to a sunny, bay-windowed breakfast room. A study and formal dining room flank the tiled entryway, which leads straight into a formal living room. Three family bedrooms are arranged across the front of the house. The master suite offers plenty of seclusion as well as two walk-in closets, a lavish bath, and direct access to the rear patio. A stairway leads to the attic.

HOME PLAN

(#) HPK1600318

Style: Tidewater

Square Footage: 2,807

Bedrooms: 3

Bathrooms: 2 ½

Width: 68' - 0"

Depth: 83' - 9"

Foundation: Unfinished Walkout Basement

eplans.com

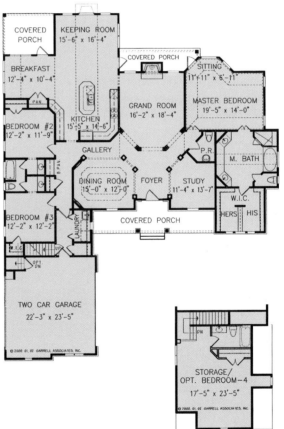

THREE COVERED PORCHES HIGHLIGHT THIS COUNTRY DESIGN. Once inside, the foyer offers three options: straight ahead is the grand room, to the left lies the kitchen and bedrooms, and to the right houses the study and the master suite. The large country kitchen, breakfast nook, and adjoining keeping room are ideal for family interaction. Two family bedrooms share a full bath with private vanities. The master suite boasts a sitting area, and a roomy bath with a dual-sink vanity, garden tub, private toilet, separate shower, and His and Hers walk-in closets. Upstairs, flex space provides a storage option or a fourth bedroom.

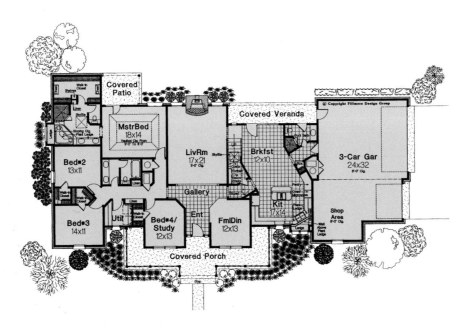

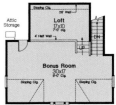

RUSTIC CORNER QUOINS, A COVERED FRONT PORCH, and interesting gables give this home its classic country character. The entry opens to the formal living areas that include a large dining room to the right and a spacious living room warmed by a fireplace straight ahead. A gallery leads the way to the efficient kitchen enhanced with a snack bar and large pantry. Casual meals can be enjoyed overlooking the covered veranda and rear grounds from the connecting breakfast room. The other side of the gallery accesses the luxurious master suite and three secondary bedrooms—all with walk-in closets. The opulent master suite enjoys a private covered patio in the rear of the plan.

HPK1600319

HOME PLAN

Style: Farmhouse

Square Footage: 2,539

Bonus Space: 636 sq. ft.

Bedrooms: 4

Bathrooms: 3

Width: 98' - 0"

Depth: 53' - 11"

Foundation: Slab

eplans.com

© 2004 by Designer, All Rights Reserved

Sitting Area
10-0x10-0

M.Bath
13-0x13-3

Master Bedroom
16-2x16-3

Sunroom
25-10x9-10

1/2 Bath

Laundry
12-4x8-5

3 Car Garage
22-2x33-3

Bedroom
13-7x12-2

Bath
8-4x7-9

Greatroom
17-3x17-9
10' Ceilings

Kitchen/ Breakfast
20-5x17-10

Bedroom
13-8x12-0

Owner's Choice
14-9x12-3

Foyer

Dining
14-9x12-3

Butler's Pantry
11-9x8-9

Desk

Stoop
14-0x4-9

HOME PLAN # HPK1600320

Style: Traditional

Square Footage: 3,084

Bedrooms: 3

Bathrooms: 2 ½

Width: 73' - 9"

Depth: 79' - 3"

Foundation: Slab, Unfinished Basement, Crawlspace

eplans.com

A STATELY NEO-CLASSICAL STOOP announces your impending entry to this home. Arched ceilings border all sides in the foyer, conjoining three rooms. A second arch separates the great room from the kitchen. A dignified butler's pantry is located between kitchen and formal dining area. The sunroom offers entry and exit via French doors, as well as an incredible and warming view. A side-loading garage fitting three cars and a laundry and half bath exist to the right of the sunroom. The sumptuous master suite, to the left of the sun room, boasts its own sitting area, and two bedrooms with shared bath occupy the opposite corner. An additional room measuring over 14' x 12' is adjacent to the foyer. Indoor columns and lots of built-in amenities add into this home's value.

WHAT A CHEERFUL COUNTRY COTTAGE! Lifted straight from the plains, you'll be amazed at all of the modern conveniences held within. A sociable porch ushers visitors to a narrow foyer with tiled flooring. The 20-foot square great room awaits as a grand surprise. To your back is a pleasing breakfast bar, emerging from the kitchen. This room and the adjacent dining room should be pleasantly filled with daylight on sunny days. Bearing left from the entry, two bedrooms with shared bath and ample closet space sit at opposite ends of the hall. The great room offers a hearth, incredible views, and acess to the patio. Across the great room is the opposite hall to the master bedroom, utility room and pantry, and double garage. There is also an optional staircase for an attic or loft; a great escape for a rainy day!

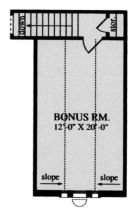

HOME PLAN

HPK1600321

Style: Prairie

Square Footage: 1,712

Bonus Space: 312 sq. ft.

Bedrooms: 3

Bathrooms: 2

Width: 57' - 8"

Depth: 53' - 10"

Foundation: Crawlspace, Slab

eplans.com

HOME PLAN
HPK1600322

Style: Traditional

Square Footage: 2,758

Bedrooms: 4

Bathrooms: 2 ½

Width: 72' - 0"

Depth: 68' - 0"

Foundation: Unfinished Basement

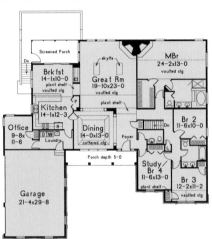

HOME PLAN
HPK1600323

Style: Tidewater

Square Footage: 3,074

Bedrooms: 3

Bathrooms: 3 ½

Width: 77' - 0"

Depth: 66' - 8"

Foundation: Island Basement

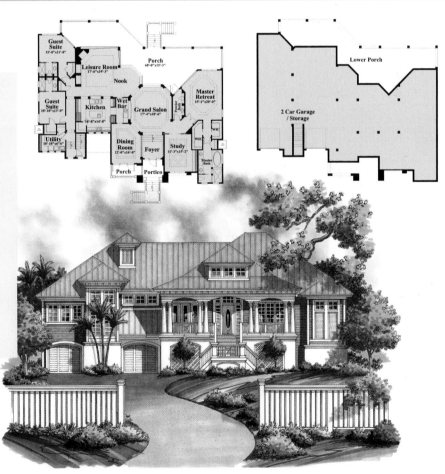

Green Style—Landscapes and Projects Complete the Home

Karen Bussolini

THE REAL BEAUTY OF A LANDSCAPE PLAN stems from how it can mature and give context to the home. Choose a plan that complements the style of the home and is appropriate to the region.

A truly gratifying landscape design takes cues from the architecture of the home, your sense of style, and the natural properties of the land. You will also need to make a decision about the kind of landscape you desire. For instance, perennials and bulbs used throughout a design will establish a garden theme and provide cutting flowers for indoor bouquets. But remember that a garden will need a lot of care and constant attention. And a neglected garden will do nothing for a home's curb appeal. Similarly, edible gardens are very appropriate in a country-inspired design—but need to be protected from the elements. More shaded parts of the landscape call for sitting areas or outdoor structures, such as storage sheds or small barns.

The right landscaping design will effectively frame your home from the rest of the neighborhood. If your lot will not allow the placement of a tall fence or natural barrier between the home and the next-door neighbor, place "retreat" areas away from property lines. That is, resist the natural urge to place quiet areas in only the corners of the yard. With the right design, owners can create a relaxing getaway right in the middle of the plan.

The virtue of predrawn landscape and project plans is that you can

Julie Maris/Semel (3)

enjoy the benefits of a professional design without paying for custom landscaping. Do-it-yourselfers can easily manage the tasks required to install a bed or build a gazebo. Your new landscape will improve your outdoor environment the day it's completed, and the initial investment will more than pay for itself by adding to the value of your home.

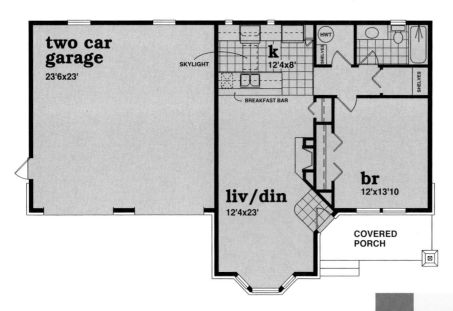

THIS DESIGN WILL HOUSE TWO MEMBERS of the family fleet and includes a comfortable apartment—great for servant's quarters or tenants. Rustic country accents enhance the siding and stone exterior. This superb design includes a spacious floor plan with a bay window in the living room and skylit kitchen. Adding to the charm of this lovely one-bedroom design are the covered porch and central fireplace. A two-car garage occupies the left half of this design and includes a separate outdoor entrance.

HOME PLAN

HPK1600324

Style: Garage
Square Footage: 1,370
Bedrooms: 1
Bathrooms: 1
Width: 52' - 0"
Depth: 34' - 0"
Foundation: Crawlspace

eplans.com

HOME PLAN

HPK1600325

Style: Garage
First Floor: 1,079 sq. ft.
Second Floor: 908 sq. ft.
Total: 1,987 sq. ft.
Bedrooms: 2
Bathrooms: 1
Width: 41' - 0"
Depth: 43' - 6"
Foundation: Slab

FIRST FLOOR

SECOND FLOOR

HOME PLAN

HPK1600326

Style: Traditional
Square Footage: 914 sq. ft.
Bonus Space: 967 sq. ft.
Bedrooms: 2
Bathrooms: 2
Width: 40' - 0"
Depth: 40' - 0"
Foundation: Crawlspace

FIRST FLOOR

SECOND FLOOR

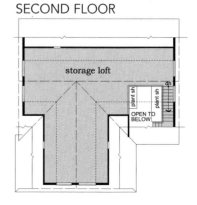

LANDSCAPES & OUTDOOR PROJECTS

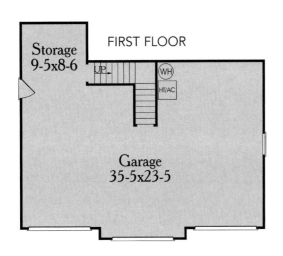

FIRST FLOOR

Storage
9-5x8-6

UP

WH

HT/AC

Garage
35-5x23-5

SECOND FLOOR

Dining
9-4x13-0

Kitchen
9-11x9-3

DN

Bedroom
10-0x13-0

Greatroom
12-5x12-4

THIS COMPACT HOME OR GUEST HOUSE is perfect for guests or a cozy vacation retreat. The entrance is via the garage, where extra storage is provided for convenience. The living quarters reside on the second floor. A dining room is on the left side of the plan next to the kitchen, allowing for easy entertainment. To the right sits the bedroom, complete with a full bath and closet. The great room faces to the front of the plan and boasts a planter box outside its window. All rooms are vaulted, lending a spacious feel to this otherwise cozy cottage.

 # HPK1600327

HOME PLAN

Style: Traditional
First Floor: 908 sq. ft.
Second Floor: 659 sq. ft.
Total: 1,567 sq. ft.
Bedrooms: 1
Bathrooms: 1
Depth: 36' - 0"
Foundation: Slab

eplans.com

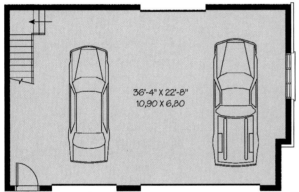

FIRST FLOOR

36'-4" X 22'-8"
10,90 X 6,80

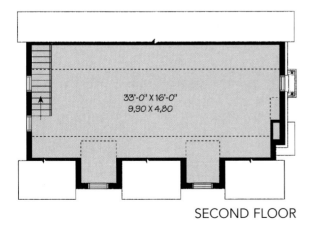

SECOND FLOOR

33'-0" X 16'-0"
9,90 X 4,80

THIS GARAGE HAS THE APPEARANCE OF A EUROPEAN COTTAGE. Two bays hold three cars with some room for a work bench or storage. An open studio provides extra flex space for guests, projects, or storage.

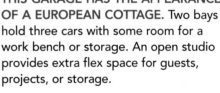

HPK1600328

HOME PLAN

Style: Contemporary

First Floor: 903 sq. ft.

Second Floor: 673 sq. ft.

Total: 1,576 sq. ft.

Width: 38' - 0"

Depth: 24' - 0"

Foundation: Slab

eplans.com

FIRST FLOOR

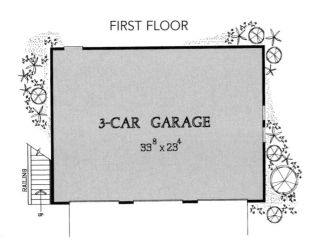

3-CAR GARAGE

$33^8 \times 23^4$

RAILING

UP

SECOND FLOOR

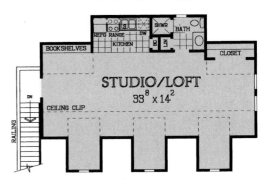

REFG RANGE | DW | SHWR | BATH
BOOKSHELVES | KITCHEN
DN
CEILING CLIP

STUDIO/LOFT

$33^8 \times 14^2$

CLOSET

RAILING

ATTRACTIVE AND FUNCTIONAL, THIS IMPRESSIVE structure has room for three cars in the garage section and 670 square feet of living area—complete with kitchen, bathroom, bookshelves, and closet—to use as a studio or a hideaway loft for guests. The treatment of the steeply pitched gable roof is repeated in three gabled dormers, each with tall, narrow windows framed with shutters. Access to the second-floor loft area is via a railed exterior stairway which leads to a small landing with its own covered roof supported by wooden columns. The clipped corners of the trim around each of the three car bays lend country charm. Four wrought-iron coach lights complete the effect.

**HPK1600329**

HOME PLAN

Style: Garage
First Floor: 824 sq. ft.
Second Floor: 670 sq. ft.
Total: 1,494 sq. ft.
Bathrooms: 1
Width: 34' - 4"
Depth: 24' - 0"
Foundation: Slab

eplans.com

A PORTICO-STYLE ENTRY IS

A WARM WELCOME to this detached three-car garage, styled to complement many of the neighborhood designs. Bonus space above offers 497 square feet of additional living area or a recreation room. With a morning kitchen, full bath, vaulted ceiling, and three dormered windows, Option A may be developed as a comfortable guest suite or a charming artist's studio. The entry vestibule provides ample storage space as well as a wrapping stair to the bonus level.

HOME PLAN

HPK1600330

Style: Garage

First Floor: 770 sq. ft.

Second Floor: 497 sq. ft.

Total: 1,267 sq. ft.

Bedrooms: 1

Bathrooms: 1

Width: 47' - 6"

Depth: 22' - 0"

Foundation: Slab

eplans.com

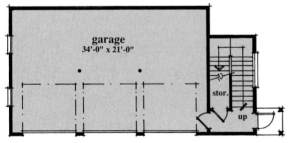

FIRST FLOOR

garage
34'-0" x 21'-0"

stor.

up

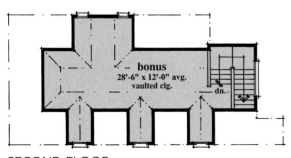

SECOND FLOOR

bonus
28'-6" x 12'-0" avg.
vaulted clg.

dn.

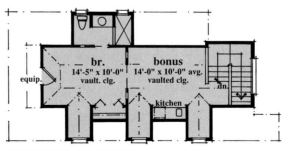

OPTIONAL LAYOUT

equip.

br.
14'-5" x 10'-0"
vault. clg.

bonus
14'-0" x 10'-0" avg.
vaulted clg.

kitchen

dn.

LANDSCAPES & OUTDOOR PROJECTS

THIS TWO-CAR GARAGE sports a low roofline topped with an open gable. Horizontal siding makes this a perfect country addition to a home. A side door and three windows provide access and plenty of natural light for working.

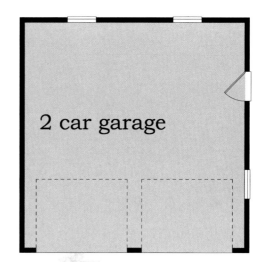

2 car garage

HOME PLAN

(#) HPK1600331

Style: Country
Width: 24' - 0"
Depth: 24' - 0"
Foundation: Slab

eplans.com

340   DreamHOMESource | **350 ONE-STORY HOME PLANS**

VENTED DORMERS and a high-pitched insulated metal roof dress up this two-car, 484-square-foot garage with quaint details that blend beautifully with any traditional neighborhood home. With three windows and a side entry, this garage is convenient and well lit.

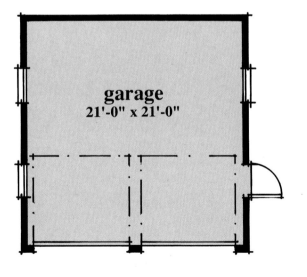

garage
21'-0" x 21'-0"

LANDSCAPES & OUTDOOR PROJECTS

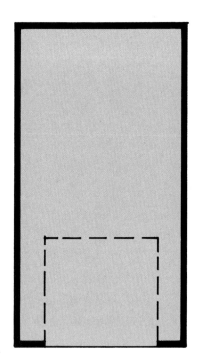

 # HPK1600333

HOME PLAN

Style: Garage
Square Footage: 264
Width: 12' - 0"
Depth: 22' - 0"
Foundation: Slab

eplans.com

A SINGLE-BAY GARAGE IS PERFECT for storing a vehicle. This space is also flexible and can be used as a storage room, garden shed, or workshop.

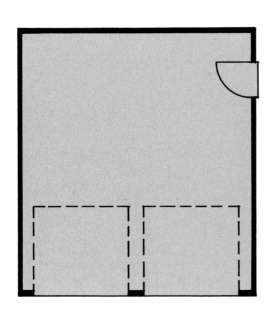

A FRONT-FACING GABLE gives this two-bay garage a traditional look. An additional side door is great for moving and accessing storage or tools. It also provides natural light for a workshop space.

HOME PLAN

HPK1600334

Style: Garage
Square Footage: 440
Width: 20' - 0"
Depth: 22' - 0"
Foundation: Slab

eplans.com

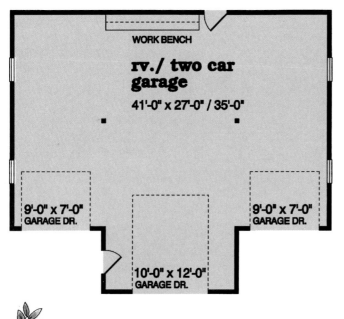

WORK BENCH

rv./ two car garage

41'-0" x 27'-0" / 35'-0"

9'-0" x 7'-0"
GARAGE DR.

9'-0" x 7'-0"
GARAGE DR.

10'-0" x 12'-0"
GARAGE DR.

HOME PLAN

HPK1600335

Style: Garage
Square Footage: 1,320
Width: 42' - 0"
Depth: 36' - 0"
Foundation: Slab

eplans.com

TWO STANDARD-SIZE CAR BAYS flank a wider and taller RV bay. No more parking and covering on the side yard or storing at an expensive facility. This garage has so much space that a workshop area is provided at the back of the plan.

HOME PLAN

#) HPK1600336

Style: Contemporary
First Floor: 995 sq. ft.
Second Floor: 928 sq. ft.
Total: 1,923 sq. ft.
Bedrooms: 2
Bathrooms: 1 ½
Width: 32' - 0"
Depth: 32' - 0"
Foundation: Slab

eplans.com

AN ENDEARING COACH-HOUSE DESIGN gives modern practicality a touch of class. The garage holds room for two cars and provides a powder room. Upstairs, a two-bedroom apartment enjoys comfortable appointments such as an open great room featuring the dining and kitchen areas. A full bath is positioned between the bedrooms.

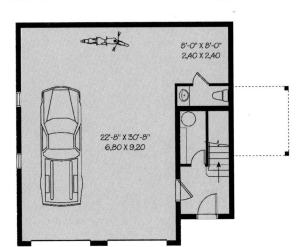

FIRST FLOOR

SECOND FLOOR

HOME PLAN

HPK1600337

Style: Garage

Square Footage: 308

Width: 14' - 0"

Depth: 22' - 0"

Foundation: Slab

eplans.com

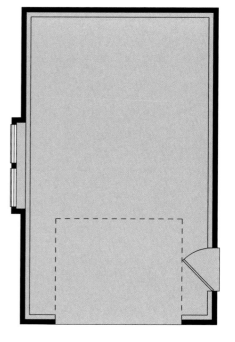

IF YOU'RE LOOKING TO ADD A SINGLE-VEHICLE garage to your property at an affordable cost, this design is for you. A stylish octagonal window above the door adorns the front and accents the gently sloping gable-style roof. A handsome box bay window is on one side, and a door that allows easy access is located on the other side. All four sides have a simple siding exterior. Ample room is available for storing garden tools or other home-maintenance supplies.

HOME PLAN

HPK1600338

Style: Garage

Square Footage: 528

Width: 24' - 0"

Depth: 22' - 0"

Foundation: Slab

eplans.com

THIS SIMPLE TWO-CAR DESIGN offers a practical approach to protecting cars from bad weather. The horizontal clapboard siding of the structure complements the horizontal panels of the twin garage doors. The side-gabled roof shelters 528 square feet of efficient space. Access the garage through the two wide doors, or through a standard entry door along the rear right wall. This plan is also available with a hip roof.

two-car garage

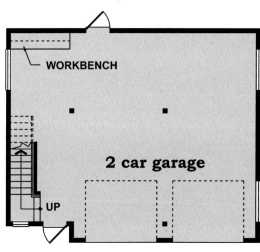

WORKBENCH

2 car garage

UP

FIRST FLOOR

HOME PLAN

HPK1600339

Style: Garage
First Floor: 816 sq. ft.
Second Floor: 618 sq. ft.
Total: 1,434 sq. ft.
Width: 32' - 0"
Depth: 26' - 0"
Foundation: Slab

eplans.com

dn

line of 8' clg

railing

loft/studio

SECOND FLOOR

THIS TRADITIONAL GUEST HOUSE AND GARAGE will complement a variety of homes in just about any neighborhood. The exterior materials can be adjusted to match any architectural style. The spacious two-car garage provides a workbench space for the handyman of the family. Upstairs, the loft/studio is perfect for a secluded guest suite, a teenage hangout, a college-student apartment, or a detached home office. Front and side windows illuminate interior spaces. Add a bathroom to give the apartment a little more independence from the main house.

TWO GABLED DORMERS ADD CHARM to this easy-to-build garage plan. A standard entry door leads to a stairway that ascends to 588 square feet of unfinished storage space. Downstairs, the garage features more than enough room for two cars and ample garden equipment storage.

HOME PLAN

(#) HPK1600340

Style: Traditional

First Floor: 672 sq. ft.

Second Floor: 588 sq. ft.

Total: 1,260 sq. ft.

Depth: 24' - 0"

Foundation: Slab

eplans.com

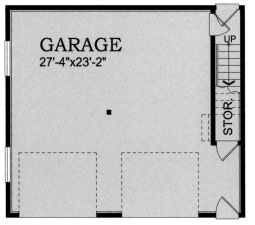

GARAGE
27'-4"x23'-2"

UP

STOR.

FIRST FLOOR

UNFIN. STORAGE

36" HIGH RAIL

LINE OF 8' CLG

dn

SECOND FLOOR

LANDSCAPES & OUTDOOR PROJECTS

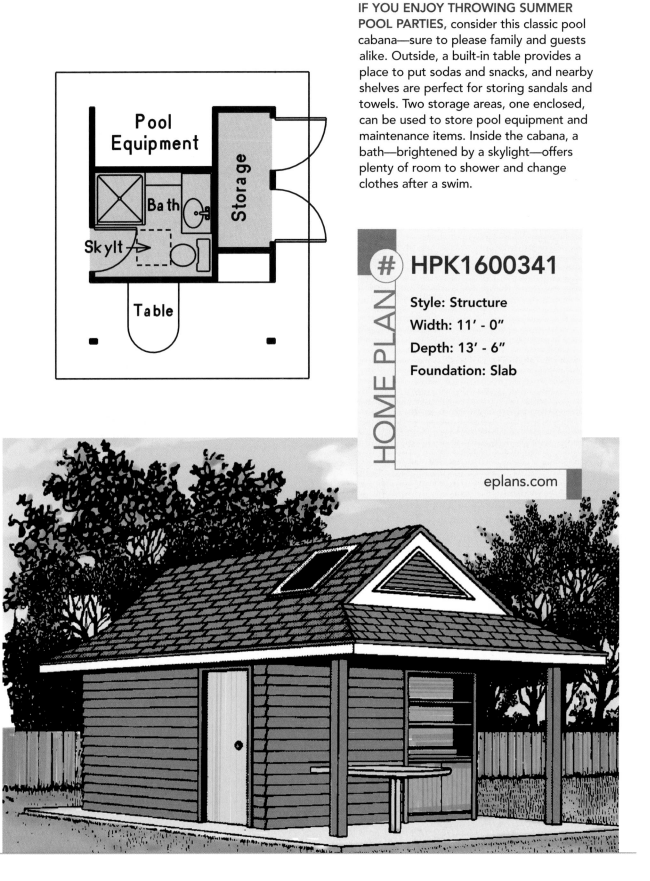

IF YOU ENJOY THROWING SUMMER POOL PARTIES, consider this classic pool cabana—sure to please family and guests alike. Outside, a built-in table provides a place to put sodas and snacks, and nearby shelves are perfect for storing sandals and towels. Two storage areas, one enclosed, can be used to store pool equipment and maintenance items. Inside the cabana, a bath—brightened by a skylight—offers plenty of room to shower and change clothes after a swim.

HPK1600341

Style: Structure
Width: 11' - 0"
Depth: 13' - 6"
Foundation: Slab

HOME PLAN

eplans.com

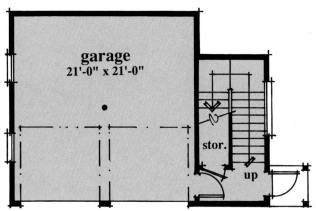

FIRST FLOOR

garage
21'-0" x 21'-0"

stor.

up

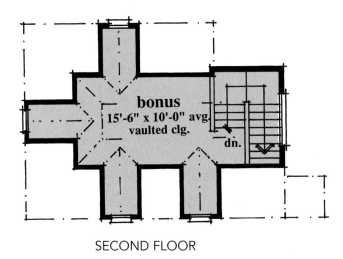

SECOND FLOOR

bonus
15'-6" x 10'-0" avg.
vaulted clg.

dn.

A ROOMY VESTIBULE OFFERS ADDITIONAL STORAGE space with this stylish two-car garage. Flexible space above may be developed into a hobby/craft area, a home office, or even guest quarters. Charming dormer windows allow views and cool breezes to enhance the bonus level.

**HPK1600342**

HOME PLAN

Style: Garage

First Floor: 484 sq. ft.

Second Floor: 264 sq. ft.

Total: 748 sq. ft.

Width: 34' - 6"

Depth: 22' - 0"

Foundation: Slab

eplans.com

(#) HPK1600343

Style: Project

Square Footage: 64

Width: 8' - 0"

Depth: 8' - 0"

Foundation: Slab

eplans.com

THIS VICTORIAN PLAYHOUSE can be the answer to a child's every dream. From the woodcut decorations to the box-bay windows—complete with hidden storage compartments—your children will enjoy hours of playtime in this petite house. Install a child-sized half-door and real windows and paint the exterior in vivid colors and presto! You have a sturdy home that could even be around for your grandchildren. Inside, you can paint the walls with cartoon characters or even paint a faux fireplace on one wall. A vaulted ceiling gives a feeling of space, and the transom windows let sunlight flood in.

**HPK1600344**

HOME PLAN

Style: Structure
Width: 20' - 0"
Depth: 30' - 0"

eplans.com

stor

LADDER TO
STORAGE
LOFT OVER

**WET
BAR**

BOOKS

FLAT CLG

FLAT CLG

**VAULTED
studio/
home office
15'x17'2**

**COVERED
PORCH**

**NEED A QUIET PLACE FOR A HOME OFFICE OR
STUDIO?** You can't go wrong by choosing the plans for
this cleverly designed structure. It is filled with amenities that make a small space seem huge. The vaulted
ceiling of the main part of the building features
clerestory windows to provide ample lighting. Bumped-
out areas on both sides are perfect for desks and work
areas. A built-in bookshelf along one wall is complemented by a large walk-in storage closet. More storage
is available in the loft overhead, reached by a ladder
nearby. A half-bath and wet bar round out the plan.
The entry is graced by a columned porch and double
French doors flanked by fixed windows.

HORIZONTAL SIDING AND A STEEPLY SLOPED ROOF highlight this eye-catching shed, and the rustic look of the siding is echoed by the wood floor inside. Its compact footprint makes it perfect for storing lawn equipment and gardening tools— or, if you choose, take advantage of the plentiful windows and use it as a greenhouse, so you can enjoy year-round gardening.

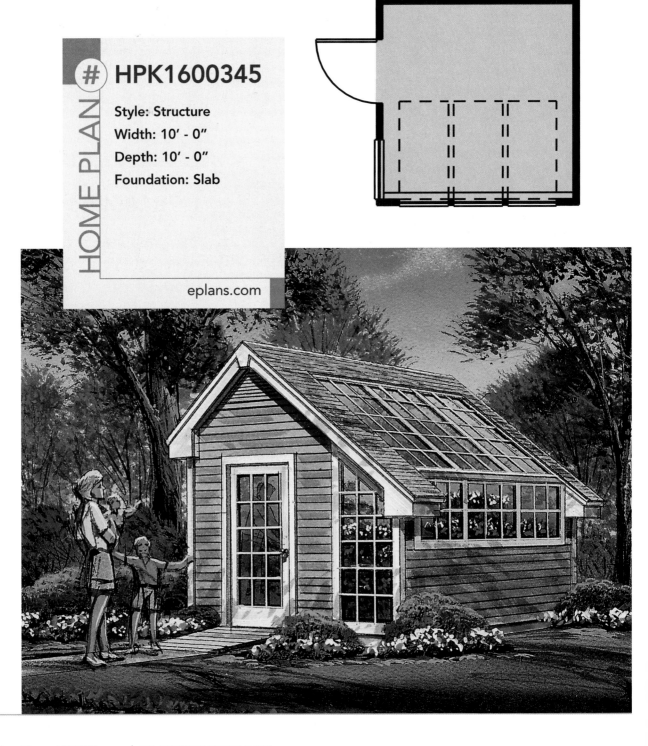

HOME PLAN

HPK1600345

Style: Structure
Width: 10' - 0"
Depth: 10' - 0"
Foundation: Slab

eplans.com

DESIGNED TO BLEND INTO THE GARDEN surroundings, this cozy little building keeps all your garden tools and supplies at your fingertips. You can vary the materials to create the appearance best suited to your site. This 72-square-foot structure is large enough to accommodate a potting bench, shelves, and an area for garden tools.

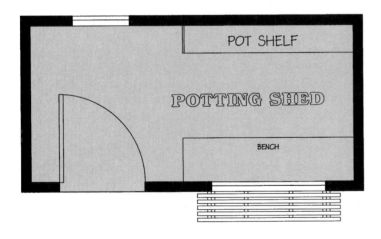

POT SHELF

POTTING SHED

BENCH

**HPK1600346**

Style: Structure

Square Footage: 72

Width: 12' - 0"

Depth: 6' - 0"

eplans.com

HOME PLAN

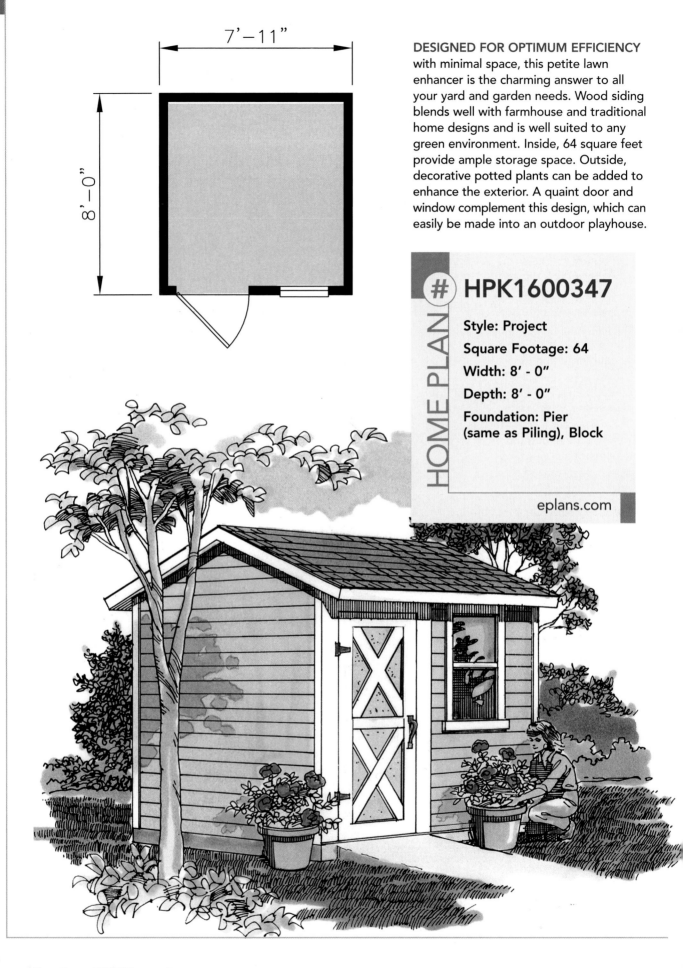

7'–11"

8'–0"

DESIGNED FOR OPTIMUM EFFICIENCY
with minimal space, this petite lawn
enhancer is the charming answer to all
your yard and garden needs. Wood siding
blends well with farmhouse and traditional
home designs and is well suited to any
green environment. Inside, 64 square feet
provide ample storage space. Outside,
decorative potted plants can be added to
enhance the exterior. A quaint door and
window complement this design, which can
easily be made into an outdoor playhouse.

 # HPK1600347

HOME PLAN

Style: Project

Square Footage: 64

Width: 8' - 0"

Depth: 8' - 0"

Foundation: Pier
(same as Piling), Block

eplans.com

STORAGE SPACE ABOUNDS IS THIS SIMPLE, yet efficiently structured lawn shed. With the look of a petite home, this wood-siding structure is a charming addition to any family yard. Tools, garden supplies, outdoor equipment, and even firewood can be accommodated with extra room to spare. The interior is well-lit by a single window and built-ins such as benches, tool cabinets, or shelves can be added to further utilize more space.

(#) HPK1600348

Style: Project

Square Footage: 144

Width: 12' - 0"

Depth: 12' - 0"

Foundation: Slab

HOME PLAN

eplans.com

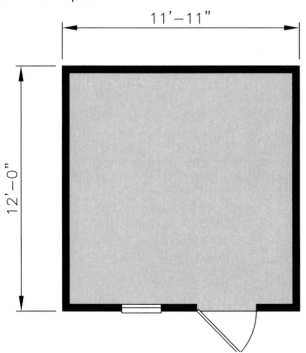

11' – 11"

12' – 0"

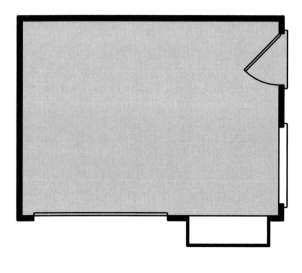

VERTICAL SIDING, A GENTLY SLOPING ROOF, and a charming boxed window make this convenient shed the perfect companion for your country home. The interior is naturally lit by the boxed window and a side window, making the shed a good place to store potted plants when the weather grows cooler. With a height of eight feet, the handy overhead door allows easy storage of bicycles, lawn equipment, or even a small boat.

ALTERNATE EXTERIOR

THOUGH SIMPLE IN DESIGN, THIS SMALLER STUDIO/HOME OFFICE provides all the right stuff for your workspace. A covered entry shelters the double-French door access to a two-room area. The smaller space features a nine-foot flat ceiling and is separated from the main studio area by a columned arch. The main area seems larger than it is thanks to a vaulted ceiling and two bumped-out windows. Define your own work area with furniture, or modify this design to include handy built-ins.

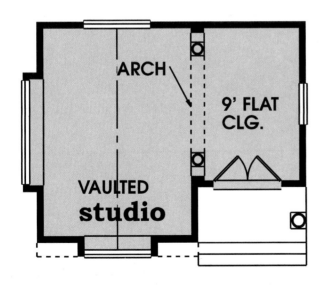

ARCH

9' FLAT CLG.

VAULTED **studio**

HOME PLAN

 # HPK1600350

Style: Structure

Square Footage: 288

Width: 20' - 0"

Depth: 16' - 0"

Foundation: Slab, Crawlspace

eplans.com

HOME PLAN #

HPK1600351

Style: Project

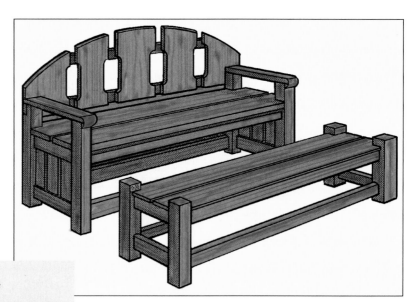

HOME PLAN #

HPK1200322

Style: Project

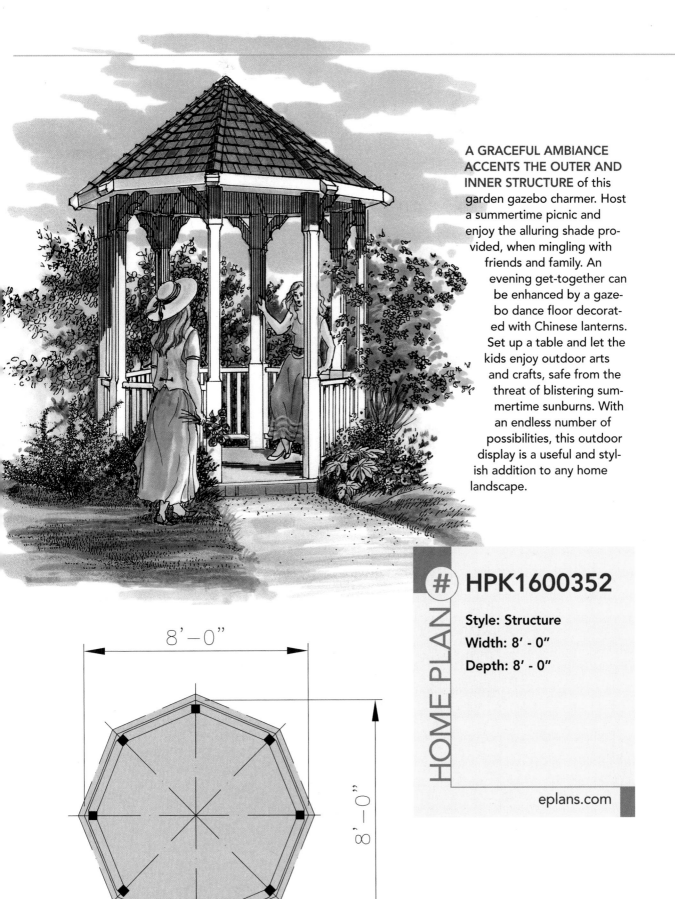

A GRACEFUL AMBIANCE ACCENTS THE OUTER AND INNER STRUCTURE of this garden gazebo charmer. Host a summertime picnic and enjoy the alluring shade provided, when mingling with friends and family. An evening get-together can be enhanced by a gazebo dance floor decorated with Chinese lanterns. Set up a table and let the kids enjoy outdoor arts and crafts, safe from the threat of blistering summertime sunburns. With an endless number of possibilities, this outdoor display is a useful and stylish addition to any home landscape.

8' – 0"

8' – 0"

HOME PLAN

HPK1600352

Style: Structure
Width: 8' - 0"
Depth: 8' - 0"

eplans.com

EYE-CATCHING PLANTINGS TURN THIS CHARMING COTTAGE into a special home, yet the yard doesn't demand much upkeep because the plants were chosen for their small size or slow growth.

Although this home sits on a narrow lot with a small front yard and an optional driveway, the designer hasn't skimped on the landscape. The tiny grounds boast a wealth of plants in a striking range of colors, textures, and shapes. The key to successfully landscaping such a small space is to use compact plants that won't outgrow their welcome. Because of the tight quarters, the designer has also chosen to plant a single deciduous tree instead of forming the more traditional triad.

The design has aspects of symmetry and formality—the flagstone walk dividing the yard in half, perennials repeated on either side of the walk, identical pools of lawn, and matching dwarf conifers flanking the porch steps—but the overall effect is informal. Flagstone pavers lead from the walk around the left side of the

HPK1600353

Season: Spring

Design by: Susan A. Roth

PLAN

eplans.com

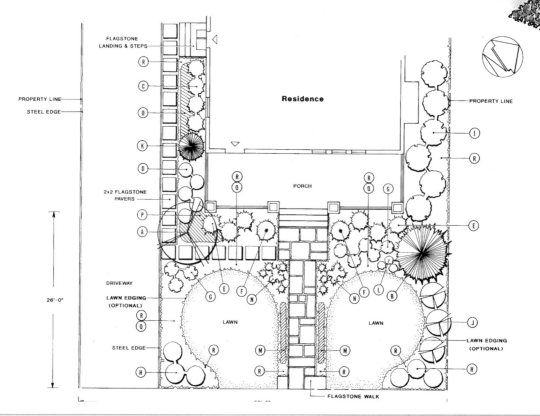

property only, providing access to cars parked in the driveway. The visual weight of this border balances that of the evergreen tree and cluster of shrubs on the opposite side of the property. This petite, but lush, landscape requires little effort to maintain, and even the patches of lawn can be cut quickly with a reel mower. However, if you wanted to reduce maintenance even further, you could eliminate the lawn and extend the groundcover. The design may also be adapted to a lot without a driveway or a garage.

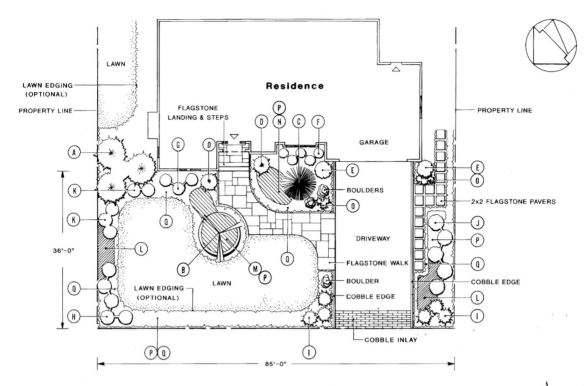

THE LANDSCAPE AROUND THIS RUSTIC STONE-FRONTED HOUSE is truly charming. The designer organizes the space into separate, easily maintained units that blend into a pleasing whole. The planting pockets—in front of the large window and the two areas bisected by pavers to the right of the drive—contain well-behaved plants that require little care to maintain their good looks. The small island of lawn can be quickly mowed, and maintenance is further reduced if lawn edging is installed, eliminating the need to edge by hand. A ribbon of small and moderate-sized shrubs, underplanted with a weed-smothering groundcover and spring bulbs, surrounds the lawn.

A single deciduous tree, set in a circle of bulbs and easy-care perennials that juts into the lawn, screens the entryway from street view and balances a triad of slow-growing, narrow conifers to the far left of the house. Shrubs in front of the windows were chosen for their low, unobtrusive growth habit. A dwarf conifer with pendulous branches forms the focus of the shrub grouping in front of the larger window.

Paving is a strong unifying force in this design. The stone in the house facade is echoed in the walk that curves from the driveway up the steps to the landing and front door. Flagstone pavers border the other side of the drive and lead around the house. The cobblestone inlay at the foot of the drive not only breaks up the monotony of the asphalt, but also visually carries the lawn border across the entire width of the property.

 # HPK1600354

PLAN

Season: Spring
Design by: Salvatore A. Masullo

eplans.com

ALTHOUGH PACKED WITH INTERESTING PLANTS, this landscape is quite manageable for the easy-care gardener. Mowing the little island of lawn is a snap, and caring for the rest of the yard is just as easy, considering the shrubs don't need pruning and fall cleanup is minimal.

AN ABUNDANCE OF TREES AND SHRUBS SUR-
ROUNDS THIS FRENCH Country home, making it look
more like a private, wooded estate in Europe rather than
a suburban lot in New York, Iowa, or California. The flow-
ering deciduous trees lined up along the front of the
property are repeated near the entrance, leading your
eye toward the front door. A single tree
with an elegant weeping form and purple
foliage provides an accent near the extension at the back of the house, and creates
a focal point from the driveway entrance.

Some aspects of formality, while creating
the grand look demanded by the architecture, are modified for ease of care. For
instance, the dense, upright conifers set in
a neat row along the driveway are allowed
to grow naturally instead of being clipped
into a formal hedge, which would require

PLAN
(#) HPK1600355

Season: Spring
**Design by: Susan A.
Roth**

eplans.com

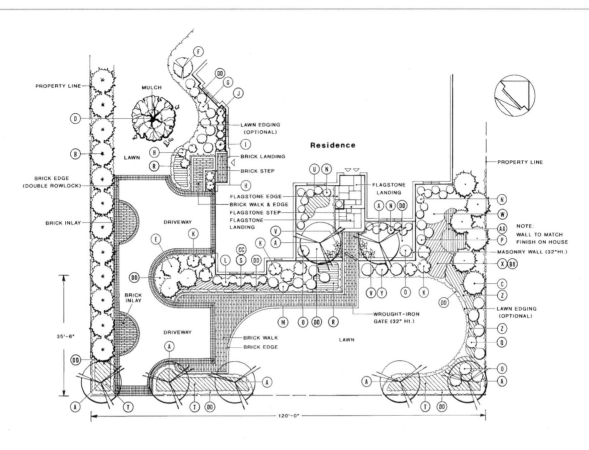

PROPERTY LINE

MULCH

F
DD
G
J

LAWN EDGING
(OPTIONAL)

D

Residence

LAWN

H
R
I

BRICK LANDING

BRICK STEP

B

PROPERTY LINE

BRICK EDGE
(DOUBLE ROWLOCK)

H

FLAGSTONE EDGE
BRICK WALK & EDGE
FLAGSTONE STEP
FLAGSTONE
LANDING

U
N

FLAGSTONE
LANDING

N
W

BRICK INLAY

DRIVEWAY

A
N
DD

NOTE:
WALL TO MATCH
FINISH ON HOUSE

E
K

V
A

AA
P

MASONRY WALL (32"Ht.)

CC
S
DD

K

X
BB

L

T

C
Z

BRICK
INLAY

DD

V
Y

O
K

DD

LAWN EDGING
(OPTIONAL)

35'-6"

DRIVEWAY

V
Y

Z
O

M
O
DD
R

WROUGHT-IRON
GATE (32" Ht.)

O
A

DD

A

BRICK WALK
BRICK EDGE

LAWN

A

O
A

A
T
T
DD
A
T
DD

120'-0"

more labor. On the opposite side of the property, a stag-
gered row of narrow conifers is also spaced for minimum
pruning. The smooth expanse of green grass at the front of
the lot gives the illusion that the house sits farther back
than it really does, yet it is small enough to maintain without professional help.

A house this size needs plenty of parking space for family
and friends. The designer breaks up the large expanse of
driveway with decorative brick inlays and with a planting
peninsula, which shields the garage from direct view. A
parking bay near the front walk provides convenient parking for visitors, who can stroll right up the front walk
toward the secluded entry courtyard after getting out of
their cars.

LOTS OF TREES AND LARGE SHRUBS
endow a suburban lot with the mood of
a French Country estate. To minimize
pruning, the plants are carefully chosen
for their upright shape, compact growth,
and ability to stay within bounds over the years.

LANDSCAPES & OUTDOOR PROJECTS

ABUNDANT FLORAL AND FOLIAGE
interest year-round, river-rock paving, and border plantings bring a wonderful, natural setting to your own backyard.

IF YOU LOOK AT THIS LANDSCAPE DESIGN and ask yourself, "Is that really a swimming pool?" then the designer is to be congratulated because he succeeded in his intention. Yes, it is a swimming pool, but the pool looks more like a natural pond and waterfall—one that you might discover in a clearing in the woods during a hike in the ilderness.

Although the pool is not included in the blueprints for this design, the surrounding landscape lends itself to its placement. Leave the pool out for a pleasing rock garden, play area, or romantic gazebo hideaway.

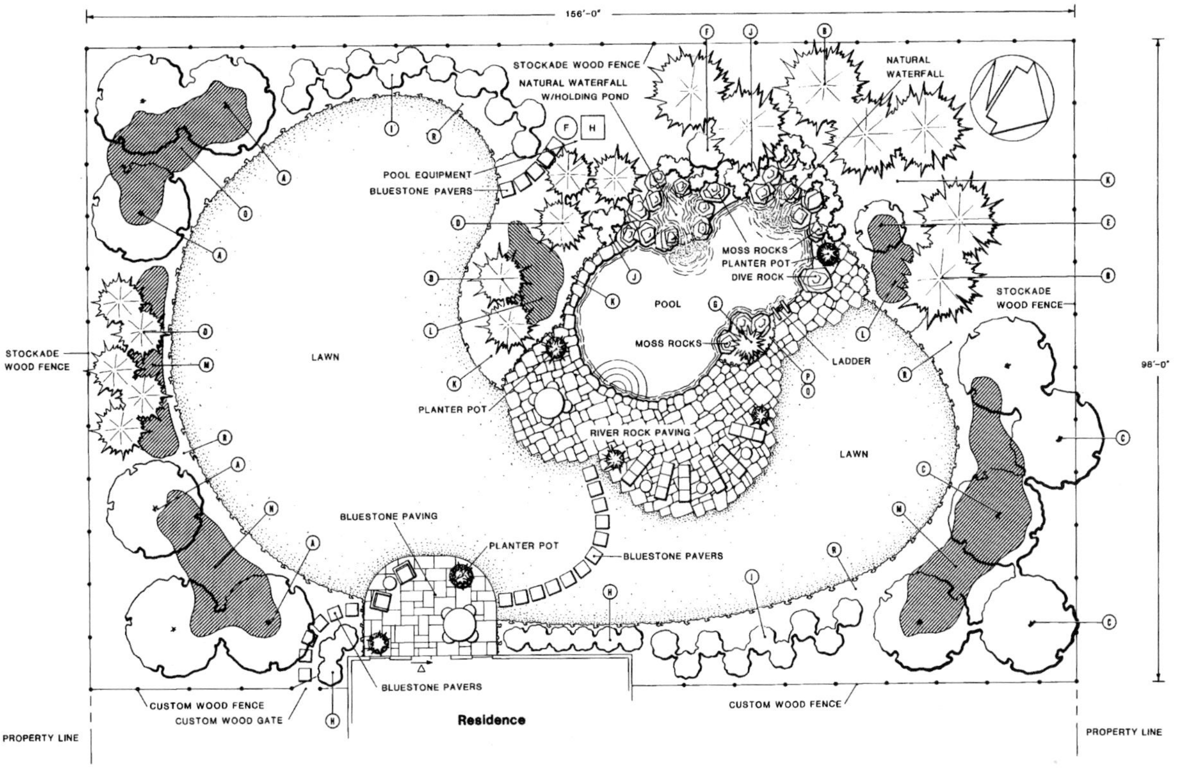

156'-0"
98'-0"
STOCKADE WOOD FENCE
NATURAL WATERFALL W/HOLDING POND
NATURAL WATERFALL
POOL EQUIPMENT
BLUESTONE PAVERS
MOSS ROCKS
PLANTER POT
DIVE ROCK
POOL
MOSS ROCKS
LADDER
STOCKADE WOOD FENCE
STOCKADE WOOD FENCE
LAWN
PLANTER POT
RIVER ROCK PAVING
LAWN
BLUESTONE PAVING
PLANTER POT
BLUESTONE PAVERS
BLUESTONE PAVERS
CUSTOM WOOD FENCE
CUSTOM WOOD GATE
Residence
CUSTOM WOOD FENCE
PROPERTY LINE
PROPERTY LINE

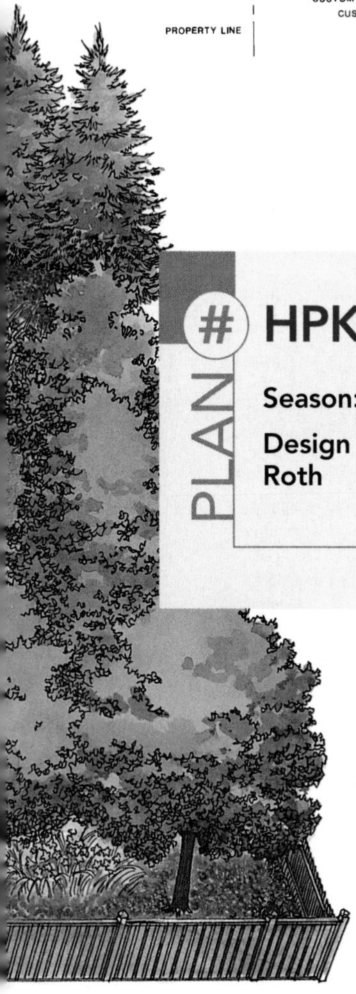

PLAN # HPK1600356

Season: Summer

Design by: Susan A. Roth

eplans.com

The designer achieves an aesthetically pleasing, natural look by employing several techniques. Large boulders form the waterfalls, one of which falls from a holding pond set among the boulders. If you do not choose to build a pool here, the boulders could empty into a pond or calming fountain. River-rock paving—the type of water-worn rocks that line the cool water of a natural spring or a rushing stream—adds a touch of wilderness.

The beautiful grassy areas of the landscape offer a serene setting with abundant floral and foliage interest throughout the year. For security reasons, a wooden stockade fence surrounds the entire backyard, yet the plantings camouflage it well. The irregular kidney shape of the lawn is pleasing to look at and beautifully integrates this naturalistic landscaping into its man-made setting.

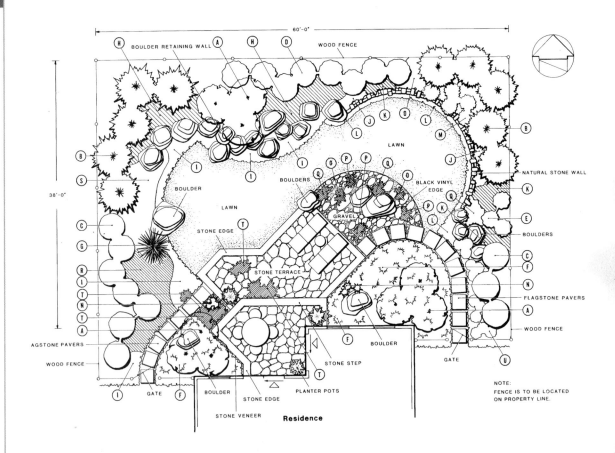

TAKE YOUR CUE FROM MOTHER NATURE: if you love the rocky outcroppings of the mountains or deserts, that may be the way to go in your garden. Boulders—single and sturdy, combined into groupings, or stacked for low walls—bring to a garden a solidity and substance that are impossible to create any other way. And rocky sites create an environment for a variety of special plants.

The designer raises the soil level of the yard slightly to create a curving contour at the back of the yard. The soil is retained by a wall of large boulders on one side and rough-chiseled natural stones forming a simple, low curvilinear dry wall on the other side. Underneath the trees and between the rocks and boulders, various creeping plants spread and spill their way toward the lawn. A combination of drought-tolerant deciduous and evergreen shrubs and trees provides softening foliage and flowers.

FOR MUCH OF ITS VISUAL EXCITEMENT, this dynamic design relies on the contrast between the overlapping curves of the pathway, gravel bed, and low rock wall on the right and the angles of the split-level stone terrace on the left. In arid areas, you may wish to substitute crushed granite or pea gravel for the lawn.

Flagstone pavers allow for circulation from the garden gates to the stone-paved terrace, which features two levels that have only a stair-step difference in height. Several types of creeping, fragrant paving plants mingle between the stones, releasing their scent when walked on. Rock garden plants mix in a chaos of color among the scattered boulders in the gravel-surfaced planting bed near the patio. The permanent structure provided by the plants, large boulders, and paving stones creates a garden of year-round beauty.

 # HPK1600357

PLAN

Season: Summer

Design by: Michael J. Opisso

eplans.com

SITE THIS BEAUTIFUL PERGOLA and its surrounding garden bed at a distance from the house, where it creates a dramatic focal point that draws visitors to come and explore.

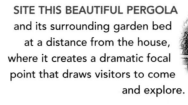

PLAN

HPK1600358

Season: Summer

Design by: Susan A. Roth

eplans.com

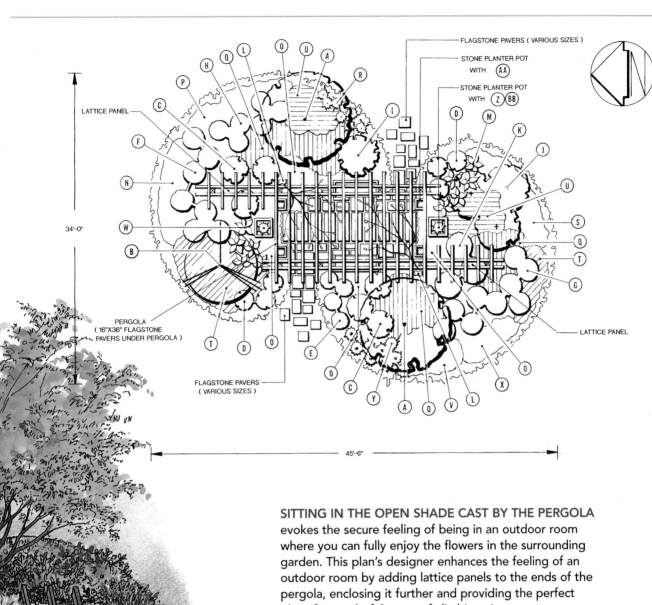

FLAGSTONE PAVERS (VARIOUS SIZES)

STONE PLANTER POT WITH (AA)

STONE PLANTER POT WITH (Z)(BB)

LATTICE PANEL

34'-0"

PERGOLA
(16"X36" FLAGSTONE
PAVERS UNDER PERGOLA)

FLAGSTONE PAVERS
(VARIOUS SIZES)

LATTICE PANEL

45'-6"

SITTING IN THE OPEN SHADE CAST BY THE PERGOLA evokes the secure feeling of being in an outdoor room where you can fully enjoy the flowers in the surrounding garden. This plan's designer enhances the feeling of an outdoor room by adding lattice panels to the ends of the pergola, enclosing it further and providing the perfect place for a colorful cover of climbing vines.

Meant to be situated in an open area of the yard, this pergola planting creates a decorative centerpiece in the lawn—you can site it in either the front- or backyard. To prevent the pergola from looking too massive and dominant, the designer adds several tall trees to the bed, offsetting and balancing its size and shape and anchoring it to the surrounding landscape.

The flagstone patio under the pergola has two entrance paths from the lawn—one on each long side—so that you can walk through the garden. That way, the large island planting becomes a lovely destination rather than an obstacle in the middle of the lawn.

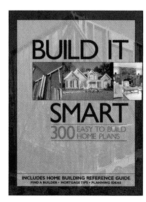
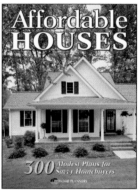

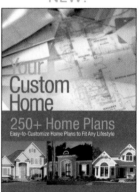

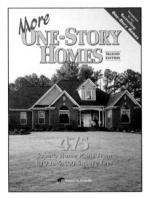

MORE ONE-STORY
HOMES, 2ND ED.
$9.95
ISBN 1-881955-81-8
(448 PAGES)

200 BUDGET-SMART
HOME PLANS
$8.95
ISBN 0-918894-97-2
(224 PAGES)

Finding the right
new home to fit

▶ Your style
▶ Your budget
▶ Your life

...has never been easier.

NEW!

BIG BOOK OF
HOME PLANS
$12.95
1-931131-36-8
(464 PAGES)

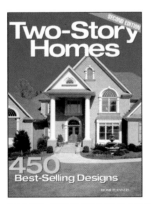

TWO-STORY HOMES,
2ND ED.
$9.95
ISBN 1-931131-15-5
(448 PAGES)

hanley▲wood
SELECTION, CONVENIENCE, SERVICE!

With more than 50 years of experience in the industry and millions of blueprints sold, Hanley Wood is a trusted source of high-quality, high-value pre-drawn home plans.

Using pre-drawn home plans is a **reliable, cost-effective way** to build your dream home, and our vast selection of plans is second-to-none. The nation's finest designers craft these plans that builders know they can trust. Meanwhile, our friendly, knowledgeable customer service representatives can help you every step of the way.

WHAT YOU'LL GET WITH YOUR ORDER

The contents of each designer's blueprint package is unique, but all contain detailed, high-quality working drawings. You can expect to find the following standard elements in most sets of plans:

I. FRONT PERSPECTIVE

This artist's sketch of the exterior of the house gives you an idea of how the house will look when built and landscaped.

2. FOUNDATION AND BASEMENT PLANS

This sheet shows the foundation layout including concrete walls, footings, pads, posts, beams, bearing walls, and foundation notes. If the home features a basement, the first-floor framing details may also be included on this plan. If your plan features slab construction rather than a basement, the plan shows footings and details for a monolithic slab. This page, or another in the set, may include a sample plot plan for locating your house on a building site. Additional sheets focus on foundation cross-sections and other details.

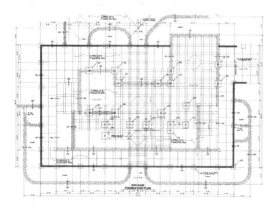

3. DETAILED FLOOR PLANS

These plans show the layout of each floor of the house. Rooms and interior spaces are carefully dimensioned, doors and windows located, and keys are given for cross-section details provided elsewhere in the plans.

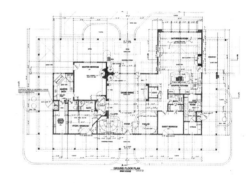

4. HOUSE AND DETAIL CROSS-SECTIONS

Large-scale views show sections or cutaways of the foundation, interior walls, exterior walls, floors, stairways, and roof details. Additional cross-sections may show important changes in floor, ceiling, or roof heights, or the relationship of one level to another. These sections show exactly how the various parts of the house fit together and are extremely valuable during construction. Additional sheets may include enlarged wall, floor, and roof construction details.

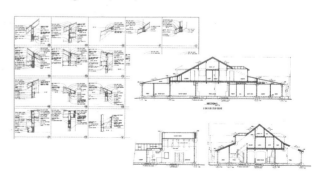

5. ROOF AND FLOOR STRUCTURAL SUPPORTS

The roof and floor framing plans provide detail for these crucial elements of your home. Each includes floor joist, ceiling joist, rafter and roof joist size, spacing, direction, span, and specifications. Beam and window headers, along with necessary details for framing connections, stairways, skylights, or dormers are also included.

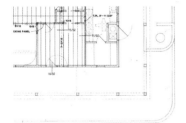

6. ELECTRICAL PLAN

The electrical plan offers a detailed outline of all wiring for your home, with notes for all lighting, outlets, switches, and circuits. A layout is provided for each level, as well as basements, garages, or other structures.

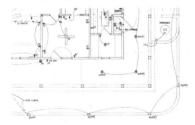

7. EXTERIOR ELEVATIONS

In addition to the front exterior, your blueprint set will include drawings of the rear and sides of your house as well. These drawings give notes on exterior materials and finishes. Particular attention is given to cornice detail, brick and stone accents, or other finish items that make your home unique.

BEFORE YOU CALL

You are making a terrific decision to use a pre-drawn house plan it is one you can make with confidence, knowing that your blueprints are crafted by national-award-winning certified residential designers and architects, and trusted by builders.

Once you ve selected the plan you want or even if you have questions along the way our experienced customer service representatives are available 24 hours a day, seven days a week to help you navigate the home-building process. To help them provide you with even better service, please consider the following questions before you call:

■ Have you chosen or purchased your lot?
If so, please review the building setback requirements of your local building authority before you call. You don t need to have a lot before ordering plans, but if you own land already, please have the width and depth dimensions handy when you call.

■ Have you chosen a builder?
Involving your builder in the plan selection and evaluation process may be beneficial. Luckily, builders know they can have confidence with pre-drawn plans because they ve been designed for livability, functionality, and typically are builder-proven at successful home sites across the country.

■ Do you need a construction loan?
Construction loans are unique because they involve determining the value of something that is not yet constructed. Several lenders offer convenient contstruction-to-permanent loans. It is important to choose a good lending partner one who will help guide you through the application and appraisal process. Most will even help you evaluate your contractor to ensure reliability and credit worthiness. Our partnership with IndyMac Bank, a nationwide leader in construction loans, can help you save on your loan, if needed.

■ How many sets of plans do you need?
Building a home can typically require a number of sets of blueprints one for yourself, two or three for the builder and subcontractors, two for the local building department, and one or more for your lender. For this reason, we offer 5- and 8-set plan packages, but your best value is the Reproducible Plan Package. Reproducible plans are accompanied by a license to make modifications and typically up to 12 duplicates of the plan so you have enough copies of the plan for everyone involved in the financing and construction of your home.

■ Do you want to make any changes to the plan?
We understand that it is difficult to find blueprints for a home that will meet all of your needs. That is why Hanley Wood is glad to offer plan Customization Services. We will work with you to design the modifications you d like to see and to adjust your blueprint plans accordingly a nything from changing the foundation; adding square footage, redesigning baths, kitchens, or bedrooms; or most other modifications. This simple, cost-effective service saves you from hiring an outside architect to make alterations. Modifications may only be made to Reproducible Plan Packages that include the license to modify.

■ Do you have to make any changes to meet local building codes?
While all of our plans are drawn to meet national building codes at the time they were created, many areas required that plans be stamped by a local engineer to certify that they meet local building codes. Building codes are updated frequently and can vary by state, county, city, or municipality. Contact your local building inspection department, office of planning and zoning, or department of permits to determine how your local codes will affect your construction project. The best way to assure that you can make changes to your plan, if necessary, is to purchase a Reproducible Plan Package.

■ Has everyone—from family members to contractors—been involved in selecting the plan?
Building a new home is an exciting process, and using pre-drawn plans is a great way to realize your dreams. Make sure that everyone involved has had an opportunity to review the plan you ve selected. While Hanley Wood is the only plans provider with an exchange policy, it s best to be sure all parties agree on your selection before you buy.

CALL TOLL-FREE 1-800-521-6797

Source Key
HPK16

CUSTOMIZE YOUR PLAN – HANLEY WOOD CUSTOMIZATION SERVICES

Creating custom home plans has never been easier and more directly accessible. Using state-of-the-art technology and top-performing architectural expertise, Hanley Wood delivers on a long-standing customer commitment to provide world-class home-plans and customization services. Our valued customers—professional home builders and individual home owners—appreciate the convenience and accessibility of this interactive, consultative service.

With the Hanley Wood Customization Service you can:

■ Save valuable time by avoiding drawn-out and frequently repetitive face-to-face design meetings

■ Communicate design and home-plan changes faster and more efficiently
■ Speed-up project turn-around time
■ Build on a budget without sacrificing quality
■ Transform master home plans to suit your design needs and unique personal style

All of our design options and prices are impressively affordable. A detailed quote is available for a $50 consultation fee. Plan modification is an interactive service. Our skilled team of designers will guide you through the customization process from start to finish making recommendations, offering ideas, and determining the feasibility of your changes. This level of service is offered to ensure the final modified plan meets your expectations. If you use our service the $50 fee will be applied to the cost of the modifications.

You may purchase the customization consultation before or after purchasing a plan. In either case, it is necessary to purchase the Reproducible Plan Package and complete the accompanying license to modify the plan before we can begin customization.

Customization Consultation $50

TOOLS TO WORK WITH YOUR BUILDER

Two Reverse Options For Your Convenience – Mirror and Right-Reading Reverse (as available)

Mirror reverse plans simply flip the design 180 degrees keep in mind, the text will also be flipped. For a minimal fee you can have one or all of your plans shipped mirror reverse, although we recommend having at least one regular set handy. Right-reading reverse plans show the design flipped 180 degrees but the text reads normally. When you choose this option, we ship each set of purchased blueprints in this format.

Mirror Reverse Fee (indicate the number of sets when ordering). . . . **$55**
Right Reading Reverse Fee (all sets are reversed). **$175**

A Shopping List Exclusively for Your Home – Materials List

A customized Materials List helps you plan and estimate the cost of your new home, outlining the quantity, type, and size of materials needed to build your house (with the exception of mechanical system items). Included are framing lumber, windows and doors, kitchen and bath cabinetry, rough and finished hardware, and much more.

Materials List. . . . . **$75 each**
Additional Materials Lists (at original time of purchase only). . **$20 each**

Plan Your Home-Building Process – Specification Outline

Work with your builder on this step-by-step chronicle of 166 stages or items crucial to the building process. It provides a comprehensive review of the construction process and helps you choose materials.
Specification Outline. . . . . **$10 each**

Get Accurate Cost Estimates for Your Home – Quote One® Cost Reports

The Summary Cost Report, the first element in the Quote One® package, breaks down the cost of your home into various categories based on building materials, labor, and installation, and includes three grades of construction: Budget, Standard, and Custom. Make even more informed decisions about your project with the second element of our package, the Material Cost Report. The material and installation cost is shown for each of more than 1,000 line items provided in the standard-grade Materials List, which is included with this tool. Additional space is included for estimates from contractors and subcontractors, such as for mechanical materials, which are not included in our packages.

Quote One® Summary Cost Report. **$35**
Quote One® Detailed Material Cost Report. **$140***
***Detailed material cost report includes the Materials List**

Learn the Basics of Building – Electrical, Plumbing, Mechanical, Construction Detail Sheets

If you want to know more about building techniques and deal more confidently with your subcontractors we offer four useful detail sheets. These sheets provide non-plan-specific general information, but are excellent tools that will add to your understanding of Plumbing Details, Electrical Details, Construction Details, and Mechanical Details.

Electrical Detail Sheet. **$14.95**
Plumbing Detail Sheet. **$14.95**
Mechanical Detail Sheet. **$14.95**
Construction Detail Sheet. **$14.95**
SUPER VALUE SETS:
Buy any 2: $26.95; Buy any 3: $34.95; Buy All 4: $39.95

Best Value

MAKE YOUR HOME TECH-READY – HOME AUTOMATION UPGRADE

Building a new home provides a unique opportunity to wire it with a plan for future needs. A Home Automation-Ready (HA-Ready) home contains the wiring substructure of tomorrow's connected home. It means that every room—from the front porch to the backyard, and from the attic to the basement—is wired for security, lighting, telecommunications, climate control, home computer networking, whole-house audio, home theater, shade control, video surveillance, entry access control, and yes, video gaming electronic solutions.

Along with the conveniences HA-Ready homes provide, they also have a higher resale value. The Consumer Electronics Association (CEA), in conjunction with the Custom Electronic Design and Installation Association (CEDIA), have developed a TechHome™ Rating system that quantifies the value of HA-Ready homes. The rating system is gaining widespread recognition in the real estate industry.

Developed by CEDIA-certified installers, our Home Automation Upgrade package includes everything you need to work with an installer during the construction of your home. It provides a short explanation of the various subsystems, a wiring floor plan for each level of your home, a detailed materials list with estimated costs, and a list of CEDIA-certified installers in your local area.

Home Automation Upgrade $250

GET YOUR HOME PLANS PAID FOR!

IndyMac Bank, in partnership with Hanley Wood, will reimburse you up to $600 toward the cost of your home plans simply by financing the construction of your new home with IndyMac Bank Home Construction Lending.

IndyMac's construction and permanent loan is a one-time close loan, meaning that one application—and one set of closing fees—provides all the financing you need.

Apply today at www.indymacbank.com, call toll free at 1-866-237-3478, or ask a Hanley Wood customer service representative for details.

DESIGN YOUR HOME – INTERIOR AND EXTERIOR FINISHING TOUCHES

Be Your Own Interior Designer! – Home Furniture Planner

Effectively plan the space in your home using our Hands-On Home Furniture Planner. It s fun and easy no more moving heavy pieces of furniture to see how the room will go together. The kit includes reusable peel-and-stick furniture templates that fit on a 12"x18" laminated layout board enough space to lay out every room in your house.

Home Furniture Planning Kit **$15.95**

Enjoy the Outdoors! – Deck Plans

Many of our homes have a corresponding deck plan, sold separately, which includes a Deck Plan Frontal Sheet, Deck Framing and Floor Plans, Deck Elevations, and a Deck Materials List. A Standard Deck Details Package, also available, provides all the how-to information necessary for building any deck. Get both the Deck Plan and the Standard Deck Details Package for one low price in our Complete Deck Building Package. See the price tier chart below and call for deck plan availability.

Deck Details (only) **$14.95**
Deck Building Package . . . . **Plan price + $14.95**

Create a Professionally Designed Landscape – Landscape Plans

Many of our homes have a front-yard Landscape Plan that is complementary in design to the house plan. These comprehensive Landscape Blueprint Packages include a Frontal Sheet, Plan View, Regionalized Plant & Materials List, a sheet on Planting and Maintaining Your Landscape, Zone Maps, and a Plant Size and Description Guide. Each set of blueprints is a full 18" x 24" with clear, complete instructions in easy-to-read type. Our Landscape Plans are available with a Plant & Materials List adapted by horticultural experts to eight regions of the country. Please specify your region when ordering your plan see region map below. Call for more information about landscape plan availability and applicable regions.

LANDSCAPE & DECK PRICE SCHEDULE

PRICE TIERS	1-SET STUDY PACKAGE	5-SET BUILDING PACKAGE	8-SET BUILDING PACKAGE	1-SET REPRODUCIBLE*
P1	$25	$55	$95	$145
P2	$45	$75	$115	$165
P3	$75	$105	$145	$195
P4	$105	$135	$175	$225
P5	$145	$175	$215	$275
P6	$185	$215	$255	$315

PRICES SUBJECT TO CHANGE   * REQUIRES A FAX NUMBER

TERMS & CONDITIONS

OUR 90-DAY EXCHANGE POLICY

BUY WITH CONFIDENCE!

Hanley Wood is committed to ensuring your satisfaction with your blueprint order, which is why a we offer a 90-day exchange policy. With the exception of Reproducible Plan Package orders, we will exchange your entire first order for an equal or greater number of blueprints from our plan collection within 90 days of the original order. The entire content of your original order must be returned before an exchange will be processed. Please call our customer service department at 1-888-690-1116 for your return authorization number and shipping instructions. If the returned blueprints look used, redlined, or copied, we will not honor your exchange. Fees for exchanging your blueprints are as follows: 20% of the amount of the original order, plus the difference in cost if exchanging for a design in a higher price bracket or less the difference in cost if exchanging for a design in a lower price bracket. (Because they can be copied, Reproducible blueprints are not exchangeable or refundable.) Please call for current postage and handling prices. Shipping and handling charges are not refundable.

ARCHITECTURAL AND ENGINEERING SEALS

Some cities and states now require that a licensed architect or engineer review and "seal" a blueprint, or officially approve it, prior to construction. Prior to application for a building permit or the start of actual construction, we strongly advise that you consult your local building official who can tell you if such a review is required.

LOCAL BUILDING CODES AND ZONING REQUIREMENTS

Each plan was designed to meet or exceed the requirements of a nationally recognized model building code in effect at the time and place the plan was drawn. Typically plans designed after the year 2000 conform to the International Residential Building Code (IRC 2000 or 2003). The IRC is comprised of portions of the three major codes below. Plans drawn before 2000 conform to one of the three recognized building codes in effect at the time: Building Officials and Code Administrators (BOCA) International, Inc.;

the Southern Building Code Congress International, (SBCCI) Inc.; the International Conference of Building Officials (ICBO); or the Council of American Building Officials (CABO).

Because of the great differences in geography and climate throughout the United States and Canada, each state, county, and municipality has its own building codes, zone requirements, ordinances, and building regulations. Your plan may need to be modified to comply with local requirements. In addition, you may need to obtain permits or inspections from local governments before and in the course of construction. We authorize the use of the blueprints on the express condition that you consult a local licensed architect or engineer of your choice prior to beginning construction and strictly comply with all local building codes, zoning requirements, and other applicable laws, regulations, ordinances, and requirements. Notice: Plans for homes to be built in Nevada must be redrawn by a Nevada-registered professional. Consult your local building official for more information on this subject.

TERMS AND CONDITIONS

These designs are protected under the terms of United States Copyright Law and may not be copied or reproduced in any way, by

any means, unless you have purchased a Reproducible Plan Package and signed the accompanying license to modify and copy the plan, which clearly indicates your right to modify, copy, or reproduce. We authorize the use of your chosen design as an aid in the construction of ONE (1) single- or multifamily home only. You may not use this design to build a second dwelling or multiple dwellings without purchasing another blueprint or blueprints or paying additional design fees. Multi-use fees vary by designer—please call one of experienced sales representatives for a quote.

DISCLAIMER

The designers we work with have put substantial care and effort into the creation of their blueprints. However, because we cannot provide on-site consultation, supervision, and control over actual construction, and because of the great variance in local building requirements, building practices, and soil, seismic, weather, and other conditions, WE MAKE NO WARRANTY OF ANY KIND, EXPRESS OR IMPLIED, WITH RESPECT TO THE CONTENT OR USE OF THE BLUEPRINTS, INCLUDING BUT NOT LIMITED TO ANY WARRANTY OF MERCHANTABILITY OR OF FITNESS FOR A PARTICULAR PURPOSE. ITEMS, PRICES, TERMS, AND CONDITIONS ARE SUBJECT TO CHANGE WITHOUT NOTICE.

BEFORE YOU ORDER

IMPORTANT COPYRIGHT NOTICE

From the Council of Publishing Home Designers

Blueprints for residential construction (or working drawings, as they are often called in the industry) are copyrighted intellectual property, protected under the terms of the United States Copyright Law and, therefore, cannot be copied legally for use in building. The following are some guidelines to help you get what you need to build your home, without violating copyright law:

1. HOME PLANS ARE COPY-RIGHTED

Just like books, movies, and songs, home plans receive protection under the federal copyright laws. The copyright laws prevent anyone, other than the copyright owner, from reproducing, modifying, or reusing the plans or design without permission of the copyright owner.

2. DO NOT COPY DESIGNS OR FLOOR PLANS FROM ANY PUBLICATION, ELECTRONIC MEDIA, OR EXISTING HOME

It is illegal to copy, change, or redraw home designs found in a plan book, CDROM or on the Internet. The right to modify plans is one of the exclusive rights of copyright. It is also illegal to copy or redraw a constructed home that is protected by copyright, even if you have never seen the plans for the home. If you find a plan or home that you like, you must purchase a set of plans from an authorized source. The plans may not be lent, given away, or sold by the purchaser.

3. DO NOT USE PLANS TO BUILD MORE THAN ONE HOUSE

The original purchaser of house plans is typically licensed to build a single home from the plans. Building more than one home from the plans without permission is an infringement of the home designer's copyright. The purchase of a multiple-set package of plans is for the construction of a single home only. The purchase of additional sets of plans does not grant the right to construct more than one home.

4. HOUSE PLANS IN THE FORM OF BLUEPRINTS OR BLACKLINES CANNOT BE COPIED OR REPRODUCED

Plans, blueprints, or blacklines, unless they are reproducibles, cannot be copied or reproduced without prior written consent of the copyright owner. Copy shops and blueprinters are prohibited from making copies of these plans without the copyright release letter you receive with reproducible plans.

5. HOUSE PLANS IN THE FORM OF BLUEPRINTS OR BLACKLINES CANNOT BE REDRAWN

Plans cannot be modified or redrawn without first obtaining the copyright owner's permission. With your purchase of plans, you are licensed to make non-structural changes by red-lining the purchased plans. If you need to make structural changes or need to redraw the plans for any reason, you must purchase a reproducible set of plans (see topic 6) which includes a license to modify the plans. Blueprints do not come with a license to make structural changes or to redraw the plans. You may not reuse or sell the modified design.

6. REPRODUCIBILE HOME PLANS

Reproducible plans (for example sepias, mylars, CAD files, electronic files, and vellums) come with a license to make modifications to the plans. Once modified, the plans can be taken to a local copy shop or blueprinter to make up to 10 or 12 copies of the plans to use in the construction of a single home. Only one home can be constructed from any single purchased set of reproducible plans either in original form or as modified. The license to modify and copy must be completed and returned before the plan will be shipped.

7. MODIFIED DESIGNS CANNOT BE REUSED

Even if you are licensed to make modifications to a copyrighted design, the modified design is not free from the original designer's copyright. The sale or reuse of the modified design is prohibited. Also, be aware that any modification to plans relieves the original designer from liability for design defects and voids all warranties expressed or implied.

8. WHO IS RESPONSIBLE FOR COPYRIGHT INFRINGEMENT?

Any party who participates in a copyright violation may be responsible including the purchaser, designers, architects, engineers, drafters, homeowners, builders, contractors, sub-contractors, copy shops, blueprinters, developers, and real estate agencies. It does not matter whether or not the individual knows that a violation is being committed. Ignorance of the law is not a valid defense.

9. PLEASE RESPECT HOME DESIGN COPYRIGHTS

In the event of any suspected violation of a copyright, or if there is any uncertainty about the plans purchased, the publisher, architect, designer, or the Council of Publishing Home Designers (www.cphd.org) should be contacted before proceeding. Awards are sometimes offered for information about home design copyright infringement.

10. PENALTIES FOR INFRINGEMENT

Penalties for violating a copyright may be severe. The responsible parties are required to pay actual damages caused by the infringement (which may be substantial), plus any profits made by the infringer commissions to include all profits from the sale of any home built from an infringing design. The copyright law also allows for the recovery of statutory damages, which may be as high as $150,000 for each infringement. Finally, the infringer may be required to pay legal fees which often exceed the damages.

BLUEPRINT PRICE SCHEDULE

PRICE TIERS	1-SET STUDY PACKAGE	5-SET BUILDING PACKAGE	8-SET BUILDING PACKAGE	1-SET REPRODUCIBLE*
A1	$450	$500	$555	$675
A2	$490	$545	$595	$735
A3	$540	$605	$665	$820
A4	$590	$660	$725	$895
C1	$640	$715	$775	$950
C2	$690	$760	$820	$1025
C3	$735	$810	$875	$1100
C4	$785	$860	$925	$1175
L1	$895	$990	$1075	$1335
L2	$970	$1065	$1150	$1455
L3	$1075	$1175	$1270	$1600
L4	$1185	$1295	$1385	$1775
SQ1				.40/SQ. FT.
SQ3				.55/SQ. FT.
SQ5				.80/SQ. FT.

PRICES SUBJECT TO CHANGE

* REQUIRES A FAX NUMBER

PLAN #	PRICE TIER	PAGE	MATERIALS LIST	QUOTE ONE®	DECK	DECK PRICE	LANDSCAPE	LANDSCAPE PRICE	REGIONS
HPK1600001	SQ1	313							
HPK1600004	C4	266							
HPK1600007	A2	16							
HPK1600008	A4	17							
HPK1600009	A2	18	Y						
HPK1600010	A2	19	Y						
HPK1600011	A2	20							
HPK1600012	A3	21	Y	Y			OLA091	P3	12345678
HPK1600013	A4	22							
HPK1600014	A4	23	Y						
HPK1600015	A4	24	Y						
HPK1600016	A2	25	Y						
HPK1600017	A4	26	Y						
HPK1600018	A4	27	Y						
HPK1600019	A3	28	Y	Y	ODA025	P3	OLA085	P3	12345678
HPK1600020	A2	29	Y						
HPK1600021	A3	30	Y	Y			OLA001	P3	123568
HPK1600022	A4	31	Y						
HPK1600023	A4	32							
HPK1600024	A4	33	Y						
HPK1600025	A2	34	Y						
HPK1600026	A2	35							
HPK1600027	A2	36	Y						
HPK1600028	A4	37	Y						
HPK1600029	A3	38	Y						
HPK1600030	A1	39	Y						
HPK1600031	A2	40	Y						
HPK1600032	A1	41	Y						
HPK1600033	A1	42	Y						
HPK1600034	A2	43	Y						
HPK1600035	A3	44	Y						
HPK1600036	A3	45	Y						
HPK1600037	A2	46							
HPK1600038	A3	47	Y						
HPK1600039	A2	48							
HPK1600040	A2	49	Y						
HPK1600041	A4	50							
HPK1600042	A2	51	Y						

PLAN #	PRICE TIER	PAGE	MATERIALS LIST	QUOTE ONE®	DECK	DECK PRICE	LANDSCAPE	LANDSCAPE PRICE	REGIONS
HPK1600043	A4	52							
HPK1600044	A2	53	Y						
HPK1600045	A4	54							
HPK1600046	A4	55							
HPK1600047	A2	56	Y						
HPK1600048	A4	57	Y						
HPK1600049	A4	58							
HPK1600050	A2	59	Y						
HPK1600051	A1	60	Y						
HPK1600052	A2	61	Y						
HPK1600053	A2	62	Y						
HPK1600054	A2	63	Y						
HPK1600055	A4	64	Y				OLA012	P3	12345678
HPK1600056	A4	65							
HPK1600057	A2	66							
HPK1600058	A2	67	Y						
HPK1600059	A2	68	Y						
HPK1600060	A4	69	Y						
HPK1600061	A3	70							
HPK1600062	A3	71							
HPK1600063	A4	72							
HPK1600064	A3	73	Y						
HPK1600065	A2	74	Y						
HPK1600066	A2	75	Y	Y	ODA014	P2	OLA027	P3	12345678
HPK1600067	A2	76	Y						
HPK1600068	A2	77	Y						
HPK1600069	A2	78	Y						
HPK1600070	A4	79	Y						
HPK1600071	A2	80							
HPK1600072	A3	81	Y	Y	ODA014	P2	OLA003	P3	123568
HPK1600073	A2	82	Y						
HPK1600074	A3	83	Y						
HPK1600075	A1	84	Y						
HPK1600076	A4	85	Y						
HPK1600077	A2	86	Y						
HPK1600078	A2	87	Y						
HPK1600079	A2	87	Y						
HPK1600080	C1	90	Y						

PLAN #	PRICE TIER	PAGE	MATERIALS LIST	QUOTE ONE®	DECK	DECK PRICE	LANDSCAPE	LANDSCAPE PRICE	REGIONS
HPK1600081	C1	90	Y						
HPK1600082	C1	91							
HPK1600083	A3	92	Y	Y					
HPK1600084	A4	93	Y	Y					
HPK1600085	A3	94							
HPK1600086	A3	95							
HPK1600087	C1	96							
HPK1600088	C1	97							
HPK1600089	A3	98							
HPK1600090	A3	99							
HPK1600091	C1	100							
HPK1600092	C1	101							
HPK1600093	C1	102							
HPK1600094	A3	103							
HPK1600095	C1	104							
HPK1600096	C1	105	Y	Y					
HPK1600097	C1	106							
HPK1600098	C1	107	Y	Y					
HPK1600099	A3	108	Y						
HPK1600100	A3	109	Y						
HPK1600101	A3	110							
HPK1600102	A3	111	Y						
HPK1600103	A3	112	Y						
HPK1600104	A3	113							
HPK1600105	A3	114							
HPK1600106	A3	115	Y						
HPK1600107	A3	116							
HPK1600108	C1	117	Y	Y					
HPK1600109	C1	118							
HPK1600110	C1	119							
HPK1600111	C1	120							
HPK1600112	C1	121	Y						
HPK1600113	A3	122	Y						
HPK1600114	A4	123	Y	Y					
HPK1600115	A3	124	Y						
HPK1600116	C1	125							
HPK1600117	A3	126	Y						
HPK1600118	A3	127	Y						
HPK1600119	C1	128	Y						
HPK1600120	C1	129	Y						
HPK1600121	C1	130	Y						
HPK1600122	C1	131	Y						
HPK1600123	C1	132	Y						
HPK1600124	C1	133	Y						
HPK1600125	C1	134	Y						
HPK1600126	A3	135							
HPK1600127	A3	136	Y						
HPK1600128	A4	137	Y		ODA013	P2	OLA001	P3	123568
HPK1600129	A3	138	Y						
HPK1600130	C1	139	Y						
HPK1600131	A3	140	Y						
HPK1600132	A3	141	Y						
HPK1600133	A4	142	Y						
HPK1600134	A3	143	Y						
HPK1600135	A3	144	Y						
HPK1600136	A3	145	Y						
HPK1600137	C1	146	Y						
HPK1600138	A3	147							
HPK1600139	C1	148	Y						
HPK1600140	C1	149	Y						
HPK1600141	C1	150	Y						
HPK1600142	C1	151							
HPK1600143	C1	152	Y						
HPK1600144	C1	153							
HPK1600145	C1	154	Y						
HPK1600146	C1	155	Y						
HPK1600147	A3	156	Y						
HPK1600148	A3	157	Y						
HPK1600149	A3	158							
HPK1600150	A3	159	Y						

PLAN #	PRICE TIER	PAGE	MATERIALS LIST	QUOTE ONE®	DECK	DECK PRICE	LANDSCAPE	LANDSCAPE PRICE	REGIONS
HPK1600151	C1	160	Y						
HPK1600152	C1	161	Y						
HPK1600153	C1	162	Y						
HPK1600154	C1	163							
HPK1600155	C1	164	Y						
HPK1600156	C1	165							
HPK1600157	C1	166	Y						
HPK1600158	C1	167							
HPK1600159	C1	168	Y	Y					
HPK1600160	A4	169	Y	Y			OLA088	P4	12345678
HPK1600161	C1	170	Y						
HPK1600162	C1	171	Y						
HPK1600163	C1	171	Y						
HPK1600164	C2	174	Y						
HPK1600165	C2	174							
HPK1600166	A4	175							
HPK1600167	A4	176	Y						
HPK1600168	A4	177							
HPK1600169	C1	178							
HPK1600170	C2	179							
HPK1600171	C1	180							
HPK1600172	A4	181							
HPK1600173	C2	182							
HPK1600174	A4	183							
HPK1600175	A4	184	Y						
HPK1600176	A4	185							
HPK1600177	C2	186	Y						
HPK1600178	C2	187	Y						
HPK1600179	A4	188	Y						
HPK1600180	C2	189							
HPK1600181	C2	190	Y						
HPK1600182	C2	191							
HPK1600183	C1	192	Y		ODA012	P3	OLA010	P3	1234568
HPK1600184	C2	193	Y						
HPK1600185	A4	194							
HPK1600186	C2	195							
HPK1600187	C2	196	Y						
HPK1600188	C2	197	Y						
HPK1600189	C2	198							
HPK1600190	C2	199							
HPK1600191	A4	200	Y						
HPK1600192	A4	201	Y						
HPK1600193	A4	202							
HPK1600194	A4	203	Y						
HPK1600195	A4	204							
HPK1600196	C2	205							
HPK1600197	A4	206	Y						
HPK1600198	A4	207							
HPK1600199	A4	208	Y						
HPK1600200	C1	209	Y						
HPK1600201	A4	210	Y						
HPK1600202	A4	211	Y						
HPK1600203	A4	212	Y						
HPK1600204	A4	213	Y						
HPK1600205	A4	214							
HPK1600206	A4	215	Y						
HPK1600207	A4	216							
HPK1600208	C1	217	Y	Y	ODA006	P2	OLA021	P3	123568
HPK1600209	A4	218							
HPK1600210	A4	219	Y						
HPK1600211	A4	220	Y						
HPK1600212	A4	221	Y				OLA010	P3	1234568
HPK1600213	A4	222							
HPK1600214	C2	223	Y	Y					
HPK1600215	C2	224	Y	Y					
HPK1600216	C2	225	Y	Y					
HPK1600217	C2	226							
HPK1600218	C2	227	Y	Y					
HPK1600219	C2	228	Y						
HPK1600220	C2	229							

PLAN #	PRICE TIER	PAGE	MATERIALS LIST	QUOTE ONE®	DECK	DECK PRICE	LANDSCAPE	LANDSCAPE PRICE	REGIONS
HPK1600221	A4	230							
HPK1600222	C1	231							
HPK1600223	A4	232	Y						
HPK1600224	A4	233							
HPK1600225	A4	234							
HPK1600226	A4	235							
HPK1600227	A4	236							
HPK1600228	A4	237	Y						
HPK1600229	C1	238	Y						
HPK1600230	C1	239							
HPK1600231	A4	240							
HPK1600232	C1	241							
HPK1600233	A4	242							
HPK1600234	C2	243	Y						
HPK1600235	A4	244							
HPK1600236	C2	245							
HPK1600237	C1	246							
HPK1600238	C1	247	Y						
HPK1600239	SQ1	248	Y	Y		OLA038	P3	7	
HPK1600240	C1	249	Y	Y					
HPK1600241	A4	250							
HPK1600242	A4	251							
HPK1600243	C1	251							
HPK1600244	C3	254	Y	Y		OLA037	P4	347	
HPK1600245	C3	254	Y						
HPK1600246	C4	255	Y						
HPK1600247	SQ1	256	Y	Y					
HPK1600248	C4	257							
HPK1600249	C2	258	Y	Y		OLA038	P3	7	
HPK1600250	C3	259	Y	Y		OLA038	P3	7	
HPK1600251	C2	260	Y			OLA015	P4	123568	
HPK1600252	C2	261							
HPK1600253	SQ1	262							
HPK1600254	L1	263							
HPK1600255	SQ1	264							
HPK1600256	C3	265							
HPK1600259	SQ1	268							
HPK1600260	C3	269				OLA001	P3	123568	
HPK1600261	C1	270							
HPK1600262	L1	271	Y						
HPK1600263	C2	272	Y						
HPK1600264	C1	273	Y						
HPK1600265	C1	274							
HPK1600266	C3	275	Y			OLA004	P3	123568	
HPK1600267	SQ1	276							
HPK1600268	SQ1	277							
HPK1600269	C4	278							
HPK1600270	SQ3	279							
HPK1600271	C1	280							
HPK1600272	C3	281				OLA012	P3	12345678	
HPK1600273	C1	282							
HPK1600274	C1	283							
HPK1600275	C2	284							
HPK1600276	C3	285							
HPK1600277	SQ1	286	Y						
HPK1600278	SQ1	287	Y						
HPK1600279	C4	288				OLA012	P3	12345678	
HPK1600280	C1	289	Y			OLA001	P3	123568	
HPK1600281	C1	290							
HPK1600282	C4	291	Y						
HPK1600283	SQ1	292	Y						
HPK1600284	C3	293							
HPK1600285	C3	294							
HPK1600286	L1	295							
HPK1600287	C1	296							
HPK1600288	SQ3	297	Y						
HPK1600289	C3	298	Y	Y					
HPK1600290	SQ1	299							
HPK1600291	C1	300							
HPK1600292	C2	301							
HPK1600293	C1	302							
HPK1600294	C2	303							
HPK1600295	C1	304							
HPK1600296	C3	305	Y						
HPK1600297	L2	306							
HPK1600298	C4	307							
HPK1600299	C1	308							
HPK1600300	C1	309							
HPK1600301	C2	310	Y	Y		OLA007	P4	1234568	
HPK1600302	SQ1	311							
HPK1600303	C3	312	Y						
HPK1600305	C1	314	Y						
HPK1600306	C3	315	Y						
HPK1600307	C1	316	Y						
HPK1600308	C3	317	Y						
HPK1600309	C2	318							
HPK1600310	C2	319							
HPK1600311	C2	320							
HPK1600312	C1	321	Y						
HPK1600313	C3	322							
HPK1600314	C3	323	Y	Y		OLA036	P4	12356	
HPK1600315	C1	324							
HPK1600316	A4	325							
HPK1600317	C3	326							
HPK1600318	C1	327							
HPK1600319	C3	328							
HPK1600320	C2	329							
HPK1600321	A3	330							
HPK1600322	C1	331	Y						
HPK1600323	C4	331							
HPK1600324	A1	334	Y						
HPK1600325	P6	335							
HPK1600326	P1	335							
HPK1600327	P5	336							
HPK1600328	P6	337							
HPK1600329	P6	338							
HPK1600330	P6	339							
HPK1600331	P4	340							
HPK1600332	P4	341							
HPK1600333	P4	342							
HPK1600334	P4	343							
HPK1600335	P5	344	Y						
HPK1600336	A2	345							
HPK1600337	P4	346							
HPK1600338	P4	347							
HPK1600339	P5	348	Y						
HPK1600340	P6	349							
HPK1600341	P2	350							
HPK1600342	P5	351							
HPK1600343	P4	352	Y						
HPK1600344	P4	353							
HPK1600345	P2	354							
HPK1600346	P1	355							
HPK1600347	P1	356							
HPK1600348	P2	357							
HPK1600349	P2	358							
HPK1600350	P4	359							
HPK1600351	P1	360							
HPK1600352	P2	361							
HPK1600353	P3	362				OLA083	P3	12345678	
HPK1600354	P3	364				OLA085	P3	12345678	
HPK1600355	P4	366				OLA086	P4	12345678	
HPK1600356	P4	368				OLA049	P4	12345678	
HPK1600357	P3	370				OLA060	P3	123467	
HPK1600358	P3	372				OLA137	P3	1234678	
HPK1600359	SQ1	6							
HPK1600360	P1	360							
HPK1600361	A2	267							